Sams **Teach Yourself**

JavaScript™

Fifth Edition

in **24**
Hours

SAMS   800 East 96th Street, Indianapolis, Indiana, 46240 USA

Sams Teach Yourself JavaScript™ in 24 Hours, Fifth Edition

Copyright © 2013 by Pearson Education, Inc.

ISBN-13: 978-0-672-33608-9
ISBN-10: 0-672-33608-1

Library of Congress Cataloging-in-Publication Data is on file.

Printed in the United States of America

First Printing October 2012

Trademarks

Warning and Disclaimer

Bulk Sales

Sams Publishing offers excellent discounts on this book when ordered in quantity for bulk purchases or special sales. For more information, please contact

U.S. Corporate and Government Sales
1-800-382-3419
corpsales@pearsontechgroup.com

For sales outside of the U.S., please contact

International Sales
international@pearsoned.com

Editor-in-Chief
Mark Taub

Acquisitions Editor
Mark Taber

Managing Editor
Kristy Hart

Project Editor
Anne Goebel

Copy Editor
Geneil Breeze

Indexer
Erika Millen

Proofreader
Chrissy White,
Language Logistics

Publishing Coordinator
Vanessa Evans

Technical Editor
Joseph Greenspan

Cover Designer
Anne Jones

Compositor
Nonie Ratcliff

Contents at a Glance

Table of Contents

About the Authors

Phil Ballard, the author of *Sams Teach Yourself Ajax in 10 Minutes*, graduated in 1980 with an honors degree in electronics from the University of Leeds, England. Following an early career as a research scientist with a major multinational, he spent a few years in commercial and managerial roles within the high technology sector, later working full time as a software engineering consultant.

Operating as "The Mouse Whisperer" (www.mousewhisperer.co.uk), Ballard has spent recent years involved solely in website and intranet design and development for an international portfolio of clients.

Michael Moncur is a freelance webmaster and author. He runs a network of websites, including the Web's oldest site about famous quotations, online since 1994. He wrote *Sams Teach Yourself DHTML in 24 Hours* and has also written several bestselling books about networking, certification programs, and databases. He lives with his wife in Salt Lake City.

We Want to Hear from You!

As the reader of this book, *you* are our most important critic and commentator. We value your opinion and want to know what we're doing right, what we could do better, what areas you'd like to see us publish in, and any other words of wisdom you're willing to pass our way.

We welcome your comments. You can email or write to let us know what you did or didn't like about this book—as well as what we can do to make our books better.

Please note that we cannot help you with technical problems related to the topic of this book.

When you write, please be sure to include this book's title and author as well as your name and email address. We will carefully review your comments and share them with the author and editors who worked on the book.

Email: feedback@samspublishing.com

Mail: Sams Publishing
           ATTN: Reader Feedback
           800 East 96th Street
           Indianapolis, IN 46240 USA

Reader Services

Visit our website and register this book at www.informit.com/register for convenient access to any updates, downloads, or errata that might be available for this book.

Introduction

Who This Book Is For

If you're interested in learning JavaScript, chances are that you've already gained at least a basic understanding of HTML and web page design in general and want to move on to adding some extra interactivity to your pages. Or maybe you currently code in another programming language and want to see what additional capabilities JavaScript can add to your armory.

If you've never tinkered with HTML at all, nor done any computer programming, it would be helpful to browse through an HTML primer before getting into the book. Don't worry—HTML is very accessible, and you don't need to be an HTML expert to start experimenting with the JavaScript examples in this book.

JavaScript is an ideal language to use for your first steps in programming, and in case you get bitten by the bug, pretty much all of the fundamental concepts that you learn in JavaScript will later be applicable in a wide variety of other languages such as C, Java, or PHP.

The Aims of This Book

When JavaScript was first introduced, it was somewhat limited in what it could do. With basic features and rather haphazard browser support, it gained a reputation in some quarters as being something of a toy or gimmick. Now, due to much better browser support for W3C standards and improvement in the JavaScript implementations used in recent browsers, JavaScript is finally beginning to be treated as a serious programming language.

Many advanced programming disciplines used in other programming languages can readily be applied to JavaScript, for example, object oriented programming promotes the writing of solid, readable, maintainable, and reusable code.

So-called "unobtrusive" scripting techniques and the use of DOM scripting focus on adding interaction to web pages while keeping the HTML simple to read and well separated from the program code.

This book aims to teach the fundamental skills relevant to all of the important aspects of JavaScript as it's used today. In the course of the book, you start from basic concepts and gradually learn the best practices for writing JavaScript programs in accordance with current web standards.

Conventions Used

All of the code examples in the book are written to validate correctly as HTML5. In the main, though, the code avoids using HTML5-specific syntax because at the time of writing its support in web browsers is still not universal. The code examples should work correctly in virtually any recent web browser, regardless of the type of computer or operating system.

In addition to the main text of each lesson, you will find a number of boxes labeled as Notes, Tips, and Cautions.

NOTE

These sections provide additional comments that might help you to understand the text and examples.

TIP

These blocks give additional hints, shortcuts, or workarounds to make coding easier.

CAUTION

Avoid common pitfalls by using the information in these blocks.

TRY IT YOURSELF

Each hour contains at least one section that walks you through the process of implementing your own script. This will help you to gain confidence in writing your own JavaScript code based on the techniques you've learned.

Q&A, Quiz, and Exercises

After each hour's lesson, you'll find three final sections.

Q&A tries to answer a few of the more common questions about the hour's topic.

The Quiz tests your knowledge of what you learned in that lesson.

Exercises offer suggestions for further experimentation, based on the lesson, that you might like to try on your own.

How the Book Is Organized

The book is divided into six parts, gradually increasing in the complexity of the techniques taught.

▶ **Part I—First Steps with JavaScript**

Part I is an introduction to the JavaScript language and how to write simple scripts using the language's common functions. This part of the book is aimed mainly at readers with little or no prior programming knowledge and no knowledge of the JavaScript language.

▶ **Part II—More Advanced JavaScript**

Here more sophisticated programming paradigms are introduced, such as program control loops and event handling, object oriented programming, JSON notation, and cookies.

▶ **Part III—Working with the Document Object Model (DOM)**

This part of the book concentrates on navigating and editing the DOM (Document Object Model) tree, using CSS stylesheets, and styling and animating page elements. There is emphasis on using good coding practice such as unobtrusive JavaScript.

▶ **Part IV—Ajax**

Here you learn how to make background calls to the server using the XMLHTTPRequest object and handle the server responses, build a simple Ajax library, and learn about debugging Ajax applications.

▶ **Part V—Using JavaScript Libraries**

In this part, you learn how to simplify cross-browser development using third-party libraries such as Prototype and jQuery.

▶ **Part VI—Using JavaScript with Other Web Technologies**

In the final part examples are given of how to use JavaScript to control multimedia, exploit HTML5 capabilities, write browser add-ons, and more.

Tools You'll Need

Writing JavaScript does not require any expensive and complicated tools such as Integrated Development Environments (IDEs), compilers, or debuggers.

The examples in this book can all be created in a text editing program, such as Windows' Notepad. At least one such application ships with just about every operating system, and countless more are available for no or low cost via download from the Internet.

NOTE

Appendix A, "Tools for JavaScript Development," lists some additional easily obtainable tools and resources for use in JavaScript development.

To see your program code working, you'll need a web browser such as Internet Explorer, Mozilla Firefox, Opera, Safari, or Google Chrome. It is recommended that you upgrade your browser to the latest current stable version.

The vast majority of the book's examples do not need an Internet connection to function. Simply storing the source code file in a convenient location on your computer and opening it with your chosen browser is generally sufficient. The exceptions to this are the hour on cookies and the section of the book about Ajax; to explore all of the example code will require a web connection (or a connection to a web server on your Local Area Network) and a little web space in which to post the example code. If you've done some HTML coding, you may already have that covered; if not, a hobby-grade web hosting account costs very little and will be more than adequate for trying out the examples in this book. (Check that your web host allows you to run scripts written in the PHP language if you want to try out the Ajax examples in Part IV. Nearly all hosts do).

PART I
First Steps with JavaScript

Introducing JavaScript

The modern Web has little to do with its original, text-only ancestor. Modern web pages can involve audio, video, animated graphics, interactive navigation, and much more—and more often than not, JavaScript plays a big part in making it all possible.

In this first hour we describe what JavaScript is, briefly review the language's origins, and consider the kinds of things it can do to improve your web pages. You also dive right in and write some working JavaScript code.

Web Scripting Fundamentals

Given that you've picked up this book, there's a pretty good chance that you're already familiar with using the World Wide Web and have at least a basic understanding of writing web pages in some variant of HTML.

HTML is not a programming language but (as the name indicates) a markup language; we can use it to mark parts of our page to indicate to the browser that these parts should be shown in a particular way—bold or italic text, for instance, or as a heading, a list of bullet points, arranged as a table of data, or using many other markup options.

Once written, these pages by their nature are *static*. They can't respond to user actions, make decisions, or modify the display of their page elements. The markup they contain will always be interpreted and displayed in the same way whenever the page is visited by a user.

As you know from using the World Wide Web, websites can do much more; the pages we routinely visit are often far from static. They can contain "live" data, such as share prices or flight arrival times, animated dis-

NOTE

The term *script* has no doubt
been borrowed from the world of
theater and TV, where the *script*
defines the actions of the pre-
senters or performers. In the
case of a web page, the protago-
nists are the elements on the
page, with a *script* provided by a
scripting language such as, in
this case, JavaScript. *Program*
and *script* are, for our purposes,
pretty much interchangeable
terms, as are *programming* and
scripting. You'll find all of these
used in the course of the book.

NOTE

There is, in fact, an elegant way
to incorporate output from
server-side scripts into your
client-side JavaScript programs.
We look at this in Part IV of this
book, when we study a technique called *Ajax*.

NOTE

Although the names are similar,
JavaScript doesn't have much, if
anything, to do with the Java language developed by Sun
Microsystems. The two languages share some aspects of
syntax, but no more so than
either of them do with a whole
host of other programming
languages.

plays with changing colors and fonts, or interactive capabilities such as the ability to click through a gallery of photographs or sort a column of data.

These clever capabilities are provided to the user by programs—often known as scripts—operating behind the scenes to manipulate what's displayed in the browser.

Server- Versus Client-Side Programming

There are two fundamental ways of adding scripts to otherwise static web content:

▶ You can have the web server execute a script before delivering your page to the user. Such scripts can define what information is sent to the browser for display to the user—for example, by retrieving product prices from the database of an online store, checking a user's identity credentials before logging her into a private area of the website, or retrieving the contents of an email mailbox. These scripts are generally run at the web server *before* generating the requested web page and serving it to the user. You won't be surprised to learn that we refer to this as *server-side scripting*.

▶ Alternatively the scripts themselves, rather than being run on the server, can be delivered to the user's browser along with the page's content. Such scripts are then executed by the browser and operate on the page's already-delivered content. The many functions such scripts can perform include animating page sections, reformatting page layouts, allowing the user to drag-and-drop items within a page, validating user input on forms, redirecting users to other pages, and much more. You have probably already guessed that this is referred to as *client-side scripting*, and you're correct.

This book is all about JavaScript, the most-used language for client-side scripting on the Internet.

JavaScript in a Nutshell

A program written in JavaScript can access the elements of a web page, and the browser window in which it is running, and perform actions on those elements, as well as creating new page elements. A few examples of JavaScript's capabilities include

▶ Opening new windows with a specified size, position, and style (for example, whether the window has borders, menus, toolbars, and so on)

▶ Providing user-friendly navigation aids such as drop-down menus

▶ Validation of data entered into a web form to make sure that they are of an acceptable format before the form is submitted to the web server

▶ Changing how page elements look and behave when particular events occur, such as the mouse cursor moving over them

▶ Detecting and exploiting advanced features supported by the particular browser being used, such as third-party plug-ins, or native support for new technologies

Because JavaScript code runs locally inside the user's browser, the page tends to respond quickly to JavaScript instructions, enhancing the user's experience and making the application seem more like one of the computer's native applications rather than simply a web page. Also, JavaScript can detect and utilize certain user actions that HTML can't, such as individual mouse clicks and keyboard actions.

Virtually every web browser in common use has support for JavaScript.

Where JavaScript Came From

The ancestry of JavaScript dates back to the mid-1990s, when version 1.0 was introduced for Netscape Navigator 2.

The European Computer Manufacturers Association (ECMA) became involved, defining ECMAScript, the great-granddaddy of the current language. At the same time, Microsoft introduced jScript, its own version of the language, for use in its Internet Explorer range of browsers.

The Browser Wars

In the late 1990s, Netscape Navigator 4 and Internet Explorer 4 both claimed to offer major improvements over earlier browser versions in terms of what could be achieved with JavaScript.

NOTE

JavaScript is not the only client-side scripting language. Microsoft browsers have supported (in addition to jScript, Microsoft's version of JavaScript) a scripting-oriented version of the company's own Visual Basic language, called VBScript.

JavaScript, however, has much better browser support; a version of JavaScript is supported by nearly every modern browser.

NOTE

The World Wide Web Consortium (W3C) is an international community that exists to develop open standards to support the long-term growth of the World Wide Web. Its website at http://www.w3.org/ is a vast resource of information and tools relating to web standards.

Unfortunately, the two sets of developers had gone in separate directions, each defining its own additions to the JavaScript language and how it interacted with your web page.

This ludicrous situation forced developers to essentially write two versions of each of their scripts and use some clumsy and often error-prone routines to try to determine which browser was being used to view the page and subsequently switching to the most appropriate version of their JavaScript code.

Thankfully, the World Wide Web Consortium (the W3C) worked hard with the individual browser manufacturers to standardize the way web pages were constructed and manipulated, by means of the Document Object Model or DOM. Level 1 of the new standardized DOM was completed in late 1998, and Level 2 in late 2000.

Don't worry if you're not sure what the DOM is or what it does—you learn a lot about it later this hour and through the course of this book.

The `<script>` Tag

NOTE

JavaScript is an *interpreted* language, rather than a *compiled* language such as C++ or Java. The JavaScript instructions are passed to the browser as plain text and are interpreted sequentially; they do not need to first be "compiled" into condensed machine code only readable by the computer's processor. This offers big advantages in that JavaScript programs are easy to read, can be edited swiftly, and their operation can be retested simply by reloading the web page in the browser.

Whenever the page is requested by a user, any JavaScript programs it contains are passed to the browser along with page content.

You can include JavaScript statements directly into your HTML code by placing them between `<script>` and `</script>` tags within the HTML:

```
<script>
    ... JavaScript statements ...
</script>
```

The examples in this book are all written to validate correctly as HTML5, in which no obligatory attributes are specified for the `<script>` element (the `type` attribute is optional in HTML5 and has been excluded from the examples in this book to aid clarity). However, if you write JavaScript for inclusion in HTML 4.x or XHTML pages, you should add the `type` attribute to your `<script>` elements:

```
<script type="text/javascript">
    ... JavaScript statements ...
</script>
```

You'll also occasionally see `<script>` elements having the attribute `language="JavaScript"`. This has long been deprecated, so unless you think you need to support ancient browsers such as Navigator and Mosaic, there's no need to continue writing code like this.

The examples in this hour place their JavaScript code within the body section of the document, but JavaScript code can appear elsewhere in the document too; you can also use the `<script>` element to load JavaScript code saved in an external file. We be discussing in much more detail how to include JavaScript in your pages in Hour 2, "Writing Simple Scripts."

Introducing the DOM

A Document Object Model or DOM is a conceptual way of visualizing a document and its contents.

Each time your browser is asked to load and display a page, it needs to interpret (we usually use the word "parse") the source code contained in the HTML file comprising the page. As part of this parsing process, the browser creates a type of internal model known as a DOM representation based on the content of the loaded document. It is this model that the browser then refers to when rendering the visible page. You can use JavaScript to access and edit the various parts of the DOM representation, at the same time changing the way the user sees and interacts with the page in view.

In the early days, JavaScript provided rather primitive access to certain parts of a web page. JavaScript programs could gain access, for example, to the images and forms contained in a web page; a JavaScript program could contain statements to select "the second form on the page" or "the form called 'registration.'"

Web developers sometimes refer to this as DOM Level 0, in backward-compatible homage to the W3C's subsequent Level 1 DOM definition. As well as DOM Level 0, you might also see reference to the BOM, or Browser Object Model. Since DOM Level 0, the W3C has gradually extended and improved the DOM specification. The W3C's much more ambitious definition has produced a DOM that is valid not just for web pages and JavaScript, but for any programming language and for XML, in addition to HTML, documents.

NOTE

The use of early browsers such as Netscape Navigator (any version) and Internet Explorer up to version 5.5 has now virtually disappeared. This book concentrates on more modern browsers that are compatible with DOM Level 1 or better, such as Internet Explorer 7+, Firefox, Google Chrome, Apple Safari, Opera, and Konqueror. You are recommended to upgrade your browser to the latest stable version.

The W3C and Standards Compliance

The browser vendors have incorporated much-improved support for DOM in their most recent versions. At the time of writing, Internet Explorer is shipping in version 9, Netscape Navigator has been reborn as Mozilla Firefox (currently in version 9), and other competitors in the market include Opera, Konqueror, Apple's Safari, and Google's Chrome and Chromium. All of these offer excellent support for the DOM.

The situation has improved markedly for web developers. Apart from a few irritating quirks, we can now largely forget about writing special code for individual browsers provided that we follow the DOM standards.

The window and document Objects

Each time your browser loads and displays a page, it creates in memory an internal representation of the page and all its elements, the Document Object Model or DOM. In the DOM, elements of your web page have a logical, hierarchical structure, like a tree of interconnected parent and child *objects*. These objects, and their interconnections, form a conceptual model of the web page and the browser that contains and displays it. Each object also has a list of *properties* that describe it and a number of *methods* we can use to manipulate those properties using JavaScript.

Right at the top of the hierarchical tree is the browser window object. This object is a parent or ancestor to everything else in the DOM representation of your page.

The window object has various child objects, some of which are visualized in Figure 1.1. The first child object shown in Figure 1.1, and the one we'll use most in this book, is the document object. Any HTML page loaded into the browser creates a document object containing all of the HTML and other resources that go to make up the displayed page. All of this information is accessible via JavaScript as a parent-child hierarchy of objects, each with its own properties and methods.

The other children of the window object visible in Figure 1.1 are the location object (containing details of the URL of the currently loaded page), the history object (containing details of the browser's previously visited pages), and the navigator object (which stores details of the browser type, version, and capabilities). We look in detail at these objects in Hour 4, "DOM Objects and Built-In Objects," and using them again at intervals throughout the book, but for now let's concentrate on the document object.

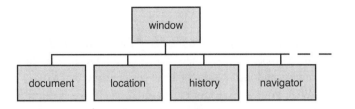

FIGURE 1.1
The window object and some of its children

Object Notation

The notation we use to represent objects within the tree uses the dot or period:

```
parent.child
```

As an example, referring to Figure 1.1, the location object is a child of the window object, so in the DOM it is referred to like this:

```
window.document
```

The <body> section of your HTML page is represented in the DOM as a child element of the document object; we would access it like this:

```
window.document.body
```

The last item in the sequence can also be, instead of another object, a *property* or *method* of the parent object:

```
object1.object2.property
```

```
object1.object2.method
```

For example, let's suppose that we want to access the title property of the current document, as specified by the HTML <title>...</title> tags. We can simply use

```
window.document.title
```

Talking to the User

Let's take a look at some of the methods associated with the window and document objects. We begin with two methods, each of which provides a means to talk to the user.

TIP

This notation can be extended as many times as necessary to represent any object in the tree. For example

`object1.object2.object3`

represents object3, whose parent is object2, which is itself a child of object1.

NOTE

Don't worry if object hierarchy and dot notation don't seem too clear right now. You'll be seeing many examples in the course of the book!

TIP

The window object always contains the current browser window, so you can refer to window.document to access the current document. As a shortcut, you can also simply use document instead of window.document—this also refers to the current window.

If you have several windows open, or if you are using a frameset, there will be a separate window and document object for each window or frame. To refer to one of these documents, you need to use the relevant window name and document name belonging to the window or frame in question.

window.alert()

Even if you don't realize it, you've seen the results of the `window` object's `alert` method on many occasions. The `window` object, you'll recall, is at the top of the DOM hierarchy, and represents the browser window that's displaying your page. When you call the `alert()` method, the browser pops open a dialog displaying your message, along with an OK button. Here's an example:

```
<script>window.alert("Here is my message");</script>
```

This is our first working example of the dot notation. Here we are calling the `alert()` method of the `window` object, so our `object.method` notation becomes `window.alert`.

Notice that the line of text inside the parentheses is contained within quotation marks. These can be single or double quotes, but they must be there, or an error will be produced.

This line of code, when executed in the browser, pops up a dialog like the one in Figure 1.2

TIP

In practice, you can leave out the `window.` part of the statement. Because the `window` object is the top of the DOM hierarchy (it's sometimes referred to as the *global object*), any methods called without direct reference to their parent object are assumed to belong to `window`. So

```
<script>alert("Here is my
message");</script>
```

works just as well.

FIGURE 1.2
A `window.alert()` dialog

TIP

Figure 1.2 shows the alert generated by the Chromium browser running on Ubuntu Linux. The appearance of the dialog box changes in detail depending on the particular browser, operating system, and display options you are using, but it always contains the message along with a single OK button.

TIP

Until the user clicks OK, he is prevented from doing anything else with the page. A dialog that behaves this way is known as a *modal* dialog.

document.write()

You can probably guess what the `write` method of the document object does, simply from its name. This method, instead of popping up a dialog, writes characters directly into the HTML of the document, as shown in Figure 1.3.

```
<script>document.write("Here is another message");</script>
```

FIGURE 1.3
Using document.write()

NOTE

In fact, `document.write` is a pretty dumb way to write content to the page—it has a lot of limitations, both in terms of its function and in terms of coding style and maintainability. It has largely fallen into disuse for "serious" JavaScript programming. By the time you come to write more advanced JavaScript programs, you'll have learned much better ways to put content into your pages using JavaScript and the DOM. However, we use `document.write` quite a lot during Part I of the book, while you come to grips with some of the basic principles of the language.

TRY IT YOURSELF ▼

"Hello World!" in JavaScript

It seems almost rude to introduce a programming language without presenting the traditional "Hello World" example. Have a look at the simple HTML document of Listing 1.1.

LISTING 1.1   "Hello World!" in an `alert()` Dialog

```
<!DOCTYPE html>
<html>
<head>
    <title>Hello from JavaScript!</title>
</head>
<body>
    <script>
        alert("Hello World!");
    </script>
</body>
</html>
```

Create a document called hello.html in your text editor and enter this code. Save it to a convenient place on your computer and then open it with your web browser.

▼ TRY IT YOURSELF

"Hello World!" in JavaScript

continued

Many popular operating systems allow you to right-click the icon of the HTML file and choose Open With..., or similar wording. Alternatively, fire up your chosen browser and use the **File > Open** options from the menu bar to navigate to your file and load it into the browser.

You should see a display similar to Figure 1.2, but with the message "Hello World!" in the dialog. If you have more than one browser installed on your computer, try them all, and compare the display—the dialogs will probably look a little different, but the message and the operation of the OK button should be just the same.

Reading a Property of the document Object

You may recall from earlier in the hour that objects in the DOM tree have properties and methods. You saw how to use the `write` method of the document object to output text to the page—now let's try *reading* one of the properties of the document object. We're going to use the `document.title` property, which contains the title as defined in the HTML `<title>` element of the page.

CAUTION

Some text editor programs might try to add a .txt extension to the filename you specify. Be sure your saved file has the extension .html or the browser will probably not open it correctly.

Edit hello.html in your text editor, and change the call to the `window.alert()` method:

```
alert(document.title);
```

CAUTION

The default security settings in some browsers cause them to show a security warning when they are asked to open local content, such as a file on your own computer. If your browser does this, just choose the option that allows the content to be shown.

Notice that `document.title` is *not* now enclosed in quotation marks—if it were, JavaScript would infer that we wanted to output the string "document.title" as literal text. Without the quote marks, JavaScript sends to the `alert()` method the *value* contained in the `document.title` property. The result is shown in Figure 1.4.

FIGURE 1.4
Displaying a property of the document object

Summary

In this hour, you were introduced to the concepts of server-side and client-side scripting and had a brief history lesson about JavaScript and the Document Object Model. You had an overview of the sorts of things JavaScript can do to enhance your web pages and improve the experience for your users.

Additionally, you learned about the basic structure of the Document Object Model and how JavaScript can access particular objects and their properties, and use the methods belonging to those objects.

In the lessons that follow, we build on these fundamental concepts to carry out more advanced scripting projects.

Q&A

Q. If I use server-side scripting (in a language such as PHP or ASP), can I still use JavaScript on the client side?

A. Most definitely. In fact, the combination of server-side and client-side scripting provides a potent platform, capable of producing powerful applications. Google Mail is a good example.

Q. How many different browsers should I test in?

A. As many as you practically can. Writing standards-compliant code that avoids browser-specific features will go a long way toward making your code run smoothly in different browsers. However, one or two minor differences between browser implementations of certain features are likely to always exist.

Q. Won't the inclusion of JavaScript code slow down the load time of my pages?

A. Yes, though usually the difference is small enough not to be noticeable. If you have a particularly large piece of JavaScript code, you may feel it's worthwhile testing your page on the slowest connection a user is likely to have. Except for in extreme circumstances, it's unlikely to be a serious issue.

Workshop

Try to answer all the questions before reading the subsequent "Answers" section.

Quiz

1. Is JavaScript a compiled or an interpreted language?

    a. A compiled language

    b. An interpreted language

    c. Neither

    d. Both

2. What extra tags must be added to an HTML page to include JavaScript statements?

    a. `<script>` and `</script>`

    b. `<type="text/javascript">`

    c. `<!--` and `-->`

3. The top level of the DOM hierarchy is occupied by

    a. The `document` property

    b. The `document` method

    c. The `document` object

    d. The `window` object

Answers

1. b. JavaScript is an interpreted language. The program code is written in plain text, and the statements are read and executed one at a time.

2. a. JavaScript statements are added between `<script>` and `</script>` tags.

3. d. The `window` object is at the top of the DOM tree, and the `document` object is one of its child objects.

Exercises

In the "Try It Yourself" section of this hour, we used the line

```
alert(document.title);
```

to output the `title` property of the document object. Try rewriting that script to instead output the `document.lastModified` property, which contains the date and time that the web page was last changed. (Be careful—property names are case sensitive. Note the capital M.) See whether you can then modify the code to use `document.write()` in place of `alert()`, to write the property directly into the page like in Figure 1.3.

Try the example code from this hour in as many different browsers as you have access to. What differences do you note in how the example pages are displayed?

Writing Simple Scripts

You learned in Hour 1, "Introducing JavaScript," that JavaScript is a scripting language capable of making web pages more interactive.

In this hour you learn more about how JavaScript can be added to your web page and then about some of the fundamental syntax of your JavaScript programs such as statements, variables, operators, and comments. You'll also get your hands dirty with more worked examples.

Including JavaScript in Your Web Page

In the previous hour we said that JavaScript programs are passed to the browser along with page content—but how do we achieve that? Actually there are two basic methods for associating JavaScript code with your HTML page, both of which use the <script></script> element introduced in Hour 1.

One method is to include the JavaScript statements directly into the HTML file, just like we did in the previous hour:

```
<script>
    ... Javascript statements are written here ...
</script>
```

A second and usually preferable way to include your code is to save your JavaScript into a separate file and use the <script> element to include that file by name using the src (source) attribute:

```
<script src='mycode.js'></script>
```

WHAT YOU'LL LEARN IN THIS HOUR

- ▶ Various ways to include JavaScript in your web pages
- ▶ The basic syntax of JavaScript statements
- ▶ How to declare and use variables
- ▶ Using mathematical operators
- ▶ How to comment your code
- ▶ Capturing mouse events

The previous example includes a file `mycode.js`, which contains our JavaScript statements. If your JavaScript file is not in the same folder as the calling script, you can also add a (relative or absolute) path to it:

```
<script src='/path/to/mycode.js'></script>
```

or

```
<script src='http://www.example.com/path/to/mycode.js'></script>
```

Placing your JavaScript code in a separate file offers some important advantages:

▶ When the JavaScript code is updated, the updates are immediately available to any page using that same JavaScript file. This is particularly important in the context of JavaScript libraries, which we look at later in the book.

▶ The code for the HTML page is kept cleaner and therefore easier to read and maintain.

▶ Performance is slightly improve because your browser caches the included file, therefore having a local copy in memory next time it is needed by this or another page.

Listing 2.1 shows the simple web page we used in Hour 1, but now with a file of JavaScript code included in the <body> section. JavaScript can be placed in either the head or body of the HTML page. In fact, it is more common—and generally recommended—for JavaScript code to be placed in the head of the page, where it provides a number of *functions* that can be called from elsewhere in the document. You learn about functions in Hour 3, "Using Functions"; until then we limit ourselves to adding our example code into the body of the document.

LISTING 2.1   An HTML Document with a JavaScript File Included

```
<!DOCTYPE html>
<html>
<head>
    <title>A Simple Page</title>
</head>
<body>
    <p>Some content ...</p>
    <script src='mycode.js'></script>
</body>
</html>
```

When JavaScript code is added into the body of the document, the code statements are interpreted and executed as they are encountered while the page is being rendered. After reading and executing the code, page rendering continues until the page is complete.

TIP

You're not limited to using a single `script` element—you can have as many of them on your page as you need.

NOTE

You sometimes see HTML-style comment notation `<!--` and `-->` inside `script` elements, surrounding the JavaScript statements, like this:

```
<script>
    <!--
    ... Javascript statements are written here ...
    -->
</script>
```

This is for the benefit of ancient browsers that didn't recognize the `<script>` tag. This HTML "comment" syntax prevented such browsers from displaying the JavaScript source code on the screen along with the page content. Unless you have a reason to support very old browsers, this technique is no longer required.

JavaScript Statements

JavaScript programs are lists of individual instructions that we refer to as *statements*. To interpret statements correctly, the browser expects to find statements written either each on a separate line:

```
this is statement 1
this is statement 2
```

or combined in the same line by terminating each with a semicolon:

```
this is statement 1; this is statement 2;
```

To ease the readability of your code, and to help prevent hard-to-find syntax errors, it's good practice to combine both methods by giving each statement its own line and terminating the statement with a semicolon too:

```
this is statement 1;
this is statement 2;
```

Commenting Your Code

Some statements are not intended to be executed by the browser's JavaScript interpreter but are there for the benefit of anybody who may be reading the code. We refer to such lines as *comments*, and there are specific rules for adding comments to our code.

A comment that occupies just a single line of code can be written by placing a double forward slash before the content of the line:

```
// This is a comment
```

NOTE

JavaScript can also use the HTML comment syntax for single-line comments:

```
<!-- this is a comment -->
```

However, this is not commonly used in JavaScript programs.

To add a multiline comment in this way, we need to prefix every line of the comment:

```
// This is a comment
// spanning multiple lines
```

A more convenient way of entering multiline comments to your code is to prefix your comment with /* and terminate it with */. A comment written using this syntax can span multiple lines:

```
/*  This comment can span
    multiple lines
    without needing
    to mark up every line   */
```

NOTE

It's true that comments add a little to the size of your JavaScript source file, and this can have an adverse effect on page loading times. Generally the difference is so small as to be barely noticeable, but if it really matters you can always strip out all the comments from a "production" version of your JavaScript file—that is, a version to use with live rather than development websites.

Adding comments to your code is really a good thing to do, especially when you're writing larger or more complex JavaScript applications. Comments can act as reminders to you and also as instructions and explanations to anybody else reading your code at a later date.

Variables

A variable can be thought of as a named "pigeon-hole" where we keep a particular piece of data. Such data can take many different forms—an integer or decimal number, a string of characters, or various other data types discussed later in this hour or in those that follow. Our variables can be called pretty much anything we want, so long as we only use alphanumeric characters, the dollar sign $, or underscores in the name.

Let's suppose we have a variable called `netPrice`. We can set the value stored in `netPrice` with a simple statement:

```
netPrice = 8.99;
```

We call this *assigning a value* to the variable. Note that we don't have to declare the existence of this variable before assigning a value, as we would have to in some other programming languages. However, doing so is possible in JavaScript by using the `var` keyword and in most cases is good programming practice:

```
var netPrice;
netPrice = 8.99;
```

Alternatively we can combine these two statements conveniently and readably into one:

```
var netPrice = 8.99;
```

To assign a *character string* as the value of a variable, we need to include the string in single or double quotes:

```
var productName = "Leather wallet";
```

We could then, for example, write a line of code sending the value contained in that variable to the `window.alert` method:

```
alert(productName);
```

The generated dialog would evaluate the variable and display it as in Figure 2.1.

JavaScript is case sensitive—a variable called `mypetcat` is a different variable from `Mypetcat` or `MYPETCAT`.

Many coders of JavaScript, and other programming languages, like to use the so-called *CamelCase* convention (also called mixedCase, BumpyCaps, and various other names) for variable names. In CamelCase, compound words or phrases have the elements joined without spaces, with each element's initial letter capitalized except the first letter, which can be either upper- or lowercase. In this example, the variable would be named `MyPetCat` or `myPetCat`.

FIGURE 2.1
Displaying the value of variable `productName`

TIP

Choose readable variable names. Having variable names such as `productName` and `netPrice` makes code much easier to read and maintain than if the same variables were called `var123` and `myothervar49`, even though the latter names are entirely valid.

Operators

The values we have stored in our variables aren't going to be much use to us unless we can manipulate them in calculations.

Arithmetic Operations

First, JavaScript allows us to carry out operations using the standard arithmetic operators of addition, subtraction, multiplication, and division.

```
var theSum = 4 + 3;
```

As you'll have guessed, after this statement has been executed, the variable theSum will contain a value of 7. We can use variable names in our operations too:

```
var productCount = 2;
var subtotal = 14.98;
var shipping = 2.75;
var total = subtotal + shipping;
```

We can use JavaScript to subtract (-), multiply (*), and divide (/) in a similar manner:

```
subtotal = total - shipping;
var salesTax = total * 0.15;
var productPrice = subtotal / productCount;
```

To calculate the remainder from a division, we can use JavaScript's *modulus division* operator. This is denoted by the % character:

```
var itemsPerBox = 12;
var itemsToBeBoxed = 40;
var itemsInLastBox = itemsToBeBoxed % itemsPerBox;
```

In this example, the variable itemsInLastBox would contain the number 4 after the last statement completes.

JavaScript also has convenient operators to increment (++) or decrement (--) the value of a variable:

```
productCount++;
```

is equivalent to the statement

```
productCount = productCount + 1;
```

Similarly

```
items--;
```

is just the same as

```
items = items - 1;
```

A more comprehensive list of JavaScript's arithmetic operators appears in Appendix B, "JavaScript Quick Reference."

Operator Precedence

When you use several operators in the same calculation, JavaScript uses *precedence rules* to determine in what order the calculation should be done. For example, consider the statement

```
var average = a + b + c / 3;
```

If, as the variable's name implies, you're trying to calculate an average, this would not give the desired result; the division operation would be carried out on c before adding the values of a and b to the result. To calculate the average correctly, we would have to add parentheses to our statement, like this:

```
var average = (a + b + c) / 3;
```

If you have doubts about the precedence rules, I would recommend that you always use parentheses liberally. There is no cost to doing so, it makes your code easier to read (both for you and for anyone else who later has to edit or decipher it), and it ensures that precedence issues don't spoil your calculations.

Using the + operator with Strings

Arithmetic operators don't make much sense if the variables they operate on contain strings rather than numeric values. The exception is the + operator, which JavaScript interprets as an instruction to concatenate (join together sequentially) two or more strings:

```
var firstname = "John";
var surname = "Doe";
var fullname = firstname + " " + surname;
// the variable fullname now contains the value "John Doe"
```

If you try to use the + operator on two variables one of which is a string and the other numeric, JavaScript converts the numeric value to a string and concatenates the two:

```
var name = "David";
var age = 45;
alert(name + age);
```

Figure 2.2 shows the result of using the + operator on a string and a numeric value.

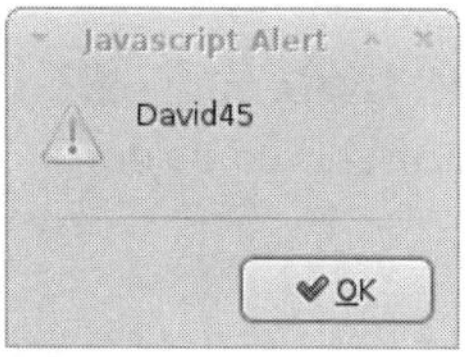

FIGURE 2.2
Concatenating a string and a numeric value

We talk about JavaScript data types, and string operations in general, much more in Hour 5, "Different Types of Data."

▼ TRY IT YOURSELF

Convert Celsius to Fahrenheit

To convert a temperature in degrees Celsius to one measured in degrees Fahrenheit, we need to multiply by 9, divide by 5, and then add 32. Let's do that in JavaScript:

```
var cTemp = 100;  // temperature in Celsius
// Let's be generous with parentheses
var hTemp = ((cTemp * 9) /5 ) + 32;
```

In fact, we could have omitted all of the parentheses from the calculation, and it would still have worked fine:

```
var hTemp = cTemp*9/5 + 32;
```

However, the parentheses make the code easier to understand and help prevent errors caused by operator precedence.

Let's test the code in a web page:

LISTING 2.2   Calculating Fahrenheit from Celsius

TRY IT YOURSELF ▼

Convert Celsius to Fahrenheit

continued

```
<!DOCTYPE html>
<html>
<head>
    <title>Fahrenheit From Celsius</title>
</head>
<body>
    <script>
        var cTemp = 100;   // temperature in Celsius
        // Let's be generous with parentheses
        var hTemp = ((cTemp * 9) /5 ) + 32;
        document.write("Temperature in Celsius: " + cTemp + "
degrees<br/>");
        document.write("Temperature in Fahrenheit: " + hTemp + "
degrees");
    </script>
</body>
</html>
```

Save this code as a file `temperature.html` and load it into your browser. You should get the result shown in Figure 2.3.

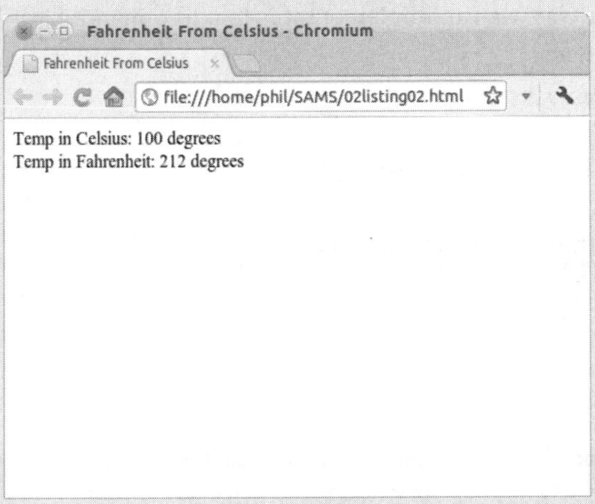

FIGURE 2.3
The output of Listing 2.2

Edit the file a few times to use different values for cTemp and check that everything works okay.

Capturing Mouse Events

One of the fundamental purposes of JavaScript is to help make your web pages more interactive for the user. To achieve this, we need to have some mechanisms to detect what the user and the program are doing at any given moment—where the mouse is in the browser window, whether the user has clicked a mouse button or pressed a keyboard key, whether a page has fully loaded in the browser, and so on.

All of these occurrences we refer to as *events*, and JavaScript has a variety of tools to help us work with them. In Hour 9, "Responding to Events," we look closely at events and learn some advanced techniques for dealing with them. For the moment, though, let's take a look at some of the ways we can detect a user's mouse actions using JavaScript.

JavaScript deals with events by using so-called *event handlers*. We are going to investigate three of these, onClick, onMouseOver, and onMouseOut.

The onClick Event Handler

The onClick event handler can be applied to nearly all HTML elements visible on a page. One way we can implement it is to add one more attrib-ute to the HTML element:

```
onclick=" ...some JavaScript code... "
```

Let's see an example; have a look at Listing 2.3.

LISTING 2.3   Using the onClick Event Handler

```
<!DOCTYPE html>
<html>
<head>
    <title>onClick Demo</title>
</head>
<body>
    <input type="button" onclick="alert('You clicked the button!')"
➥value="Click Me" />
</body>
</html>
```

The HTML code adds a button to the `<body>` element of the page and sup-plies that button with an onclick attribute. The value given to the onclick attribute is the JavaScript code we want to run when the HTML element (in this case a button) is clicked. When the user clicks the button, the `onclick` *event* is activated (we normally say the event has been "fired"), and the JavaScript statement(s) listed in the value of the attribute are executed.

In this case, there's just one statement:

```
alert('You clicked the button!')
```

Figure 2.4 shows the result of clicking the button.

FIGURE 2.4
Using the `onClick` event handler

NOTE

You may have noticed that we call the handler `onClick` but that we write this in lowercase as `onclick` when adding it to an HTML element. This convention has arisen because although HTML is case insensitive, XHTML is case *sensitive* and requires all HTML elements and attribute names to be written in lowercase.

onMouseOver and onMouseOut Event Handlers

When we simply want to detect where the mouse pointer is on the screen with reference to a particular page element, `onMouseOver` and `onMouseOut` can help us to do that.

The `onMouseOver` event is fired when the user's mouse cursor enters the region of the screen occupied by the element in question. The `onMouseOut` event, as I'm sure you've already guessed, is fired when the cursor leaves that same region.

Listing 2.4 gives a simple example of the `onMouseOver` event in action:

LISTING 2.4 Using onMouseOver

```
<!DOCTYPE html>
<html>
<head>
    <title>onMouseOver Demo</title>
</head>
<body>
```

LISTING 2.4   Continued

```
    <img src="image1.png" alt="image 1" onmouseover="alert('You entered
➥the image!')" />
</body>
</html>
```

The result of running the script is shown in Figure 2.5. Replacing onmouseover with onmouseout in Listing 2.4 will, of course, simply fire the event handler—and therefore pop up the alert dialog—as the mouse *leaves* the image, rather than doing so as it enters.

FIGURE 2.5
Using the onMouseOver event handler

▼ TRY IT YOURSELF

Creating an Image Rollover

We can use the onMouseOver and onMouseOut events to change how an image appears while the mouse pointer is above it. To achieve this, we use onMouseOver to change the src attribute of the HTML <img> element as the mouse cursor enters and onMouseOut to change it back as the mouse cursor leaves. The code is shown in Listing 2.5.

LISTING 2.5   An Image Rollover Using onMouseOver and onMouseOut

```
<!DOCTYPE html>
<html>
<head>
    <title>OnMouseOver Demo</title>
</head>
<body>
    <img src="tick.gif" alt="tick" onmouseover="this.src='tick2.gif';"
onmouseout="this.src='tick.gif';" />
</body>
</html>
```

You may notice something new in the syntax we used here. Within the JavaScript statements for onMouseOver and onMouseOut, we use the keyword this.

When using this within an event handler added via an attribute of an HTML element, this refers to the HTML element itself; in this case, you can read it as "this image," and this.src refers (using the "dot" notation that we've already met) to the src (source) property of this image object.

In this example we used two images, tick.gif and tick2.gif—you can use any images you have on hand, but the demonstration works best if they are the same size and not too large.

Use your editor to create an HTML file containing the code of Listing 2.5. You can change the image names tick.gif and tick2.gif to the names of your two images, if different; just make sure the images are saved in the same folder as your HTML file. Save the HTML file and open it in your browser.

You should see that the image changes as the mouse pointer enters and changes back as it leaves, as depicted in Figure 2.6.

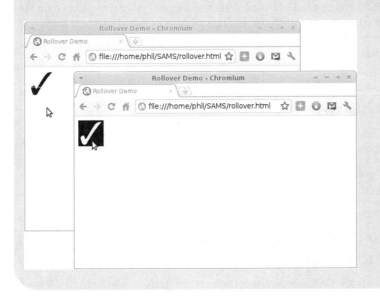

TRY IT YOURSELF ▼

Creating an Image Rollover
continued

FIGURE 2.6
An image rollover using onMouseOver and onMouseOut

NOTE

There was a time when image rollovers were regularly done this way, but these days they can be achieved much more efficiently using Cascading Style Sheets (CSS). Still, it's a convenient way to demonstrate the use of the onMouseOver and onMouseOut event handlers.

Summary

You covered quite a lot of ground this hour.

First of all you learned various ways to include JavaScript code in your HTML pages.

You studied how to declare variables in JavaScript, assign values to those variables, and manipulate them using arithmetic operators.

Finally, you were introduced to some of JavaScript's event handlers and you learned how to detect certain actions of the user's mouse.

Q&A

Q. **Some of the listings and code snippets list opening and closing `<script>` tags are on the same line; other times they are on separate lines. Does it matter?**

A. Empty spaces such as the space character, tabs, and blank lines are completely ignored by JavaScript. You can use such blank space, which programmers usually call *whitespace*, to lay out your code in such a way that it's more legible and easy to follow.

Q. **Can I use the same `<script>` element both to include an external JavaScript file and to contain JavaScript statements?**

A. No. If you use the `script` element to include an external JavaScript file by using the `src` attribute, you cannot also include JavaScript statements between `<script>` and `</script>`—this region must be left empty.

Workshop

Try to answer the following questions before looking at the "Answers" section that follows.

Quiz

1. What is an `onClick` event handler?

   a. An object that detects the mouse's location in the browser

   b. A script that executes in response to the user clicking the mouse

   c. An HTML element that the user can click

2. How many `<script>` elements are permitted on a page?

   a. None

   b. Exactly one

   c. Any number

3. Which of these is *not* a true statement about variables?

    a. Their names are case sensitive.

    b. They can contain numeric or non-numeric information.

    c. Their names may contain spaces.

Answers

1. b. An onClick event handler is fired when the user clicks the mouse.

2. c. You can use as many <script> elements as you need.

3. c. Variable names in JavaScript must not contain spaces.

Exercises

Starting with Listing 2.4, remove the onMouseOver and onMouseOut handlers from the <img> element. Instead, add an onClick handler to set the title property of the image to My New Title. [Hint: You can access the image title using this.title.]

Can you think of an easy way to test whether your script has correctly set the new image title?

Using Functions

Commonly, programs carry out the same or similar tasks repeatedly during the course of their execution. For you to avoid rewriting the same piece of code over and over again, JavaScript has the means to parcel up parts of your code into reusable modules, called *functions*. After you've written a function, it is available for the rest of your program to use, as if it were itself a part of the JavaScript language.

Using functions also makes your code easier to debug and maintain. Suppose you've written an application to calculate shipping costs; when the tax rates or haulage prices change, you'll need to make changes to your script. There may be 50 places in your code where such calculations are carried out. When you attempt to change every calculation, you're likely to miss some instances or introduce errors. However, if all such calculations are wrapped up in a few functions used throughout the application, then you just need to make changes to those functions. Your changes will automatically be applied all through the application.

Functions are one of the basic building blocks of JavaScript and will appear in virtually every script you write. In this hour you see how to create and use functions.

WHAT YOU'LL LEARN IN THIS HOUR

▶ How to define functions

▶ How to call (execute) functions

▶ How functions receive data

▶ Returning values from functions

▶ About the scope of variables

General Syntax

Creating a function is similar to creating a new JavaScript command that you can use in your script.

Here's the basic syntax for creating a function:

```
function sayHello() {
    alert("Hello");
    // ... more statements can go here ...
}
```

CAUTION

The keyword `function` must always be used in lowercase, or an error will be generated.

You begin with the keyword `function`, followed by your chosen function name with parentheses appended, then a pair of curly braces {}. Inside the braces go the JavaScript statements that make up the function. In the case of the preceding example, we simply have one line of code to pop up an `alert` dialog, but you can add as many lines of code as are necessary to make the function...well, function!

To keep things tidy, you can collect together as many functions as you like into one `<script>` element:

```
<script>
    function doThis() {
        alert("Doing This");
    }
    function doThat() {
        alert("Doing That");
    }
</script>
```

Calling Functions

TIP

Function names, like variable names, are case-sensitive. A function called `MyFunc()` is different from another called `myFunc()`. Also, as with variable names, it's really helpful to the readability of your code to choose meaningful function names.

TIP

You've already seen numerous examples of using the *methods* associated with JavaScript objects, such as `document.write()` and `window.alert()`.

Methods are simply functions that "belong" to a specific object. You learn much more about objects in Hour 4, "DOM Objects and Built-In Objects."

Code wrapped up in a function definition will not be executed when the page loads. Instead, it waits quietly until the function is *called*.

To call a function, you simply use the function name (with the parentheses) wherever you want to execute the statements contained in the function:

```
sayHello();
```

For example, you may want to add a call to your new function `sayHello()` to the `onClick` event of a button:

```
<input type="button" value="Say Hello" onclick="sayHello()" />
```

Putting JavaScript Code in the Page `<head>`

Up to now, our examples have all placed the JavaScript code into the `<body>` part of the HTML page. Using functions lets you employ the much more common, and usually preferable, practice of storing our JavaScript code in the `<head>` of the page. Functions contained within a `<script>` element in the page head, or in an external file included via the `src` attribute of a `<script>` element in the page head, are available to be called from anywhere on the page. Putting functions in the document's head section ensures that they have been defined prior to any attempt being made to execute them.

Listing 3.1 has an example.

LISTING 3.1   Functions in the Page Head

```
<!DOCTYPE html>
<html>
<head>
    <title>Calling Functions</title>
    <script>
        function sayHello() {
            alert("Hello");
        }
    </script>
</head>
<body>
    <input type="button" value="Say Hello" onclick="sayHello()" />
</body>
</html>
```

In this listing, you can see that the function definition itself has been placed inside a `<script>` element in the page head, but the call to the function has been made from a different place entirely—on this occasion, from the `onClick` event handler of a button in the body section of the page.

The result of clicking the button is shown in Figure 3.1.

FIGURE 3.1
Calling a JavaScript function

Arguments

It would be rather limiting if your functions could only behave in an identical fashion each and every time they were called, as would be the case in the preceding example.

Fortunately, you can extend the capabilities of functions a great deal by passing data to them. You do this when the function is called, by passing to it one or more *arguments*:

```
functionName(arguments)
```

Let's write a simple function to calculate the cube of a number and display the result:

```
function cube(x) {
    alert(x * x * x);
}
```

Now we can call our function, replacing the variable x with a number. Calling the function like this

```
cube(3);
```

NOTE

You'll sometimes see or hear the word *parameters* used in place of arguments, but it means exactly the same thing.

results in a dialog box being displayed that contains the result of the calculation, in this case 27.

Of course, you could equally pass a variable name as an argument. The following code would also generate a dialog containing the number 27:

```
var length = 3;
cube(length);
```

Multiple Arguments

CAUTION

Make sure that your function calls contain enough argument values to match the arguments specified in the function definition. If any of the arguments in the definition are left without a value, JavaScript may issue an error, or the function may perform incorrectly. If your function call is issued with too many arguments, the extra ones will be ignored by JavaScript.

Functions are not limited to a single argument. When you want to send multiple arguments to a function, all you need to do is separate them with commas:

```
function times(a, b) {
    alert(a * b);
}
times(3, 4); // alerts '12'
```

You can use as many arguments as you want.

It's important to note that the names given to arguments in the definition of your function have nothing to do with the names of any variables whose values are passed to the function. The variable names in the argument list act like placeholders for the actual values that will be passed when the function is called. The names that you give to arguments are only used inside the function definition to specify how it works.

We talk about this in more detail later in the hour when we discuss variable *scope*.

A Function to Output User Messages

Let's use what we've learned so far in this hour by creating a function that can send the user a message about a button he or she has just clicked. We place the function definition in the <head> section of the page and call it with multiple arguments.

Here's our function:

```
function buttonReport(buttonId, buttonName, buttonValue) {
    // information about the id of the button
    var userMessage1 = "Button id: " + buttonId + "\n";
    // then about the button name
    var userMessage2 = "Button name: " + buttonName + "\n";
    // and the button value
    var userMessage3 = "Button value: " + buttonValue;
    // alert the user
    alert(userMessage1 + userMessage2 + userMessage3);
}
```

The function buttonReport takes three arguments, those being the id, name, and value of the button element that has been clicked. With each of these three pieces of information, a short message is constructed. These three messages are then concatenated into a single string, which is passed to the alert() method to pop open a dialog containing the information.

To call our function, we put a button element on our HTML page, with its id, name, and value defined:

```
<input type="button" id="id1" name="Button 1" value="Something" />
```

We need to add an onClick event handler to this button from which to call our function. We're going to use the this keyword, as discussed in Hour 2, "Writing Simple Scripts":

```
onclick = "buttonReport(this.id, this.name, this.value)"
```

TIP

You may have noticed that the first two message strings have an element "\n" appended to the string; this is a "new line" character, forcing the message within the alert dialog to return to the left and begin a new line. Certain special characters like this one must be prefixed with \ if they are to be correctly interpreted when they appear in a string. Such a prefixed character is known as an *escape sequence*. You learn more about escape sequences in Hour 5, "Different Types of Data."

▼ TRY IT YOURSELF

**A Function to Output
User Messages**

continued

The complete listing is shown in Listing 3.2.

LISTING 3.2   Calling a Function with Multiple Arguments

```
<!DOCTYPE html>
<html>
<head>
    <title>Calling Functions</title>
    <script>
        function buttonReport(buttonId, buttonName, buttonValue) {
            // information about the id of the button
            var userMessage1 = "Button id: " + buttonId + "\n";
            // then about the button name
            var userMessage2 = "Button name: " + buttonName + "\n";
            // and the button value
            var userMessage3 = "Button value: " + buttonValue;
            // alert the user
            alert(userMessage1 + userMessage2 + userMessage3);
        }
    </script>
</head>
<body>
    <input type="button" id="id1" name="Left Hand Button" value="Left"
➥onclick = "buttonReport(this.id, this.name, this.value)"/>
    <input type="button" id="id2" name="Center Button" value="Center"
➥onclick = "buttonReport(this.id, this.name, this.value)"/>
    <input type="button" id="id3" name="Right Hand Button" value="Right"
➥onclick = "buttonReport(this.id, this.name, this.value)"/>
</body>
</html>
```

Use your editor to create a file buttons.html and enter the preceding code. You
should find that it generates output messages like the one shown in Figure
3.2, but with different message content depending on which button has been
clicked.

TRY IT YOURSELF ▼

A Function to Output User Messages

continued

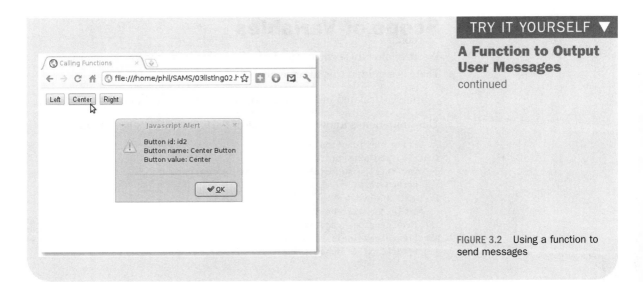

FIGURE 3.2   Using a function to send messages

Returning Values from Functions

Okay, now you know how to pass information to functions so that they can act on that information for you. But how can you get information back from your function? You won't always want your functions to be limited to popping open a dialog box!

Luckily, there is a mechanism to collect data from a function call—the *return value*. Let's see how it works:

```
function cube(x) {
    return x * x * x;
}
```

Instead of using an alert() dialog within the function, as in the previous example, this time we prefixed our required result with the return keyword. To access this value from outside the function, we simply assign to a variable the value *returned* by the function:

```
var answer = cube(3);
```

The variable answer will now contain the value 27.

NOTE

The values returned by functions are not restricted to numerical quantities as in this example. In fact, functions can return values having any of the data types supported by JavaScript. We discuss data types in Hour 5.

TIP

Where a function returns a value, we can use the function call to pass the return value directly to another statement in our code. For example, instead of

```
var answer = cube(3);
alert(answer);
```

we could simply use

```
alert(cube(3));
```

The value of 27 returned from the function call cube(3) immediately becomes the argument passed to the alert() method.

Scope of Variables

We have already seen how to declare variables with the var keyword. There is a golden rule to remember when using functions:

"Variables declared inside a function only exist inside that function."

This limitation is known as the *scope* of the variable. Let's see an example:

```
// Define our function addTax()
function addTax(subtotal, taxRate) {
    var total = subtotal * (1 + (taxRate/100));
    return total;
}
// now let's call the function
var invoiceValue = addTax(50, 10);
alert(invoiceValue); // works correctly
alert(total);  // doesn't work
```

If we run this code, we first see an alert() dialog with the value of the variable invoiceValue (which should be 55 but in fact will probably be something like 55.000000001 as we have not asked JavaScript to round the result).

We will not, however, then see an alert() dialog containing the value of the variable total. Instead, JavaScript simply produces an error. Whether you see this error reported depends on your browser settings—we learn more about error handling later in the book—but JavaScript will be unable to display an alert() dialog with the value of your variable total.

This is because we placed the declaration of the variable total *inside* the addTax() function. Outside the function the variable total simply doesn't exist (or, as JavaScript puts it, "is not defined"). We used the return keyword to pass back just the *value* stored in the variable total, and that value we then stored in another variable, invoice.

We refer to variables declared inside a function definition as being *local* variables, that is, *local to that function*. Variables declared outside any function are known as *global* variables. To add a little more confusion, local and global variables can have the same name, but still be different variables!

The range of situations where a variable is defined is known as the *scope* of the variable—we can refer to a variable as having *local scope* or *global scope*.

To illustrate the issue of a variable's scope, take a look at the following piece of code:

```
var a = 10;
var b = 10;
function showVars() {
    var a = 20; // declare a new local variable 'a'
    b = 20;     // change the value of global variable 'b'
    return "Local variable 'a' = " + a + "\nGlobal variable 'b' = " + b;
}
var message = showVars();
alert(message + "\nGlobal variable 'a' = " + a);
```

Within the showVars() function we manipulate two variables, a and b. The variable a we define inside the function; this is a local variable that only exists inside the function, quite separate from the global variable (also called a) that we declare at the very beginning of the script.

The variable b is not declared inside the function, but outside; it is a *global* variable.

Listing 3.3 shows the preceding code within an HTML page.

LISTING 3.3   Global and Local Scope

```
<!DOCTYPE html>
<html>
<head>
    <title>Variable Scope</title>
</head>
<body>
    <script>
        var a = 10;
        var b = 10;
        function showVars() {
            var a = 20; // declare a new local variable 'a'
            b = 20;     // change the value of global variable 'b'
            return "Local variable 'a' = " + a + "\nGlobal variable 'b' =
➥" + b;
        }
        var message = showVars();
        alert(message + "\nGlobal variable 'a' = " + a);
    </script>
</body>
</html>
```

When the page is loaded, showVars() returns a message string containing information about the updated values of the two variables a and b, as they exist inside the function—a with local scope, and b with global scope.

▼ TRY IT YOURSELF

Demonstrating the Scope of Variables
continued

A message about the current value of the other, *global* variable a is then appended to the message, and the message displayed to the user.

Copy the code into a file scope.html and load it into your browser. Compare your results with Figure 3.3.

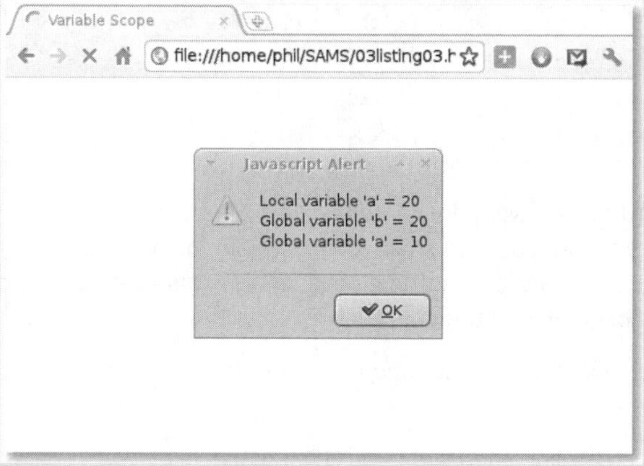

FIGURE 3.3
Local and global scope

Summary

In this hour you learned about what functions are and how to create them in JavaScript. You learned how to call functions from within your code and pass information to those functions in the form of arguments. You also found out how to return information from a function to its calling statement.

Finally, you learned about the local or global scope of a variable and how the scope of variables affects how functions work with them.

Q&A

Q. Can one function contain a call to another function?

A. Most definitely; in fact, such calls can be nested as deeply as you need them to be.

Q. What characters can I use in function names?

A. Function names must start with a letter or an underscore and can contain letters, digits, and underscores in any combination. They cannot contain spaces, punctuation, or other special characters.

Workshop

Try to answer all the questions before reading the subsequent "Answers" section.

Quiz

1. Functions are called using

   a. The function keyword

   b. The `call` command

   c. The function name, with parentheses

2. What happens when a function executes a return statement?

   a. An error message is generated.

   b. A value is returned and function execution continues.

   c. A value is returned and function execution stops.

3. A variable declared inside a function definition is called

   a. A local variable

   b. A global variable

   c. An argument

Answers

1. c. A function is called using the function name.

2. c. After executing a return statement, a function returns a value and then ceases function execution.

3. a. A variable defined within a function has local scope.

Exercises

Write a function to take a temperature value in Celsius as an argument and return the equivalent temperature in Fahrenheit, basing it on the code from Hour 2.

Test your function in an HTML page.

DOM Objects and Built-In Objects

In Hour 1, "Introducing JavaScript," we talked a little about the DOM and introduced the top level object in the DOM tree, the window object. We also looked at one of its child objects, document.

In this hour, we introduce some more of the utility objects and methods that you can use in your scripts.

Interacting with the User

Among the methods belonging to the window object, there are some designed specifically to help your page communicate with the user by assisting with the input and output of information.

alert()

You've already used the alert() method to pop up an information dialog for the user. You'll recall that this modal dialog simply shows your message with a single OK button. The term *modal* means that script execution pauses and all user interaction with the page is suspended until the user clears the dialog. The alert() method takes a message string as its argument:

```
alert("This is my message");
```

alert() does not return a value.

confirm()

The confirm() method is similar to alert(), in that it pops up a modal dialog with a message for the user. The confirm() dialog, though, provides the user with a choice; instead of a single OK button, the user may select between OK and Cancel, as shown in Figure 4.1. Clicking either button clears the dialog and allows the calling script to continue, but the confirm() method returns a different value depending on which button was clicked—Boolean true in the case of OK, or false in the case of Cancel. We look at JavaScript's data types in the next hour, but for the moment you just need to know that a Boolean variable can only take one of two values, *true* or *false*.

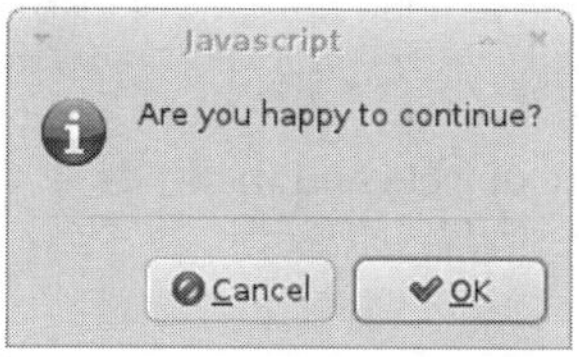

FIGURE 4.1
The confirm() dialog

The confirm() method is called in a similar way to alert(), passing the required message as an argument:

```
var answer = confirm("Are you happy to continue?");
```

Note that here, though, we pass the returned value of true or false to a variable so we can later test its value and have our script take appropriate action depending on the result.

prompt()

The prompt() method is yet another way to open up a modal dialog. In this case, though, the dialog invites the user to enter information.

A prompt() dialog is called in just the same manner as confirm():

```
var answer = prompt("What is your full name?");
```

The prompt method also allows for an optional second argument, giving a default response in case the user clicks OK without typing anything:

```
var answer = prompt("What is your full name?", "John Doe");
```

The return value from a `prompt()` dialog depends on what option the user takes.

NOTE

The `null` value is used by JavaScript on certain occasions to denote an empty value. When treated as a number it takes the value 0, when used as a string it evaluates to the empty string `""`, and when used as a Boolean value it becomes *false*.

▶ If the user types in input and clicks OK or presses Enter, the user input string is returned.

▶ If the user clicks OK or presses Enter without typing anything into the prompt dialog, the method returns the default response (if any), as optionally specified in the second argument passed to `prompt()`.

▶ If the user dismisses the dialog box (e.g., by clicking Cancel or pressing Escape), then the prompt method returns *null*.

The `prompt()` dialog generated by the previous code snippet is shown in Figure 4.2.

FIGURE 4.2
The `prompt()` dialog

Selecting Elements by Their `id`

In Part III, "Working with the Document Object Model (DOM)," you learn a lot about navigating around the DOM using the various methods of the document object. For now, we limit ourselves to looking at one in particular—the `getElementById()` method.

To select an element of your HTML page having a specific `id`, all you need to do is call the `document` object's `getElementById()` method, specifying as an argument the id of the required element. The method returns the DOM object corresponding to the page element with the specified `id`.

Let's look at an example. Suppose your web page contains a `<div>` element:

```
<div id="div1">
    ... Content of DIV element ...
</div>
```

In your JavaScript code, you can access this `<div>` element using `getElementById()`, passing the required `id` to the method as an argument:

```
var myDiv = document.getElementById("div1");
```

We now have access to the chosen page element and all of its properties and methods.

The `innerHTML` Property

A handy property that exists for many DOM objects, `innerHTML` allows us to get or set the value of the HTML content inside a particular page element. Imagine your HTML contains the following element:

```
<div id="div1">
    <p>Here is some original text.</p>
</div>
```

We can access the HTML content of the `<div>` element using a combination of `getElementById()` and `innerHTML`:

```
var myDivContents = document.getElementById("div1").innerHTML;
```

Variable `myDivContents` will now contain the string value:

```
"<p>Here is some original text.</p>"
```

We can also use `innerHTML` to *set* the contents of a chosen element:

```
document.getElementById("div1").innerHTML =
    "<p>Here is some new text instead!</p>";
```

Executing this code snippet erases the previous HTML content of the `<div>` element and replaces it with the new string.

Accessing Browser History

The browser's history is represented in JavaScript by the `window.history` object, which is essentially a list of the URLs previously visited. Its methods enable you to use the list, but not to manipulate the URLs explicitly.

The only property owned by the history object is its length. You can use this property to find how many pages the user has visited:

```
alert("You've visited " + history.length + " web pages in this browser
➥session");
```

The `history` object has three methods.

`forward()` and `back()` are equivalent to pressing the Forward and Back buttons on the browser; they take the user to the next or previous page in the history list.

```
history.next();
```

There is also a method, go, which takes a single parameter. This can be an integer, positive or negative, and if so, it takes the user to a relative place in the history list:

```
history.go(-3);  // go back 3 pages
history.go(2);   // go forward 2 pages
```

The method can alternatively accept a string, which it uses to find the first matching URL in the history list:

```
history.go("example.com");  // go to the nearest URL in the history
                 // list that contains 'example.com'
```

Using the `location` Object

The `location` object contains information about the URL of the currently loaded page.

We can think of the page URL as a series of parts:

[protocol]//[hostname]:[port]/[pathname][search][hash]

Here's an example URL:

http://www.example.com:8080/tools/display.php?section=435#list

The list of properties of the `location` object include data concerning the various parts of the URL. The properties are listed in Table 4.1.

TABLE 4.1   Properties of the `location` Object

Property	Description
`location.href`	'http://www.example.com:8080/tools/display.php? section=435#list'
`location.protocol`	'http:'
`location.host`	'www.example.com:8080'
`location.hostname`	'www.example.com'
`location.port`	'8080'

TABLE 4.1   Continued

Property	Description
location.pathname	'/tools/display.php'
location.search	'?section=435'
location.hash	'#list'

Navigating Using the location Object

There are two ways to take the user to a new page using the location object.

First, we can directly set the href property of the object:

```
location.href = 'www.newpage.com';
```

Using this technique to transport the user to a new page maintains the original page in the browser's history list, so the user can return simply by using the browser Back button. If you would rather the sending page were removed from the history list and replaced with the new URL, we can instead use the location object's replace() method:

```
location.replace('www.newpage.com');
```

This replaces the old URL with the new one both in the browser and in the history list.

Reloading the Page

To reload the current page into the browser—the equivalent to having the user click the "reload page" button—we can use the reload() method:

```
location.reload();
```

TIP
Using reload() without any arguments retrieves the current page from the browser's cache if it's available there. To avoid this and get the page directly from the server, you can call reload with the argument true:

```
document.reload(true);
```

Browser Information—The navigator Object

While the location object stores information about the current URL loaded in the browser, the navigator object's properties contain data about the browser application itself.

We're going to write a script to allow you to find out what the navigator object knows about your own browsing setup. Use your editor to create a file navigator.html containing the code from Listing 4.1. Save the file and open it in your browser.

LISTING 4.1   Using the navigator Object

```html
<!DOCTYPE html>
<html>
<head>
    <title>window.navigator</title>
    <style>
        td {border: 1px solid gray; padding: 3px 5px;}
    </style>
</head>
<body>
    <script>
        document.write("<table>");
        document.write("<tr><td>appName</td><td>"+navigator.appName +
"</td></tr>");

document.write("<tr><td>appCodeName</td><td>"+navigator.appCodeName +
"</td></tr>");
        document.write("<tr><td>appVersion</td><td>"+navigator.appVersion
+ "</td></tr>");
        document.write("<tr><td>language</td><td>"+navigator.language +
"</td></tr>");

document.write("<tr><td>cookieEnabled</td><td>"+navigator.cookieEnabled +
"</td></tr>");
        document.write("<tr><td>cpuClass</td><td>"+navigator.cpuClass +
"</td></tr>");
        document.write("<tr><td>onLine</td><td>"+navigator.onLine +
"</td></tr>");
        document.write("<tr><td>platform</td><td>"+navigator.platform +
"</td></tr>");
        document.write("<tr><td>No of
Plugins</td><td>"+navigator.plugins.length + "</td></tr>");
        document.write("</table>");
    </script>
</body>
</html>
```

Compare your results to ours, shown in Figure 4.3.

▼ TRY IT YOURSELF

**Displaying
Information Using
the navigator
Object**

continued

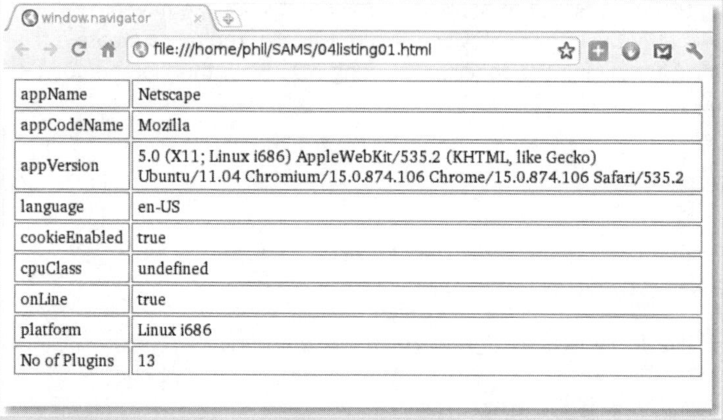

FIGURE 4.3
Browser information from the
navigator object

appName	Netscape
appCodeName	Mozilla
appVersion	5.0 (X11; Linux i686) AppleWebKit/535.2 (KHTML, like Gecko) Ubuntu/11.04 Chromium/15.0.874.106 Chrome/15.0.874.106 Safari/535.2
language	en-US
cookieEnabled	true
cpuClass	undefined
onLine	true
platform	Linux i686
No of Plugins	13

Whoa, what's going on here? We loaded the page into the Chromium browser on our Ubuntu Linux PC. Why is it reporting the `appName` property as Netscape, and the `appCodeName` property as Mozilla? Also, the `cpuClass` property has come back as `undefined`; what's that all about?

There's a lot of history and politics behind the `navigator` object. The result is that the object provides, at best, an unreliable source of information about the user's platform. Not all properties are supported in all browsers (hence the failure to report the `cpuClass` property in the example), and the names reported for browser type and version rarely match what one would intuitively expect. Figure 4.4 shows the same page loaded into Internet Explorer 9 on Windows 7.

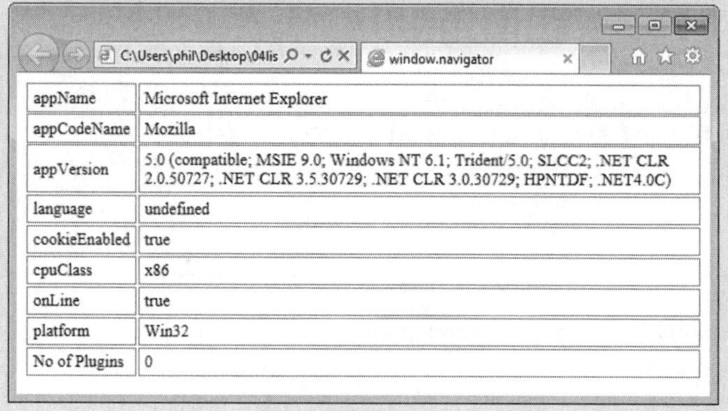

FIGURE 4.4
Browser information from the
navigator object

appName	Microsoft Internet Explorer
appCodeName	Mozilla
appVersion	5.0 (compatible; MSIE 9.0; Windows NT 6.1; Trident/5.0; SLCC2; .NET CLR 2.0.50727; .NET CLR 3.5.30729; .NET CLR 3.0.30729; HPNTDF; .NET4.0C)
language	undefined
cookieEnabled	true
cpuClass	x86
onLine	true
platform	Win32
No of Plugins	0

TRY IT YOURSELF ▼
Displaying Information Using the navigator Object
continued

We now have a value for `cpuClass`, but the `language` property is not supported in Internet Explorer and has returned `undefined`.

Although cross-browser standards compliance is closer than it was a few years ago, there still remain occasions when you need to know the capabilities of your user's browser. Querying the `navigator` object is nearly always the *wrong* way to do it.

NOTE

Later in the book we talk about *feature detection*, a much more elegant and cross-browser way to have your code make decisions based on the capabilities of the user's browser.

Dates and Times

The `Date` object is used to work with dates and times. There is no `Date` object already created for you as part of the DOM, as was the case with the examples so far. Instead, we create our own `Date` objects as and when we need them. Each `Date` object we create can represent a different date and time.

Create a `Date` Object with Current Date and Time

The simplest way to create a new date object containing information about the date and time is

```
var mydate = new Date();
```

Variable `mydate` is an object containing information about the date and time at the moment the object was created. JavaScript has a long list of methods for retrieving, setting, and editing data within `Date` objects. Let's look at a few simple examples:

```
var year = mydate.getFullYear(); // four-digit year e.g. 2012
var month = mydate.getMonth(); // month number 0 - 11; 0 is Jan, etc.
var date = mydate.getDate(); // day of the month 1 - 31
var day = mydate.getDay(); // day of the week 0 - 6; Sunday = 0, etc.
var hours = mydate.getHours(); // hours part of the time, 0 - 23
var minutes = mydate.getMinutes(); // minutes part of time, 0 - 59
var seconds = mydate.getSeconds(); // minutes part of time, 0 - 59
```

Creating a `Date` Object with a Given Date and Time

We can easily create `Date` objects representing arbitrary dates and times by passing arguments to the `Date()` statement. There are several ways to do this:

```
new Date(milliseconds) //milliseconds since January 1st 1970
new Date(dateString)
new Date(year, month, day, hours, minutes, seconds, milliseconds)
```

Here are a few examples.

Using a date string:

```
var d1 = new Date("October 22, 1995 10:57:22")
```

When using separate arguments for the parts, trailing arguments are optional; any missing will be replaced with zero:

```
var d2 = new Date(95,9,22) // 22nd October 1995 00:00:00
var d3 = new Date(95,9,22,10,57,0)  // 22nd October 1995 10:57:00
```

Setting and Editing Dates and Times

The `Date` object also has an extensive list of methods for setting or editing the various parts of the date and time.

```
var mydate = new Date();  // current date and time
document.write( "Object created on day number " + mydate.getDay() +
➥"<br />");
mydate.setDate(15);     // change day of month to the 15th
document.write("After amending date to 15th, the day number is " +
➥mydate.getDay());
```

In the preceding code snippet, we initially created an object `mydate` representing the date and time of its creation, but with the day of the month subsequently changed to the 15th; if we retrieve the day of the week before and after this operation, we'll see that it has been correctly recalculated to take account of the changed date:

```
Object created on day number 5
After amending date to 15th, the day number is 0
```

So in this example, the object was created on a Friday; whereas the 15th of the month corresponded to a Sunday.

We can also carry out date and time arithmetic, letting the `Date` object do all the heavy lifting for us:

```
var mydate=new Date();
document.write("Created: " + mydate.toDateString() + " " +
mydate.toTimeString() + "<br />");
mydate.setDate(mydate.getDate()+33); // add 33 days to the 'date' part
document.write("After adding 33 days: " + mydate.toDateString() + " " +
mydate.toTimeString());
```

The preceding example calculates a date 33 days in the future, automatically amending the day, date, month, and/or year as necessary. Note the use of toDateString() and toTimeString(); these are useful methods for converting dates into a readable format. The preceding example produces output like the following:

```
Created: Fri Jan 06 2012 14:59:24 GMT+0100 (CET)
After adding 33 days: Wed Feb 08 2012 14:59:24 GMT+0100 (CET)
```

The set of methods available for manipulating dates and times is way too large for us to explore them all here. A full list of the methods of the Date object is available in Appendix B, "JavaScript Quick Reference."

Simplifying Calculation with the Math Object

JavaScript's Math object can save you a lot of work when performing many sorts of calculations that frequently occur.

Unlike the Date object, the Math object does not need to be created before use; it already exists, and you can call its methods directly.

A full list of the available methods is available in Appendix B, but Table 4.2 shows some examples.

TABLE 4.2   Some Methods of the Math Object

Method	Description
ceil(n)	Returns n rounded up to the nearest whole number
floor(n)	Returns n rounded down to the nearest whole number
max(a,b,c,...)	Returns the largest number
min(a,b,c,...)	Returns the smallest number
round(n)	Returns n rounded up or down to the nearest whole number
random()	Returns a random number between 0 and 1

Let's work through some examples.

Rounding

The methods `ceil()`, `floor()`, and `round()` are useful for truncating the decimal parts of numbers:

```
var myNum1 = 12.55;
var myNum2 = 12.45;
alert(Math.floor(myNum1));  // shows 12
alert(Math.ceil(myNum1));   // shows 13
alert(Math.round(myNum1));  // shows 13
alert(Math.round(myNum2));  // shows 12
```

Note that when using `round()`, if the fractional part of the number is .5 or greater, the number is rounded to the next highest integer. If the fractional part is less than .5, the number is rounded to the next lowest integer.

Finding Minimum and Maximum

We can use `min()` and `max()` to pick the largest and smallest number from a list:

```
var ageDavid = 23;
var ageMary = 27;
var ageChris = 31;
var ageSandy = 19;
document.write("The youngest person is "
    + Math.min(ageDavid, ageMary, ageChris, ageSandy)
    + " years old<br />");
document.write("The oldest person is "
    + Math.max(ageDavid, ageMary, ageChris, ageSandy)
    + " years old<br />");
```

The output as written to the page looks like this:

```
The youngest person is 19 years old
The oldest person is 31 years old
```

Random Numbers

To generate a random number, we can use `Math.random()`, which generates a random number between 0 and 1.

Normally we like to specify the possible range of our random numbers; for example, we might want to generate a random integer between 0 and 100.

As `Math.random()` generates a random number between 0 and 1, it's helpful to wrap it in a small function that suits our needs. The following function takes the `Math` object's randomly generated number, scales it up by multiplying by variable range (passed to the function as an argument), and finally uses round() to remove any fractional part.

```
function myRand(range) {
    return Math.round(Math.random() * range);
}
```

To generate a random integer between 0 and 100, we can then simply call

```
myRand(100);
```

Mathematical Constants

Various often-used mathematical constants are available as properties of Math. They are listed in Table 4.2

TABLE 4.2   Mathematical Constants

Constant	Description
E	Base of natural logs, approx 2.718.
LN2	Natural log of 2, approx 0.693.
LN10	Natural log of 10, approx 2.302.
LOG2E	Base 2 log of E, approx 1.442.
LOG10E	Base 10 log of E, approx 0.434.
PI	Approx 3.14159.
SQRT1_2	1 over the square root of 2, approx 0.707.
SQRT2	Square root of 2, approx 1.414.

These constants can be used directly in your calculations:

```
var area = Math.PI * radius * radius;   // area of circle
var circumference = 2 * Math.PI * radius;   // circumference
```

The with Keyword

Although you can use the with keyword with any object, the Math object is an ideal object to use an example. By using with you can save yourself some tedious typing.

The keyword with takes an object as an argument and is followed by a code block wrapped in braces. The statements within that code block can call methods without specifying an object, and JavaScript assumes that those methods belong to the object passed as an argument.

CAUTION

You always use Math methods directly, for example, Math.floor(), rather than as a method of an object you created. In other words, the following is wrong:

```
var myNum = 24.77;
myNum.floor();
```

The code would provoke a JavaScript error.

Instead you simply need

```
Math.floor(myNum);
```

Here's an example:

```
with (Math) {
    var myRand = random();
    var biggest = max(3,4,5);
    var height = round(76.35);
}
```

In this example, we call `Math.random()`, `Math.max()`, and `Math.round()` simply by using the method names because all method calls in the code block have been associated with the `Math` object.

▼ TRY IT YOURSELF

Reading the Date and Time

We put into practice some of what we covered in this hour by creating a script to get the current day and date when the page is loaded. We also implement a button to reload the page, refreshing the time and date information.

Take a look at Listing 4.2.

LISTING 4.2   Getting Date and Time Information

```
<!DOCTYPE html>
<html>
<head>
    <title>Current Date and Time</title>
    <style>
        p {font: 14px normal arial, verdana, helvetica;}
    </style>
    <script>
        function telltime() {
            var out = "";
            var now = new Date();
            out += "<br />Date: " + now.getDate();
            out += "<br />Month: " + now.getMonth();
            out += "<br />Year: " + now.getFullYear();
            out += "<br />Hours: " + now.getHours();
            out += "<br />Minutes: " + now.getMinutes();
            out += "<br />Seconds: " + now.getSeconds();
            document.getElementById("div1").innerHTML = out;
        }
    </script>
</head>
<body>
    The current date and time are:<br/>
    <div id="div1"></div>
    <script>
        telltime();
```

TRY IT YOURSELF ▼

**Reading the Date
and Time**
continued

```
        </script>
        <input type="button" onclick="location.reload()" value="Refresh" />
    </body>
</html>
```

The first statement in the function `telltime()` creates a new `Date` object
called now. As you will recall, because the object is created without passing
any parameters to `Date()`, it will have properties pertaining to the current
date and time at the moment of its creation.

```
var now = new Date();
```

We can access the individual parts of the time and date using `getDate()`,
`getMonth()`, and similar methods. As we do so, we assemble the output
message as a string stored in a variable out.

```
out += "<br />Date: " + now.getDate();
out += "<br />Month: " + now.getMonth();
out += "<br />Year: " + now.getFullYear();
out += "<br />Hours: " + now.getHours();
out += "<br />Minutes: " + now.getMinutes();
out += "<br />Seconds: " + now.getSeconds();
```

Finally, we use `getElementById()` to select the (initially empty) `<div>` element having `id="div1"` and write the contents of variable out into it using
the `innerHTML` method.

```
document.getElementById("div1").innerHTML = out;
```

The function `telltime()` is called by a small script embedded in the `<body>`
part of the page:

```
<script>
    telltime();
</script>
```

To refresh the date and time information, we simply need to reload the page
into the browser. At that point the script runs again, creating a new instance
of the `Date` object with the current date and time. We could just hit Refresh
on the browser's menu, but because we know how to reload the page using
the `location` object, we do that by calling

```
location.reload()
```

from a button's `onClick` method.

▼ TRY IT YOURSELF

Reading The Date and Time
continued

Figure 4.5 shows the script in action. Note that the month is displayed as 0—remember that JavaScript counts months starting at 0 (January) and ending in 11 (December).

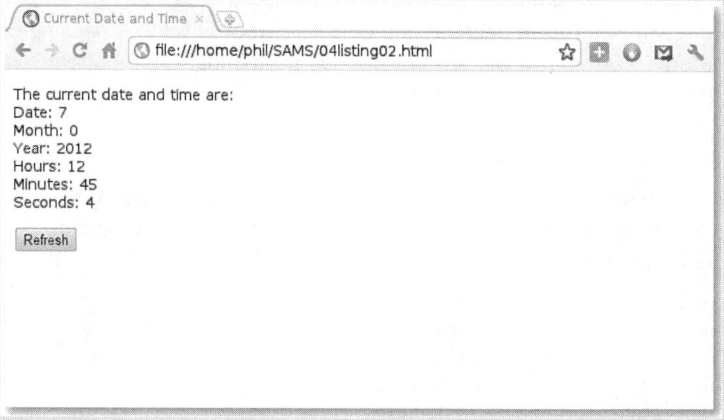
Current Date and Time
file:///home/phil/SAMS/04listing02.html
The current date and time are:
Date: 7
Month: 0
Year: 2012
Hours: 12
Minutes: 45
Seconds: 4
Refresh

FIGURE 4.5
Getting date and time information

Summary

In this hour you looked at some useful objects either built into JavaScript or available via the DOM and how their properties and methods can help you write code more easily.

You saw how to use the `window` object's modal dialogs to exchange information with the user.

You learned how to select page elements by their `id` using the `document.getElementById` method, and how to get and set the HTML inside a page element using the `innerHTML` property.

You worked with browser information from the `navigator` object and page URL information from the `location` object.

Finally, you saw how to use the `Date` and `Math` objects.

Q&A

Q. Does `Date()` have methods to deal with time zones?

A. Yes, it does. In addition to the `get...()` and `set...()` methods discussed in this hour (such as `getDate()`, `setMonth()`, etc.) there are UTC (Universal Time, previously called GMT) versions of the same methods (`getUTCDate()`, `setUTCMonth()`, and so on). You can retrieve the difference between your local time and UTC time by using the `getTimezoneOffset()` method. See Appendix B for a full list of methods.

Q. Why does `Date()` have the methods called `getFullYear()` and `setFullYear()` instead of just `getYear()` and `setYear()`?

A. The methods `getYear()` and `setYear()` do exist; they deal with 2-digit years instead of the 4-digit years used by `getFullYear()` and `setFullYear()`. Because of the potential problems with dates spanning the millennium, these functions have been deprecated. You should use `getFullYear()` and `setFullYear()` instead.

Workshop

Try to answer all the questions before reading the subsequent "Answers" section.

Quiz

1. What happens when a user clicks OK in a confirm dialog?

    a. A value of true is returned to the calling program.

    b. The displayed message is returned to the calling program.

    c. Nothing.

2. Which method of the `Math()` object always rounds a number up to the next integer?

    a. `Math.round()`

    b. `Math.floor()`

    c. `Math.ceil()`

3. If my loaded page is http://www.example.com/documents/letter.
htm?page=2, what will the `location.pathname` property of the location
object contain?

    a. `http`

    b. `www.example.com`

    c. `/documents/letter.htm`

    d. `page=2`

Answers

1. a. A value of true is returned when OK is clicked. The dialog box is
cleared, and control is returned to the calling program.

2. c. `Math.ceil()` always rounds a number up to the next higher integer.

3. c. The `location.pathname` property contains `/documents/`
`letter.htm`.

Exercises

Modify Listing 4.3 to output the date and time as a single string, such as:

25 Dec 2011 12:35

Use the `Math` object to write a function to return the volume of a round chim-
ney, given its radius and height in meters as arguments. The volume returned
should be rounded up to the nearest cubic meter.

Use the `history` object to create a few pages with their own Forward and
Back buttons. After you've navigated to these pages (to put them in your
browser's history list), do your Forward and Back buttons operate exactly like
the browser's?

Different Types of Data

We use the term *data type* to talk about the nature of the data that a variable contains. A string variable contains a string, a number variable a numerical value, and so forth. However, the JavaScript language is what's called a *loosely typed* language, meaning that JavaScript variables can be interpreted as different data types in differing circumstances.

In JavaScript, you don't have to declare the data type of a variable before using it, as the JavaScript interpreter will make its best guess. If you put a string into your variable and later want to interpret that value as a number, that's okay with JavaScript, provided that the variable actually contains a string that's "like" a numerical value (e.g., "200px" or "50 cents" but not something such as your name). Later you can use it as a string again if you want.

In this hour you learn about the JavaScript data types of number, string, and Boolean, and about some built-in methods for handling values of these types. We also mention *escape sequences* in strings and two special JavaScript data types—*null* and *undefined*. You also learn about one of JavaScript's most powerful and useful data constructs, the *array* object.

Numbers

Mathematicians have all sorts of names for different types of numbers. From the so-called *natural numbers* 1, 2, 3, 4 ... you can add 0 to get the *whole numbers* 0, 1, 2, 3, 4 ..., and then include the negative values -1, -2, -3, -4 ... to form the set of *integers*.

WHAT YOU'LL LEARN IN THIS HOUR

- About the various data types supported by JavaScript
- Conversion between data types
- How to manipulate strings
- How to declare and populate arrays
- Managing array contents

To express numbers falling between the integers, we commonly use a decimal point with one or more digits following it:

3.141592654

Calling such numbers *floating-point* indicates that they can have an arbitrary number of digits before and after the decimal point, that is, the decimal point can "float" to any location in the number.

JavaScript supports both integer and floating-point numbers.

Integers

An integer is a whole number—positive, negative, or zero. To put it another way, an integer is any numerical value without a fractional part.

All of the following are valid integers:

- ▶ 33
- ▶ -1,000,000
- ▶ 0
- ▶ -1

Floating-Point Numbers

Unlike integers, floating-point numbers have a fractional part, even if that fractional part is zero. They can be represented in the traditional way, like 3.14159, or in exponential notation, like 35.4e5.

All the following are valid floating-point numbers:

- ▶ 3.0
- ▶ 0.00001
- ▶ -99.99
- ▶ 2.5e12
- ▶ 1e-12

Not a Number (NaN)

NaN is the value returned when your script tries to treat something non-numerical as a number but can't make any sense of it as a numerical value. For instance the result of trying to multiply a string by an integer is not numerical. You can test for non-numerical values with the isNaN() function:

```
isNaN(3);       // returns false
isNaN(3.14159);    // returns false
isNaN("horse");    // returns true;
```

Using parseFloat() and parseInt()

JavaScript offers us two functions with which we can force the conversion of a string into a number format.

The parseFloat() function parses a string and returns a floating-point number.

If the first character in the specified string is a number, it parses the string until it reaches the end of that number and returns the value as a number, not a string:

```
parseFloat("21.4") // returns 21.4
parseFloat("76 trombones") // returns 76
parseFloat("The magnificent 7") // returns NaN
```

Using parseInt() is similar but returns either an integer value or NaN. This function allows us to optionally include as a second argument, the base (radix) of the number system we're using, and can therefore be used to return the base 10 values of binary, octal, or other number formats:

```
parseInt(18.95, 10); // returns 18
parseInt("12px", 10); // returns 12
parseInt("1110", 2); // returns 14
parseInt("Hello") // returns NaN
```

Infinity

Infinity is a value larger than the largest number that JavaScript can represent. In most JavaScript implementations, this is an integer of plus or minus 2^{53}. Okay, that's not quite infinity, but it is pretty big.

There is also the keyword literal -Infinity to signify the negative infinity.

You can test for infinite values with the isFinite() function. The isFinite() function takes the value to test as an argument and tries to convert that argument into a number. If the result is NaN, positive infinity (Infinity) or negative infinity (-Infinity), the isFinite() function returns *false*; otherwise it returns *true*. (False and true are known as Boolean values, discussed later in this hour.)

```
isFinite(21); // true
isFinite("This is not a numeric value"); // false
isFinite(Math.sqrt(-1)); // false
```

Strings

A string is a sequence of characters from within a given character set (e.g., the ASCII or Unicode character sets) and is usually used to store text.

You define a string by enclosing it in single or double quotes:

```
var myString = "This is a string";
```

You can define an empty string by using two quote marks with nothing between them:

```
var myString = "";
```

Escape Sequences

Some characters that you want to put in a string may not have associated keys on the keyboard or may be special characters that for other reasons can't occur in a string. Examples include the tab character, the new line character, and the single or double quote that encloses the string itself. To use such a character in a string, it must be represented by a character preceded by a backslash (\ ), a combination that JavaScript interprets as the desired special character. Such a combination is known as an *escape sequence*.

Suppose that you wanted to enter some "new line" characters into a string so that when the string is shown by a call to the alert() method, it will be split into several lines:

```
var message = "IMPORTANT MESSAGE:\n\nError detected!\nPlease check your
➥data";
alert(message);
```

The result of inserting these escape sequences is shown in Figure 5.1

The more common escape sequences are shown in Table 5.1.

FIGURE 5.1
Using escape sequences in a string

TABLE 5.1   Some Common Escape Sequences

Escape Sequence	Character
\t	Tab
\n	New line; inserts a line break at the point where it appears in the string
\"	Double quote
\'	Single quote or apostrophe
\\	The backslash itself
\x99	2-digit number specifying the hexadecimal value of an ASCII character
\u9999	4-digit hexadecimal number specifying a Unicode character

String Methods

A full list of the properties and methods of the string object is given in Appendix B, "JavaScript Quick Reference," but for now let's look at some of the important ones, listed in Table 5.2.

TABLE 5.2   Some Popular Methods of the string Object

Method	Description
concat	Joins strings and returns a copy of the joined string
indexOf	Returns the position of the first occurrence of a specified value in a string
lastIndexOf	Returns the position of the last occurrence of a specified value in a string
replace	Searches for a match between a substring and a string and replaces the substring with a new substring
split	Split a string into an array of substrings and returns the new array

TABLE 5.2   Continued

Method	Description
substr	Extracts a substring from a string, beginning at a specified start position, and through the specified number of character
toLowerCase	Converts a string to lowercase letters
toUpperCase	Converts a string to uppercase letters

concat()

You've already had experience in earlier hours of joining strings together using the + operator. This is known as string concatenation, and JavaScript strings have a concat() method offering additional capabilities:

```
var string1 = "The quick brown fox ";
var string2 = "jumps over the lazy dog";
var longString = string1.concat(string2);
```

indexOf()

TIP

Remember that the index of the first character in a string is 0, not 1.

We can use indexOf() to find the first place where a particular substring of one or more characters occurs in a string. The method returns the index (the position) of the searched-for substring, or -1 if it isn't found anywhere in the string:

```
var string1 = "The quick brown fox ";
string1.indexOf('fox') // returns 16
string1.indexOf('dog') // returns -1
```

lastIndexOf()

As you'll have guessed, lastIndexOf() works just the same way as indexOf() but finds the last occurrence of the substring, rather than the first.

replace()

Searches for a match between a substring and a string and replaces the substring with a new substring:

```
var string1 = "The quick brown fox ";
string1.replace("brown", "orange"); // string1 is now "the quick orange
➥fox"
```

split()

Used to split a string into an array of substrings and return the new array:

```
var string1 = "The quick brown fox ";
var newArray = string1.split(" ")
```

substr()

The substr() method takes one or two arguments.

The first is the starting index—substr() extracts the characters from a string, beginning at the starting index, for the specified number of characters, returning the new substring. The second parameter (number of characters) is optional, and if omitted, all of the remaining string will be extracted:

```
var string1 = "The quick brown fox ";
var sub1 = string1.substr(4, 11); // extracts "quick brown"
var sub2 = string1.substr(4); // extracts "quick brown fox"
```

toLowerCase() **and** toUpperCase()

Puts the string into all uppercase or all lowercase:

```
var string1 = "The quick brown fox ";
var sub1 = string1.toLowerCase(); // sub1 contains "the quick brown fox "
var sub2 = string1.toUpperCase(); // sub2 contains "THE QUICK BROWN FOX "
```

TIP

You learn about arrays later in this hour. Make a note to refer back to this method after you've read the section on arrays.

Boolean Values

Data of Boolean type can have one of only two values, *true* or *false*. Boolean variables are most often used to store the result of a logical operation in your code that returns a true/false or yes/no result:

```
var answer = confirm("Do you want to continue?"); // answer will contain
➥true or false
```

If you write code that expects Boolean values in computations, JavaScript automatically converts true to 1 and false to 0.

```
var answer = confirm("Do you want to continue?"); // answer will contain
➥true or false
alert(answer * 1); // will display either 0 or 1
```

CAUTION

When you want to assign a Boolean value of true or false, it's important to remember *not* to enclose the value in quotes, or the value will be interpreted as a string literal:

```
var success = false;   //
correct
var success = "false"; //
incorrect
```

It works the other way, too. JavaScript interprets any nonzero value as *true* and zero as *false*. JavaScript interprets all of the following values as false.

- ▶ Boolean false (you don't say?)
- ▶ undefined
- ▶ null
- ▶ 0 (zero)
- ▶ NaN
- ▶ "" (empty string)

The Negation Operator (!)

JavaScript interprets the ! character, when placed before a Boolean variable, as "not," that is, "the opposite value." Take a look at this code snippet:

```
var success = false;
alert(!success);  // alerts 'true'
```

In Hour 6, "Scripts That Do More," we use this and other operators to test the values of JavaScript variables, and have our programs make decisions based on the results.

Arrays

Arrays are a type of object used for storing multiple values in a single variable. Each value has a numeric index that may contain data of any data type—Booleans, numbers, strings, functions, objects, even other arrays.

Creating a New Array

The syntax used for creating an array will already be familiar to you; after all, an array is simply another object:

```
var myArray = new Array();
```

However, for arrays there is a shorthand version—simply use square brackets [] like this:

```
var myArray = [];
```

Initializing an Array

You can optionally preload data into your array at the time it is created:

```
var myArray = ['Monday', 'Tuesday', 'Wednesday'];
```

Alternatively, items can be added after the array has been created:

```
var myArray = [];
myArray[0] = 'Monday';
myArray[1] = 'Tuesday';
myArray[2] = 'Wednesday';
```

`array.length`

All arrays have a `length` property that tells how many items the array contains. The length property is automatically updated when you add or remove items to the array. For the just shown array:

```
myArray.length  // returns 3
```

Array Methods

Table 5.3 contains some of the more commonly used methods of the array object.

TABLE 5.3   Some Useful Array Methods

Method	Description
concat	Joins multiple arrays
join	Joins all the array elements together into a string.
toString	Returns array as a string.
indexOf	Searches the array for specific elements.
lastIndexOf	Returns the last item in the array that matches the search criteria.
slice	Returns a new array from the specified index and length.

CAUTION

The length is always 1 higher than the highest index, even if there are actually fewer items in the array. Suppose we add a new item to the above array:

```
myArray[50] = 'Ice cream day';
```

`myArray.length` now returns 51, even though the array only has 4 entries.

CAUTION

Some of the array methods have the same name—and almost the same function—as string methods of the same name. Be aware of what data type you are working with, or your script might not function as you would like.

TABLE 5.3   Continued

Method	Description
sort	Sorts the array alphabetically or by the supplied function.
splice	Adds or deletes the specified index(es) from/to the array.

concat()

You've already had experience of string concatenation, and JavaScript arrays have a concat() method too:

```
var myOtherArray = ['Thursday','Friday'];
var myWeek = myArray.concat(myOtherArray);
// myWeek will contain 'Monday', 'Tuesday', 'Wednesday', 'Thursday',
➥'Friday'
```

join()

To join all of an array's elements together into a single string, we can use the join() method:

```
var longDay = myArray.join(); // returns MondayTuesdayWednesday
```

Optionally, we can pass a string argument to this method; the passed string will then be inserted as a separator in the returned string:

```
var longDay = myArray.join("-"); // returns Monday-Tuesday-Wednesday
```

toString()

toString() is almost a special case of join()—it returns the array as a string with the elements separated by commas:

```
var longDay = myArray.toString(); // returns Monday,Tuesday,Wednesday
```

indexOf()

We can use indexOf() to find the first place where a particular element occurs in an array. The method returns the index of the searched-for element, or -1 if it isn't found anywhere in the array:

```
myArray.indexOf('Tuesday')  // returns 1 (remember, arrays start with
➥index 0)
myArray.indexOf('Sunday') // returns -1
```

lastIndexOf()

As you might expect, `lastIndexOf()` works just the same way as `indexOf()` but finds the last occurrence in the array of the search term, rather than the first occurrence.

slice()

When we need to create an array that is a subset of our starting array, we can use `slice()`, passing to it the starting index and the number of elements we want to retrieve:

```
var myShortWeek = myWeek.slice(1, 3);
//myShortWeek contains 'Tuesday', 'Wednesday', 'Thursday'
```

sort()

We can use `sort()` to carry out an alphabetical sort:

```
myWeek.sort()  // returns 'Friday', 'Monday', 'Thursday', 'Tuesday',
➥'Wednesday'
```

splice()

To add or delete specific items from the array, we can use `splice()`.

The syntax is a little more complex than that of the previous examples:

```
array.splice(index, howmany, [new elements]);
```

The first element sets the location in the array where we want to perform the splice; the second element, how many items to remove (if set to 0, none are deleted), and thereafter, an optional list of any new elements to be inserted.

```
myWeek.splice(2,1,"holiday")
```

The preceding line of code locates us at item with index 2 ('Wednesday'), removes 1 element ('Wednesday') and inserts a new element ('holiday'); so myWeek now contains 'Monday', 'Tuesday', 'holiday', 'Thursday', 'Friday'. The method returns any removed elements.

CAUTION

Using `splice()` changes the original array! If you need to preserve the array for use elsewhere in your code, copy the array to a new variable before executing `splice()`.

Let's put some of these methods to work. In your text editor, create the script listed in Listing 5.1 and save it as array.html.

LISTING 5.1   Array Manipulation

```html
<!DOCTYPE html>
<html>
<head>
<title>Strings and Arrays</title>
<script>
    function wrangleArray() {
        var sentence = "JavaScript is a really cool language";
        var newSentence = "";
        //Write it out
        document.getElementById("div1").innerHTML = "<p>" + sentence +
"</p>";
        //Convert to an array
        var words = sentence.split(" ");
        // Remove 'really' and 'cool', and add 'powerful' instead
        var message = words.splice(3,2,"powerful");
        // use an alert to say what words were removed
        alert('Removed words: ' + message);
        // Convert the array to a string, and write it out
        document.getElementById("div2").innerHTML = "<p>" + words.join("
") + "</p>";
    }
</script>
</head>
<body>
    <div id="div1"></div>
    <div id="div2"></div>
    <script>wrangleArray();</script>
</body>
</html>
```

As we work through this listing, you may want to refer to the definitions of the individual string and array methods given earlier in the hour and the discussion of getElementById() and innerHTML from Hour 4, "DOM Objects and Built-In Objects."

Stepping through the function wrangleArray(), we first define a string:

```
var sentence = "JavaScript is a really cool language";
```

After writing it out to any empty <div> element using innerHTML, we apply the split() method to the string, passing to it a single space as an argument. The method returns an array of elements, created by splitting the string

TRY IT YOURSELF

Array Manipulation
continued

wherever a space occurs—that is to say, splits it into individual words. We store that array in variable words.

We next apply the splice() array method to the words array, removing two words at array index 3, "really" and "cool". Because the splice() method returns any deleted words, we can display these in an alert() dialog:

```
var message = words.splice(3,2,"powerful");
alert('Removed words: ' + message);
```

Finally, we apply the join() method to the array, once more collapsing it into a string. Because we supply a single space as the argument to join(), the individual words are once more separated by spaces. Finally we output the revised sentence to a second <div> element by using innerHTML.

The wrangleArray() function is called by a small script in the body of the document:

```
<script>wrangleArray();</script>
```

The script operation is shown in Figure 5.2.

FIGURE 5.2
Output from array manipulation script

Summary

In this hour, you learned about the various different data types supported by JavaScript. You also saw some of the methods of JavaScript strings and array objects.

This concludes Hour 5 and also Part I of the book. In this first part you learned a lot about the basics of JavaScript—what it is and where it came from, what sorts of things the language can do, and how to carry out basic tasks such as declaring variables, assigning values, and performing calculations.

You also got your hands dirty with some of JavaScript's built-in objects and some of the DOM objects and carried out some exercises using their properties and methods. In Part II, "More Advanced JavaScript," you learn how you can also create your own objects with their associated properties and write methods to allow those properties to be accessed and manipulated, including a look at the basics of Object Oriented Programming (OOP).

For the sake of clarity, in Part I we used some coding techniques that are perfectly valid and were once common practice in JavaScript but nowadays are not considered "best practice." We go a long way toward correcting that in Part II, as we look at much better techniques for handling events, as well as introductions to other advanced JavaScript techniques involving program flow control, cookies, JSON notation, and more.

Q&A

Q. What is the maximum length of a string in JavaScript?

A. The JavaScript Specification does not specify a maximum string length, rather it will be specific to your browser and operating system. For certain implementations, it will be a function of available memory.

Q. Does JavaScript allow associative arrays?

A. Not directly, but there are ways to simulate their behavior by using objects. You see examples of this later in the book.

Workshop

Try to answer all the questions before reading the subsequent "Answers" section.

Quiz

1. What statement would you use to append one string `string2` to another string `string1`?

    a. `concat(string1) + concat(string2);`

    b. `string1.concat(string2);`

    c. `join(string1, string2);`

2. Which statement sets the value of variable `paid` to Boolean true?

    a. `var paid = true;`

    b. `var paid = "true";`

    c. `var paid.true();`

3. For a string `myString` containing the value "stupid is as stupid does", which of the following would return a value of -1?

    a. `myString.indexOf("stupid");`

    b. `myString.lastIndexOf("stupid");`

    c. `myString.indexOf("is stupid");`

Answers

1. b. `string1.concat(string2);` joins `string2` to the end of `string1`.

2. a. Boolean values should not be enclosed in quotes.

3. c. The substring "is stupid" does not appear in `myString`.

Exercises

Change the script in Listing 5.1 to allow the user to enter a starting string via a `prompt()` dialog. Extend your script to use some of the other string and array functions discussed in this hour.

Review the array and string methods that share a method name. Familiarize yourself with how the syntax and operation changes depending on whether these methods are applied to a string or an array.

PART II
More Advanced JavaScript

Scripts That Do More

In the last hour of Part I you took a quick trip through the data types that JavaScript variables can contain. To create anything but the simplest scripts, though, you're going to need your code to make decisions based on those values. In this hour we examine ways to recognize particular conditions and have our program act in a prescribed way as a result.

You also learn how to use browser-based tools to help debug these more complex JavaScript programs.

WHAT YOU'LL LEARN IN THIS HOUR

▸ Using conditional statements
▸ Comparing values with comparison operators
▸ Applying logical operators
▸ Writing loops and control structures
▸ Debugging your scripts

Conditional Statements

Conditional statements, as the name implies, are used to detect particular conditions arising in the values of the variables you are using in your script. JavaScript supports various such conditional statements, as outlined in the following sections.

The `if()` Statement

In the previous hour we discussed Boolean variables, which we saw could take one of only two values—*true* or *false*.

JavaScript has several ways to test such values, the simplest of which is the `if` statement. It has the following general form:

```
if(this condition is true) then do this;
```

Let's look at a trivial example:

```
var message = "";
var bool = true;
if(bool) message = "The test condition evaluated to TRUE";
```

First we declare a variable `message` and assign an empty string to it as a value. We then declare a new variable `bool`, which we set to the Boolean value of *true*. The third statement tests the value of the variable `bool` to see whether it is true; if so (as in this case) the value of the variable `message` is set to a new string. Had we assigned a value of *false* to `bool` in the second line, the test condition would not have been fulfilled, and the instruction to assign a new value to `message` would have been ignored, leaving the variable `message` containing the empty string.

Remember, we said that the general form of an `if` statement is

```
if(this condition is true) then do this.
```

In the case of a Boolean value, as in this example, we have replaced the condition with the variable itself; because its value can only be *true* or *false*, the contents of the parentheses passed back to `if` accordingly evaluate to `true` or `false`.

We can test for the Boolean value `false` by using the negation character `!` that you met in the previous hour:

```
if(!bool) message = "The value of bool is FALSE";
```

Clearly, for `!bool` to evaluate to true, `bool` must be of value `false`.

Comparison Operators

The `if()` statement is not limited to testing the value of a Boolean variable; instead, we can enter a condition in the form of an expression into the parentheses of our `if` statement, and JavaScript evaluates the expression to determine whether it is true or false:

```
var message = "";
var temperature = 60;
if(temperature < 64) message = "Turn on the heating!";
```

NOTE

A more comprehensive list of comparison operators appears in Appendix B, "JavaScript Quick Reference."

The less than operator (<) is one of a range of comparison operators available in JavaScript. Some of the comparison operators are listed in Table 6.1.

TABLE 6.1   JavaScript Comparison Operators

Operator	Meaning
==	is equal to
===	is equal to in both value and type
!=	is not equal to

TABLE 6.1   Continued

Operator	Meaning
>	is greater than
<	is less than
>=	is greater than or equal to
<=	is less than or equal to

Testing for Equality

In the previous example, how could we test to see whether the temperature *exactly equals* 64 degrees? Remember that we use the equals sign (=) to
assign a value to a variable, so this code won't work as might be expected:

```
if(temperature = 64) ....
```

Were we to use this statement, the expression within the parentheses
would be evaluated by JavaScript, and our variable `temperature` would be
assigned the value of 64. If this value assignment terminates successfully—
and why shouldn't it?—then the value assignment would return a value of
true back to the `if()` statement, and the rest of the statement would therefore be executed. This isn't the behavior we want at all.

Instead, to test for equality we must use a double equals sign (==).

```
if(temperature == 64) message = "64 degrees and holding!";
```

> CAUTION
>
> If you need to test whether two items are equal *both in value and in type*,
> JavaScript has an operator === to perform this test. For example:
> ```
> var x = 2;        //  assign a numeric value
> if(x == "2") ... //  true, as the string "2" is interpreted
> if(x === "2") ...//  false, a string is not numeric
> ```
> This can be useful when testing to see whether a returned value is
> actually false, or just a value that is "falsy" (can be interpreted
> as false):
> ```
> var x = 0;        //  assign a value of zero
> if(!x)  ...       //  evaluates to true
> if(x === false)..//  evaluates to false
> ```

More about `if()`

The previous examples carry out only a single statement when the test
condition is met. What if we want to do more than this, for instance, carry
out several statements?

TIP

There exists a shorthand form
of the syntax for the `if()` statement:

```
(condition is true)? [do if
true] : [do if false];
```

Here's an example:

```
errorMessage = count +
((count == 1)? " error ":"
errors ") + "found.";
```

In this example, if the number
of errors stored in variable
count is exactly one, the message variable will contain

`1 error found.`

If the value in count is 0 or a
number greater than 1, the
message variable will contain a
string such as

`3 errors found.`

To achieve this, we simply enclose in curly braces {} all of the code statements that we want to execute if the condition is fulfilled:

```
if(temperature < 64) {
    message = "Turn on the heating!";
    heatingStatus = "on";
    // … more statements can be added here
}
```

We can also add a clause to our `if` statement that contains code we want to
execute if the condition is *not* fulfilled. To achieve this we use the `else` construct:

```
if(temperature < 64) {
    message = "Turn on the heating!";
    heatingStatus = "on";
    // … more statements can be added here
} else {
    message = "Temperature is high enough";
    heatingStatus = "off";
    // … more statements can be added here too
}
```

Testing Multiple Conditions

You can use "nested" combinations of `if` and `else` to test multiple conditions before deciding how to act. Let's return to our heating system example and have it switch on the cooling fan if the temperature is too high:

```
if(temperature < 64) {
    message = "Turn on the heating!";
    heatingStatus = "on";
    fanStatus = "off";
} else if(temperature > 72){
    message = "Turn on the fan!";
    heatingStatus = "off";
    fanStatus = "on";
} else {
    message = "Temperature is OK";
    heatingStatus = "off";
    fanStatus = "off";
}
```

The `switch` Statement

When testing for a range of different possible outcomes of the same conditional statement, a concise syntax we can use is that of JavaScript's `switch`
statement:

```
switch(color) {
    case "red" :
        message = "Stop!";
        break;
    case "yellow" :
        message = "Pass with caution";
        break;
    case "green" :
        message = "Come on through";
        break;
    default :
        message = "Traffic light out of service. Pass only with great
➥care";
}
```

The keyword `switch` has in parentheses the name of the variable to be tested.

The tests themselves are listed within the braces { and }. Each `case` statement (with its value in quotes) is followed by a colon, then the list of actions to be executed if that case has been matched. There can be any number of code statements in each section.

Note the `break` statement after each case. This jumps us to the end of the `switch` statement after having executed the code for a matching case. If `break` is omitted, it's possible that more than one case will have its code executed.

The optional `default` case has its code executed if none of the specified cases were matched.

Logical Operators

There will be occasions when we want to test a combination of criteria to determine whether a test condition has been met, and doing so with `if ... else` or `switch` statements becomes unwieldy.

Let's return once more to our temperature control program. JavaScript allows us to combine conditions using logical AND (&&) and logical OR (||). Here's one way:

```
if(temperature >= 64 && temperature <= 72) {
    message = "The temperature is OK";
} else {
    message = "The temperature is out of range!";
}
```

We can read this condition as "If the temperature is greater than or equal to 64 AND the temperature is less than or equal to 72."

We can achieve exactly the same functionality using OR instead of AND:

```
if(temperature < 64 || temperature > 72) {
    message = "The temperature is out of range!";
} else {
    message = "The temperature is OK";
}
```

Here we have reversed the way we carry out the test; our conditional statement is now fulfilled when the temperature is *out of* range and can be read as "If the temperature is less than 64 OR greater than 72."

Loops and Control Structures

The `if` statement can be thought of as a *junction* in program execution. Depending on the result of the test performed on the data, the program may go down one route or another with its execution of statements.

There are many occasions, though, when we might want to execute some operation a number of times before continuing with the rest of our program. If the number of repeats is fixed, we could perhaps achieve this with multiple `if` statements and incrementing counter variables, though the code would be messy and hard to read. But what if we don't know how many times we need to repeat our piece of code because the number of repeats depends upon, for example, the changing value of a variable?

JavaScript has various built-in loop structures that allow us to achieve such goals.

while

The syntax of the `while` statement is very much like the syntax for the `if` statement:

```
while(this condition is true) {
    carry out these statements ...
}
```

The `while` statement *works* just like `if`, too. The only difference is that after completing the conditional statements, `while` goes back and tests the condition again. All the time the condition keeps coming up `true`, `while` keeps right on executing the conditional code. Here's an example:

```
var count = 10;
var sum = 0;
while(count > 0) {
    sum = sum + count;
    count--;
}
alert(sum);
```

Each time while evaluates the condition as *true*, the statements in the curly braces are executed over and over, adding the current value of count to the variable sum on each trip around the loop.

When count has been decremented to zero, the condition fails and the loop stops; program operation then continues from after the closing brace. By this time, the variable sum has a value of

```
10 + 9 + 8 + 7 + 6 + 5 + 4 + 3 + 2 + 1 = 55
```

do … while

The do … while structure is similar in operation to while, but with one important difference. Here's the syntax:

```
do {
    … these statements …
} while(this condition is true)
```

The only real difference here is that because the while clause appears *after* the braces, the list of conditional statements is executed once *before* the while clause is evaluated. The statements in a do … while clause will therefore always be executed at least once.

for

The for loop is another loop similar in operation to while, but with a more comprehensive syntax. With the for loop, we can specify an initial condition, a test condition (to end the loop), and a means of changing a counter variable for each pass through the loop, all in one statement. Have a look at the syntax:

```
for(x=0; x<10; x++) {
    … execute these statements ...
}
```

We interpret this as follows:

"For x initially set to zero, and while x is less than 10, and incrementing x by 1 on each pass through the loop, carry out the conditional statements."

Let's rewrite the example we gave when looking at the `while` loop, but this time using a `for` loop:

```
var count;
var sum = 0;
for(count = 10; count > 0; count--) {
    sum = sum + count;
}
```

If the counter variable has not previously been declared, it is often conven-ient to declare it with the `var` keyword within the `for` statement instead of outside:

```
var sum = 0;
for(var count = 10; count > 0; count--) {
    sum = sum + count;
}
alert(sum);
```

As in the previous example, after the loop terminates the variable `sum` has a value of

```
10 + 9 + 8 + 7 + 6 + 5 + 4 + 3 + 2 + 1 = 55
```

Leaving a Loop with `break`

The `break` command works within a loop pretty much as it does in a `switch` statement—it kicks us out of the loop and returns operation to the line of code immediately after the closing brace.

Here's an example:

```
var count = 10;
var sum = 0;
while(count > 0) {
    sum = sum + count;
    if(sum > 42) break;
    count--;
}
alert(sum);
```

We saw previously that without the break instruction, the value of sum evolved like this:

`10 + 9 + 8 + 7 + 6 + 5 + 4 + 3 + 2 + 1 = 55`

Now, we find that when the value of sum reaches

`10 + 9 + 8 + 7 + 6 + 5 = 45`

the conditional clause of the if(sum > 42) statement will come up *true* and cause the loop to terminate due to the break command.

Looping through Objects with for ... in

The for...in loop is a special sort of loop intended for stepping through the properties of an object. Let's see it in action applied to an array object in Listing 6.1.

LISTING 6.1   The for ... in Loop

```
<!DOCTYPE html>
<html>
<head>
    <title>Loops and Control</title>
</head>
<body>
    <script>
        var days = ['Sun','Mon','Tue','Wed','Thu','Fri','Sat'];
        var message = "";
        for (i in days) {
            message += 'Day ' + i + ' is ' + days[i] + '\n';
        }
        alert(message);
    </script>
</body>
</html>
```

In this sort of loop, we don't need to worry about maintaining a loop counter or devising a test to see when the loop should complete. The loop will occur once for every property of the supplied object (in our example, once for every array item) and then terminate.

The result of running this example is shown in Figure 6.1.

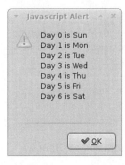

Debugging Your Scripts

As you delve into more advanced scripting, you're going to now and then create JavaScript programs that contain errors.

JavaScript errors can be caused by a variety of minor blunders, such as mismatched opening and closing parentheses, mistyping of variable names or keywords, making calls to nonexistent methods, and so on. The scripts you are encountering in this hour, with their various loops and branches, can be particularly prone to errors and tricky to debug.

How your browser presents such errors to you differs from browser to browser. Have a look at the code in Listing 6.2.

LISTING 6.2   A Program with Errors

```
<!DOCTYPE html>
<html>
<head>
    <title>Strings and Arrays</title>
</head>
<body>
    <script>
        function sayHi() {
            alert("Hello!);
        }
    </script>
    <input type="button" value="good" onclick="sayHi()" />
    <input type="button" value="bad" onclick="sayhi()" />
</body>
</html>
```

This code listing has two different types of error. First, in the call to the `alert()` method, our argument is missing its closing quotation mark.

Second, the `onclick` handler of the second button calls a function `sayhi()`—remember that function names are case sensitive, so in fact there is no function defined with the name `sayhi()`.

Loading the page into Firefox, we can see the expected two buttons, one labeled "good" and the other "bad." Neither seems to do anything. I can open Firefox's Error Console by pressing Ctrl+Shft+J, and the result is shown in Figure 6.2.

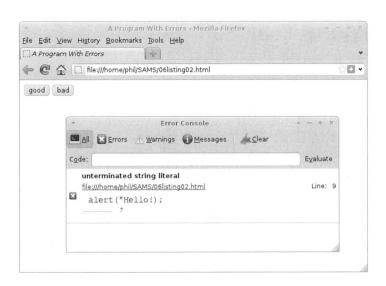

FIGURE 6.2
The Firefox Error Console

That's a helpful start. Firefox tells me it found an *unterminated string literal,* gives me the line number, and even shows me the line of code with an arrow pointed at the section where it has a problem.

With the error corrected and the file saved again, I'm ready to try again. First I click Clear on the toolbar of the Error Console to remove the old error message; then I reload my test page.

That looks better. My page comes up again, and the Error Console stays blank. Clicking the button labeled "good" opens the expected `alert()` dialog—so far, so good.

But clicking the button labeled "bad" doesn't seem to do anything—so I refer again to the Error Console, as shown in Figure 6.3.

Firefox again identifies the problem: "sayhi is not defined." Now we're well on the way to having our code fully debugged and working correctly.

Every browser has its own way of dealing with errors. Figure 6.4 shows how the Chromium browser reports the initial error of the unterminated string literal.

NOTE

Google Chrome and Chromium are almost identical browsers, differing mainly in how they are packaged and distributed. Essentially, Google Chrome is the Chromium open source browser packaged and distributed by Google.

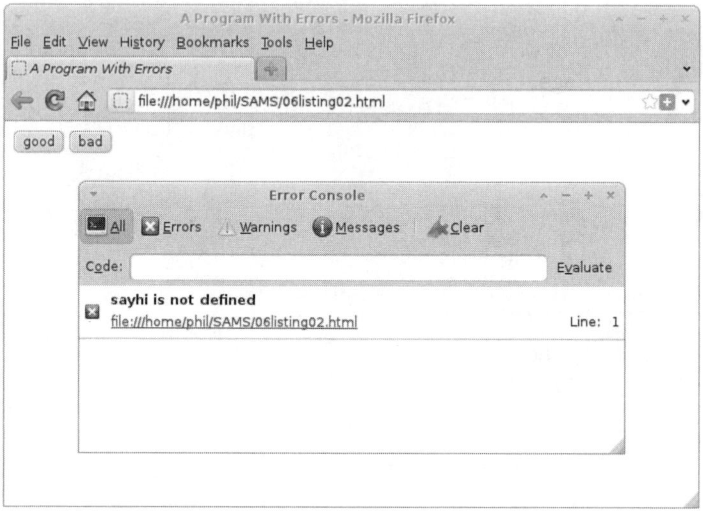

FIGURE 6.3
The second error

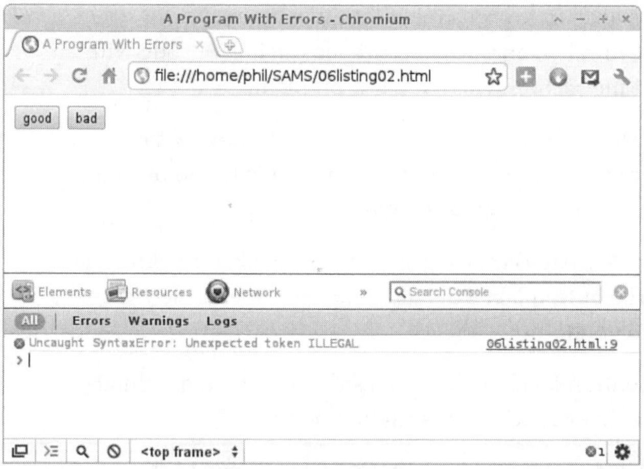

FIGURE 6.4
Google Chromium JavaScript console

TIP

It's worth getting to know the debugging tools in your favorite browser, and even think about switching browsers if you particularly prefer the tools on offer in another. If you plan to regularly write JavaScript code, it makes sense to do so in a development environment in which you feel comfortable, where you'll be more productive and less frustrated.

Chromium's message is a slightly more cryptic "Uncaught syntax error: Unexpected token ILLEGAL", but it also gives the line number in a clickable link that shows me the faulty line of code.

To open Internet Explorer 9's developer tools, press F12 or select Developer Tools from the IE9 Tools menu. Select the Console tab to view error messages returned by JavaScript.

Let's put to use some of what you learned in this hour by writing a script to
cycle images on the page. I'm sure you have seen this sort of program
before, either as an image slideshow or perhaps to rotate advertisement
banners.

First, I want to introduce you to two new items. The first is an event handler
that you haven't met before—the onLoad method of the window object. Its
operation is simple: We can attach it to the <body> element like this:

```
<body onload="somefunction()" >
```

When the page has finished loading completely, the onLoad event fires, and
the code specified in the event handler runs. We use this event handler to
run our banner rotator as soon as the page has loaded.

Second, we are going to use JavaScript's setInterval() function. This function allows us to run a JavaScript function repeatedly, with a preset delay
between successive executions.

The setInterval() function takes two arguments. The first is the name of the
function we want to run, the second the delay (in milliseconds) between successive executions of the function. As an example, the line

```
setInterval(myFunc, 5000);
```

would execute the function myFunc() every five seconds.

We use setInterval() to rotate the banner image at a regular interval.

Create a new file banner.html and enter the code from Listing 6.3.

TIP

We discuss some more
sophisticated ways to add
event handlers in Hour 9,
"Responding to Events."

LISTING 6.3   A Banner Rotator

```
<!DOCTYPE html>
<html>
<head>
    <title>Banner Cycler</title>
    <script>
        var banners = ["banner1.jpg", "banner2.jpg", "banner3.jpg"];
        var counter = 0;
        function run() {
            setInterval(cycle, 2000);
        }
        function cycle() {
            counter++;
            if(counter == banners.length) counter = 0;
            document.getElementById("banner").src = banners[counter];
        }
    </script>
</head>
```

LISTING 6.3   Continued

```
<body onload = "run();">
    <img id="banner" alt="banner" src="banner1.jpg" />
</body>
</html>
```

The HTML part of the page could hardly be simpler—the body of the page just contains an image element. This image will form the banner, which will be "rotated" by changing its src property.

Now let's take a look at the code.

The function run() contains only one statement; the setInterval() function. This function executes another function, cycle(), every two seconds (2000 milliseconds).

Every time the function cycle() executes, we carry out three operations:

▶ Increment a counter

```
counter++;
```

▶ Use a conditional statement to check whether the counter has reached the number of elements in the array of image names; if so, reset the counter to zero.

```
if(counter == banners.length) counter = 0;
```

▶ Set the src property of the displayed image to the appropriate file name selected from the array of images file names.

```
document.getElementById("banner").src = banners[counter];
```

The operation of the script is shown in Figure 6.5.

Now let's examine the script operation using browser-based debug tools. I'm using Chromium, so I open the Developer Tools console again like I did in Figure 6.4. In Chromium that's **Wrench Icon > Tools > Developer Tools** or the shortcut Ctrl+Shift+I.

This time I select the Scripts tab in the lower pane. To the left of the lower pane, the code is listed; I'm going to click the line number of line 15 to set a breakpoint, as shown in Figure 6.6.

A Banner Cycling Script
continued

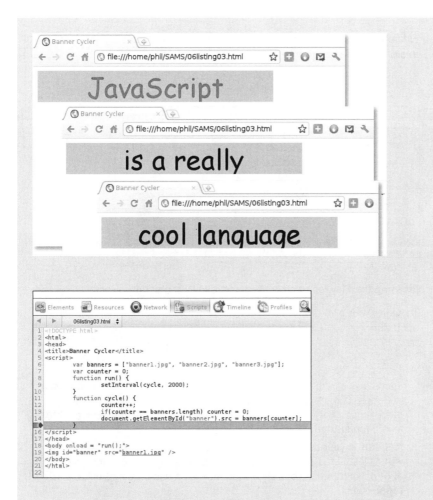

FIGURE 6.5
Our banner cycler

FIGURE 6.6
Setting a breakpoint

While this breakpoint remains set, code execution will halt every time this line of code is reached, before executing the code in the line—in this case, before completing the current execution of the function `cycle()`.

On the right-hand side of the same pane, our breakpoint now appears in the Breakpoints panel. In the same pane, I can click in the Watch Expressions panel and add the names of any variables or expressions whose values I want to examine each time the program pauses; I'm going to enter `counter` and `getElementById("Banner").src` to see what values they contain.

▼ TRY IT YOURSELF

A Banner Cycling Script

continued

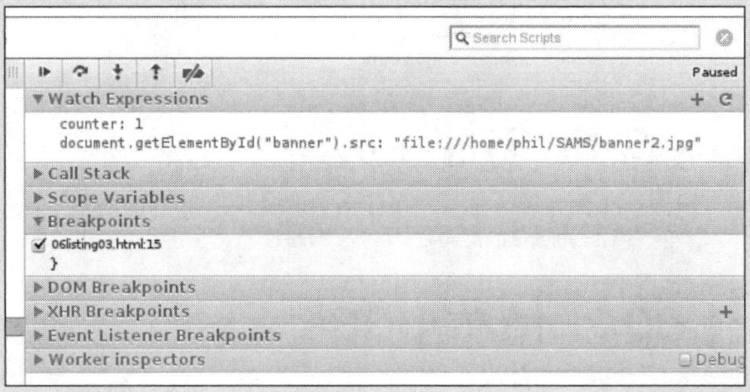

FIGURE 6.7
Showing variable values at a breakpoint

Figure 6.7 shows the display when the program next pauses, showing the values of my two chosen expressions.

Pressing the Play icon above the panel allows the script to restart.

Try using your own browser's debugging tools to explore the program's operation.

TIP

I have only scratched the surface here of the capabilities of the debugger in Google Chrome/Chromium. To learn more, there is a good tutorial at http://code.google.com/chrome/devtools/docs/scripts-breakpoints.html to get you started.

If Firefox is your browser of choice for development work, you would do well to install the popular Firebug extension, which you can read about at http://getfirebug.com/javascript and which has broadly similar capabilities.

Those using Microsoft Internet Explorer 9 will find good information on debugging with the F12 Developer Tools at http://msdn.microsoft.com/en-us/library/ie/dd565622(v=vs.85).aspx.

Opera contains the Dragonfly debugging tool, which you can read about at http://www.opera.com/dragonfly/documentation/.

Summary

In this hour, the first of Part II, "More Advanced JavaScript," you learned a lot about testing conditions and controlling program flow based on the values of variables and how to write various kinds of program loops controlled by conditions.

You also learned a little about using browser tools to help you to trace and correct errors in your programs.

Q&A

Q. Is there any particular reason why I should use one sort of loop over another?

A. It's true that there is usually more than one type of loop that will solve any particular programming problem. You can use the one you feel most comfortable with, though it's usually good practice to use whichever loop makes the most sense (in conjunction with your chosen variable names) in the context of what your code sets out to do.

Q. Is there a way to stop the current trip around a loop and move straight to the next iteration?

A. Yes, you can use the `continue` command. It works pretty much like `break`, but instead of canceling the loop and continuing code execution from after the closing brace, `continue` only cancels the current trip around the loop and moves on to the next one.

Workshop

Try to answer all the questions before reading the subsequent "Answers" section.

Quiz

1. How is "greater than or equal to" expressed in JavaScript?

   a. >

   b. >=

   c. >==

2. What command forces the cancellation of a loop and moves code operation to the statement after the closing brace?

   a. break;

   b. loop;

   c. close;

3. Which of the following is likely to cause an infinite loop to occur?

   a. The wrong sort of loop has been used.

   b. The condition to terminate the loop is never met.

   c. There are too many statements in the loop.

Answers

1. b. JavaScript interprets >= as "greater than or equal to."

2. a. The break command ends loop execution.

3. b. An infinite loop occurs if the condition to terminate the loop is never met.

Exercises

How would you modify the banner cycling script to add links to the banners, such that each image displayed linked to a different external page?

Using your knowledge of random number generation using the Math object, can you rewrite the banner cycling script to show a random banner at each change, instead of cycling through them in order? Use your browser's built-in debugging tools to help you.

Object Oriented Programming

As your programs become more complex, you need to use coding techniques that help you to maintain control and ensure that your code remains efficient, readable, and maintainable. In this hour you learn the basics of Object Oriented Programming, an important technique for writing clear and reliable code that you can reuse over and over.

What Is Object Oriented Programming (OOP)?

The code examples to date have been so-called *procedural* programming. Procedural programming is characterized by having data stored in variables, which are operated on by lists of instructions. Each instruction (or list of instructions, such as a function) can create, destroy, or modify the data, yet the data always remains somehow "separate" from the program code.

In Object Oriented Programming (OOP), the program instructions and the data on which they operate are more intertwined. OOP is a way of conceptualizing a program's data into discrete "things" referred to as *objects*—each having its own *properties* (data) and *methods* (instructions).

Suppose, for example, you wanted to write a script to help manage a car rental business. You might design a general-purpose object Car. The Car object would have certain properties (color, year, odometerReading, and make) and perhaps a few methods (e.g., a method setOdometer(newMiles) to update the odometerReading property to the current figure newMiles).

WHAT YOU'LL LEARN IN THIS HOUR

▶ What Object Oriented Programming is
▶ Two ways to create objects
▶ Instantiating an object
▶ Extending and inheriting objects using prototype
▶ Accessing object methods and properties
▶ Using feature detection

NOTE

An instance of an object is a particular application of an object "template" to create a working object based on specific data. For example, the general object template Car might have a specific instance where a Car object has been created with specific data identifying it as a "blue 1998 Ford," and another instance describing a "yellow 2004 Nissan." In most discussions of Object Oriented Programming, such an object template is referred to as a *class*. I've resisted the temptation to use that term, as JavaScript doesn't really use classes, but the JavaScript concept called a *constructor function* is similar. You learn about constructor functions during this hour.

NOTE

Some programming languages such as C++ and Smalltalk lean heavily toward OOP, and are often referred to as Object Oriented languages. JavaScript is not one of these, but it does support enough of the essentials to allow you to write useful OOP code. We could easily fill the whole book with theory and practice of OOP, but we just look at the basics here.

For each car in the rental fleet, you would create an *instance* of the Car object.

Writing OOP code offers several advantages over procedural methods:

▶ **Code reuse**—First, OOP allows you to reuse your code in a variety of scripts. You could achieve this with regular functions, but it would soon become difficult to keep track of all the variables that needed to be passed, their scope, and meaning. For objects, in contrast, you only need to document the properties and methods for each object. Providing they adhere to these rules, other programs—and even other programmers—can easily use your object definitions.

▶ **Encapsulation**—You can define the way objects interact with other parts of your scripts by carefully controlling the properties and methods that the rest of the program can "see." The *internal* workings of the object can be hidden away, forcing code external to the object to access that object's data only through the documented interfaces that the object offers.

▶ **Inheritance**—Often when coding you will have a need for some code that is nearly, but not quite, the same as something that's been coded before—maybe even something already coded in the same application. Using *inheritance*, new objects can be created based on the design of previously defined objects, optionally with additions or modifications to their methods and properties; the new object *inherits* properties and methods from the old.

In the previous hours you often used objects; either those built into JavaScript, or those that make up the DOM. However, you can also create your own objects, with their own properties and functions, to use in your programs.

Object Creation

JavaScript offers several ways to create an object. Let's look first at how to declare a *direct instance* of an object; later we create an object by using a *constructor function*.

Create a Direct Instance

JavaScript has a built-in object simply called Object, which you can use as a kind of blank canvas for creating your own objects:

```
myNewObject = new Object();
```

Okay, you now have a brand new object myNewObject. For the moment, it doesn't actually do anything, as it doesn't have any properties or methods. You can begin to rectify that by adding a property:

```
myNewObject.info = 'I am a shiny new object';
```

Now your object owns a property—in this case a text string containing some information about the object and called info. You can also easily add a method to the object too, by first defining a function and then attaching it to myNewObject as one of the object's methods:

```
function myFunc(){
        alert(this.info);
    };
myNewObject.showInfo = myFunc;
```

To call the new method, you can simply use the now-familiar dot notation:

```
myNewObject.showInfo();
```

Using the this Keyword

Note the use of the this keyword in the previous function definition. You may recall that you used such a keyword in Hour 2, "Writing Simple Scripts," and Hour 3, "Using Functions." In those previous examples, you used this in an inline event handler:

```
<img src="tick.gif" alt="tick" onmouseover="this.src='tick2.gif';"  />
```

When used in that way, this refers to the HTML element itself—in the preceding case the <img> element. When you use this inside a function (or method), the keyword this refers to the function's *parent* object.

On first declaring the function myFunc(), its parent is the global object, that is, the window object. The window object does not have a property called info, so if you were to call the myFunc() function directly, an error would occur.

However, you go on to create a method showInfo of myNewObject, and you assign myFunc() to that method:

```
 myNewObject.showInfo = myFunc;
```

In the context of the showInfo() method, myNewObject is the parent object, so this.info refers to the property myNewObject.info.

Let's see if we can clarify this a little with the code in Listing 7.1.

LISTING 7.1   Creating an Object

```
<!DOCTYPE html>
<html>
<head>
    <title>Object Oriented Programming</title>
    <script>
        myNewObject = new Object();
        myNewObject.info = 'I am a shiny new object';
        function myFunc(){
                alert(this.info);
            }
        myNewObject.showInfo = myFunc;
    </script>
</head>
<body>
    <input type="button" value="Good showInfo Call"
➥onclick="myNewObject.showInfo()" />
    <input type="button" value="myFunc Call" onclick="myFunc()" />
    <input type="button" value="Bad showInfo Call" onclick="showInfo()"
➥/>
</body>
</html>
```

Notice that in the <head> section of the page, you create the object myNewObject and assign it a property info and a method showInfo, as described earlier.

Loading this page into your browser, you are confronted with three buttons.

Clicking the first button makes a call to the showInfo method of the newly created object:

```
<input type="button" value="Good showInfo Call"
➥onclick="myNewObject.showInfo()" />
```

FIGURE 7.1
The info property is correctly called.

As you would hope, the value of the info property is passed to the alert() dialog as shown in Figure 7.1.

The second button attempts to make a call directly to the function myFunc().

```
<input type="button" value="myFunc Call" onclick="myFunc()" />
```

Because myFunc() is a method of the global object (having been defined without reference to any other object as parent), it attempts to pass to the alert() dialog the value of a nonexistent property window.info, with the result shown in Figure 7.2.

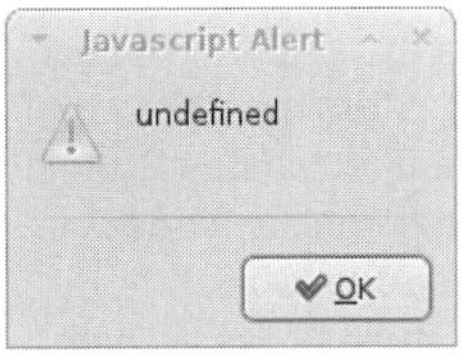

Finally, your third button attempts to call showInfo without reference to its parent object:

```
<input type="button" value="Bad showInfo Call" onclick="showInfo()" />
```

Because the method does not exist outside the object myNewObject, JavaScript reports an error, as shown in Figure 7.3.

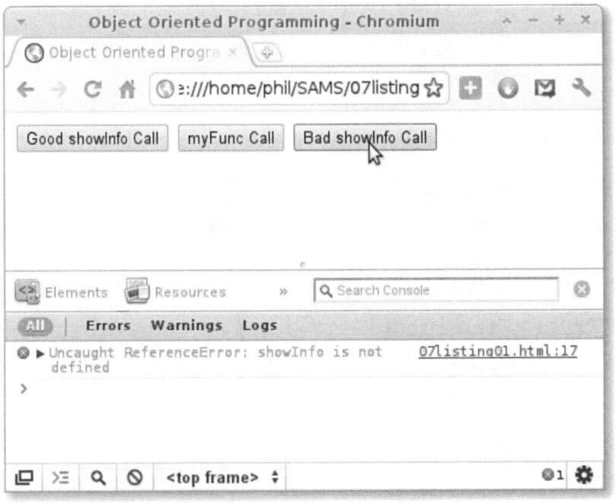

FIGURE 7.2
The global object has no property called info.

FIGURE 7.3
JavaScript reports that showInfo is not defined.

NOTE

Refer back to Hour 6, "Scripts That Do More," for more about showing JavaScript errors using your browser's JavaScript Console or Error Console.

Anonymous Functions

There is a more convenient and elegant way to assign a value to your object's showInfo method, without having to create a separate, named function and then later assign it by name to the required method. Instead of this code:

```
function myFunc(){
        alert(this.info);
    };
myNewObject.showInfo = myFunc;
```

you could simply have written:

```
myNewObject.showInfo = function() {
    alert(this.info);
}
```

TIP

JavaScript offers a further way
to create a direct instance of an
object; the technique uses
JSON (JavaScript Object
Notation). It isn't covered here,
as we explore JSON in detail in
Hour 8, "Meet JSON."

TIP

An object with only one global
instance is sometimes called a
singleton object. They are useful
sometimes, for example, a user
of your program might have only
one associated userProfile
object, perhaps containing his
or her user name, URL of last
page viewed, and similar
properties.

NOTE

Note that this syntax is identical
to using new Object(), except
you use your purpose-designed
object type in place of
JavaScript's general-purpose
Object(). In doing so, you
instantiate the object complete
with the properties and methods
defined in the constructor
function.

Because you haven't needed to give a name to your function prior to
assigning it, this technique is referred to as using an *anonymous function*.

By using similar assignment statements you can add as many properties
and methods as you need to your instantiated object.

Using a Constructor Function

Directly creating an instance of an object is fine if you think you'll only
need one object of that type. Unfortunately, if you need to create another
instance of the same type of object, you'll have to go through the same
process again; creating the object, adding properties, defining methods,
and so on.

A better way to create objects that will have multiple instances is by using
an *object constructor function*. An object constructor function creates a kind
of "template" from which further objects can be instantiated.

Take a look at the following code. Instead of using new Object(), you first
declare a function myObjectType(), and in its definition you can add properties and methods using the this keyword.

```
function myObjectType(){
    this.info = 'I am a shiny new object';
    this.showInfo = function(){
        alert(this.info);  // show the value of the property info
    }
     this.setInfo = function (newInfo) {
        this.info = newInfo; // overwrite the value of the property info
    }
}
```

In the preceding code you added a single property, info, and two methods: showInfo, which simply displays the value currently stored in the
info property, and setInfo. The setInfo method takes an argument
newInfo and uses its value to overwrite the value of the info property.

Instantiating an Object

You can now create as many instances as you want of this object type. All
will have the properties and methods defined in the myObjectType()
function. Creating an object instance is known as *instantiating* an object.

Having defined your constructor function, you can create an instance of
your object simply by using the constructor function:

```
var myNewObject = new myObjectType();
```

Now you can call its methods and examine its properties:

```
var x = myNewObject.info // x now contains 'I am a shiny new object'
myNewObject.showInfo(); // alerts 'I am a shiny new object'
myNewObject.setInfo("Here is some new information"); // overwrites the
info property
```

Creating multiple instances is as simple as calling the constructor function as many times as you need to:

```
var myNewObject1 = new myObjectType();
var myNewObject2 = new myObjectType();
```

Let's see this in action. The code in Listing 7.2 defines an object constructor function the same as the one described previously.

Two instances of the object are instantiated; clearly, both objects are initially identical. You can examine the value stored in the info property for each object by clicking one of the buttons labeled Show Info 1 and Show Info 2.

A third button calls the setInfo method of object myNewObject2, passing a new string literal as an argument to the method. This overwrites the value stored in the info property of object myNewObject2, but of course leaves myNewObject unchanged. The revised values can be checked by once again using Show Info 1 and Show Info 2.

LISTING 7.2　Creating Objects with a Constructor Function

```
<!DOCTYPE html>
<html>
<head>
    <title>Object Oriented Programming</title>
    <script>
        function myObjectType(){
            this.info = 'I am a shiny new object';
            this.showInfo = function(){
                alert(this.info);
            }
            this.setInfo = function (newInfo) {
                this.info = newInfo;
            }
        }
        var myNewObject1 = new myObjectType();
        var myNewObject2 = new myObjectType();
    </script>
</head>
<body>
    <input type="button" value="Show Info 1"
onclick="myNewObject1.showInfo()" />
```

LISTING 7.2   Continued

```
    <input type="button" value="Show Info 2"
➥onclick="myNewObject2.showInfo()" />
    <input type="button" value="Change info of object2"
➥onclick="myNewObject2.setInfo('New Information!')" />
</body>
</html>
```

Using Constructor Function Arguments

There is nothing to stop you customizing your objects at the time of instantiation, by passing one or more arguments to the constructor function. In the following code, the definition of the constructor function includes one argument personName, which is assigned to the name property by the constructor function. As you instantiate two objects, you pass a name as an argument to the constructor function for each instance.

```
function Person(personName){
    this.name = personName;
    this.info = 'I am called ' + this.name;
    this.showInfo = function(){
        alert(this.info);
    }
}
var person1 = new Person('Adam');
var person2 = new Person('Eve');
```

TIP

You can define the constructor function to accept as many or as few arguments as you want:

```
function Car(Color, Year, Make, Miles) {
    this.color = Color;
    this.year = Year;
    this.make = Make;
    this.odometerReading = Miles;
    this.setOdometer = function(newMiles) {
        this.odometerReading = newMiles;
    }
}
var car1 = new Car("blue","1998","Ford",79500);
var car2 = new Car("yellow","2004","Nissan", 56350);
car1.setOdometer(82450);
```

Extending and Inheriting Objects Using `prototype`

A major advantage of using objects is the ability to reuse already written code in a new context. JavaScript provides a means to modify objects to include new methods and/or properties or even to create brand new objects based on ones that already exist.

These techniques are known, respectively, as *extending* and *inheriting* objects.

Extending Objects

What if you want to extend your objects with new methods and properties after the objects have already been instantiated? You can do so using the keyword `prototype`. The prototype object allows you to quickly add a property or method that is then available for all instances of the object.

TRY IT YOURSELF ▼

Extend an Object Using prototype

Let's extend the `Person` object of the previous example with a new method sayHello.

```
Person.prototype.sayHello = function() {
    alert(this.name + " says hello");
}
```

Create a new HTML file in your editor, and enter the code from Listing 7.3.

LISTING 7.3   Adding a New Method with `prototype`

```
<!DOCTYPE html>
<html>
<head>
<title>Object Oriented Programming</title>
    <script>
        function Person(personName){
            this.name = personName;
            this.info = 'This person is called ' + this.name;
            this.showInfo = function(){
                alert(this.info);
            }
        }
```

```
            var person1 = new Person('Adam');
            var person2 = new Person('Eve');
            Person.prototype.sayHello = function() {
                alert(this.name + " says hello");
            }
        </script>
    </head>
    <body>
        <input type="button" value="Show Info on Adam"
    onclick="person1.showInfo()" />
        <input type="button" value="Show Info on Eve"
    onclick="person2.showInfo()" />
        <input type="button" value="Say Hello Adam"
    onclick="person1.sayHello()" />
        <input type="button" value="Say Hello Eve"
    onclick="person2.sayHello()" />
    </body>
</html>
```

Let's walk through this code and see what's happening.

First, you define a constructor function that takes a single argument
personName. Within the constructor, two properties name and info, and one
method showInfo are defined.

You create two objects, instantiating each with a different name property.
Having created these two person objects, you then decide to add a further
method sayHello to the person object definition. You do so using the
prototype keyword.

Load the HTML file into your browser. Clicking the four buttons visible on the
page shows that the initially defined showInfo method is still intact, but the
new sayHello method operates too and is available for both of the existing
instances of the object type.

Inheritance

Inheritance is the ability to create one object type from another; the new
object type inherits the properties and methods of the old, as well as
optionally having further properties and methods of its own. This can save
you a lot of work, as you can first devise "generic" classes of objects and
then refine them into more specific classes by inheritance.

JavaScript uses the `prototype` keyword to emulate inheritance, too.

Because `object.prototype` is used to add new methods and properties, you can utilize it to add *all* of the methods and properties of an existing constructor function to your new object.

Let's define another simple object:

```
function Pet() {
    this.animal = "";
    this.name = "";
    this.setAnimal = function(newAnimal) {
        this.animal = newAnimal;
    }
    this.setName = function(newName) {
        this.name = newName;
    }
}
```

A `Pet` object has properties that contain the type of animal and the name of the pet and methods to set these values:

```
var myCat = new Pet();
myCat.setAnimal = "cat";
myCat.setName = "Sylvester";
```

Now suppose you want to create an object specifically for dogs. Rather than starting from scratch, you want to inherit the `Dog` object from `Pet` but add an additional property `breed` and an additional method `setBreed`.

First, let's create the `Dog` constructor function, and in it define the new property and method:

```
function Dog() {
    this.breed = "";
    this.setBreed = function(newBreed) {
        this.breed = newBreed;
    }
}
```

That's taken care of the additional property and method. Now you can inherit the properties and methods of `Pet`. You do so using the `prototype` keyword:

```
Dog.prototype = new Pet();
```

You can now access the properties and methods of `Pet` in addition to those of `Dog`:

```
var myDog = new Dog();
myDog.setName("Alan");
myDog.setBreed("Greyhound");
alert(myDog.name + " is a " + myDog.breed);
```

Extending JavaScript's Own Objects

Prototype can also be used to extend JavaScript's built-in objects. You can implement a `String.prototype.backwards` method, for instance, that will return a reversed version of any string you supply, as in Listing 7.4.

LISTING 7.4   Extending the String Object

```
<!DOCTYPE html>
<html>
<head>
    <title>Object Oriented Programming</title>
    <script>
        String.prototype.backwards = function(){
            var out = '';
            for(var i = this.length-1; i >= 0; i--){
                out += this.substr(i, 1);
            }
            return out;
        }
    </script>
</head>
<body>
    <script>
        var inString = prompt("Enter your test string:");
        document.write(inString.backwards());
    </script>
</body>
</html>
```

Save the code of Listing 7.4 as an HTML file and open it in your browser. The script uses a `prompt()` dialog to invite you to enter a string and then shows the string reversed on the page.

Let's see how the code works.

```
String.prototype.backwards = function(){
    var out = '';
    for(var i = this.length-1; i >= 0; i--){
        out += this.substr(i, 1);
    }
    return out;
}
```

First, you declare a new variable out within the anonymous function that you are creating. This variable will hold the reversed string.

You then begin a loop, starting at the end of the input string (remember that JavaScript string character indexing starts at 0, not 1, so you need to begin at

TRY IT YOURSELF ▼

Extending JavaScript's Own Objects
continued

`this.length` - 1) and decrementing one character at a time. As you loop backwards through the string, you add characters one at a time to our output string stored in out.

When you reach the beginning of the input string, the reversed string is returned. The result is shown in Figure 7.4.

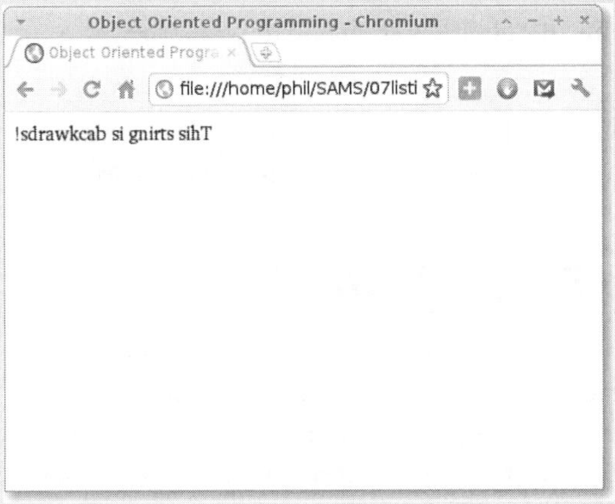

FIGURE 7.4
Method to reverse a string

Encapsulation

Encapsulation is the name given to OOP's capability to hide data and instructions inside an object. How this is achieved varies from language to language, but in JavaScript any variables declared inside the constructor function are available only from within the object; they are invisible from outside. The same is true of any function declared inside the constructor function.

Such variables and functions become accessible to the outside world only when they are assigned with the `this` keyword; they then become properties and methods, respectively, of the object.

Let's look at an example.

```
function Box(width, length, height) {
    function volume(a,b,c) {
        return a*b*c;
    }
    this.boxVolume = volume(width, length, height);
}
```

```
var crate = new Box(5,4,3);
alert("Volume = " + crate.boxVolume); // works correctly
alert(volume(5,4,3)); // fails as function volume() is invisible
```

In the preceding example, the function volume(a,b,c) cannot be called from any place outside the constructor function as it has not been assigned to an object method by using this. However, property crate.boxVolume *is* available outside the constructor function; even though it uses the function volume() to calculate its value, it only does so inside the constructor function.

If you don't "register" methods and properties using this, they are not available outside. Such methods and properties are referred to as *private*.

Using Feature Detection

Back in the dark days before the W3C DOM evolved to its current state, JavaScript developers were forced into horrible code contortions to try to cope with browsers' different DOM implementations. It was not uncommon for scripts to be written almost as two or more separate programs, the version to be executed only being decided after an attempt to detect the browser in use.

As you saw in your work with the navigator object in Hour 4, "DOM Objects and Built-In Objects," browser detection is a tricky business. The navigator object contains information that can be misleading at best (and sometimes downright incorrect). Also, when a new browser or version is introduced with new capabilities and features, your browser-detecting code is usually broken once again.

Thankfully a much better way to write cross-browser code has emerged, based on objects. Instead of attempting browser detection, it's a much better idea to have JavaScript examine whether the particular feature you need is supported. You can do this by testing for the availability of a specific object, method, or property. In many cases it's sufficient to try to use the object, method, or property in question and detect the value JavaScript returns.

Here's an example of testing for browser support of the document.getElementById() method that you've already met. Although getElementById() has been supported by all new browsers for some time now, very early browsers do not support this method.

You can test for the availability of the `getElementById()` method (or any similar method or property) by using `if()`:

```
if(document.getElementById) {
    myElement = document.getElementById(id);
} else {
    // do something else
}
```

If `document.getElementById` is not available, the `if()` conditional statement will switch code operation to avoid using that method.

Another, related method uses the `typeof` operator to check whether a JavaScript function exists before calling it:

```
if(typeof document.getElementById == 'function') {
    // you can use getElementById()
} else {
    // do something else
}
```

A number of possible values can be returned by `typeof`, as listed in Table 7.1

TABLE 7.1   Values Returned by `typeof`

Evaluates to	Indicates
"number"	Operand is a number.
"string"	Operand is a string.
"boolean"	Operand is a Boolean.
"object"	Operand is an object.
null	Operand is null.
undefined	Operand is not defined.

You can use this technique to check for the existence not only of DOM and built-in objects, methods, and properties, but also those created within your scripts.

Note that at no point in this exercise have you tried to determine what browser your user has—you simply want to know whether it supports the objects, properties, or methods you are about to try to use. Not only is such *feature detection* much more accurate and elegant than so-called *browser sniffing* (trying to infer the browser in use by interpreting properties of the `navigator` object), but it's also much more future-proof—the introduction of new browsers or browser versions won't break anything in your code's operation.

Summary

In this hour you learned about Object Oriented Programming (OOP) in JavaScript, starting with the basic concepts behind OOP and how it can help your code development, especially for more complex applications.

You learned a way to directly instantiate an object and add properties and methods to it. You then learned to create an object constructor function from which you can instantiate multiple similar objects.

You also learned about the `prototype` keyword and how it can be used to extend objects or create new objects via inheritance.

Q&A

Q. Should I always write Object Oriented code?

A. It's a matter of personal preference. Some coders prefer to always think in terms of objects, methods, and properties and write all their code with those principles in mind. Others feel that, particularly for smaller and simpler programs, the level of abstraction provided by OOP is too much and that procedural coding is OK.

Q. How would I use my objects in other programs?

A. An object's constructor function is quite a portable entity. If you link into your page a JavaScript file containing an object constructor function, you have the means to create objects and use their properties and methods throughout your code.

Workshop

Try to answer all the questions before reading the subsequent "Answers" section.

Quiz

1. A new object created from a constructor function is known as:

    a. an instance of the object

    b. a method of the object

    c. a prototype

2. Deriving new objects by using the design of currently existing objects is known as:

    a. Encapsulation

    b. Inheritance

    c. Instantiation

3. Which of the following is a valid way to create a direct instance of an object?

    a. `myObject.create();`

    b. `myObject = new Object;`

    c. `myObject = new Object();`

Answers

1. a. A new object created from a constructor function is known as an instance.

2. b. New objects are derived from existing ones through inheritance.

3. c. `myObject = new Object();`

Exercises

Write a constructor function for a `Card` object with properties `suit` (diamonds, hearts, spades, or clubs) and `face` (ace, 1, 2 ...king). Add methods to set the values of `suit` and `face`.

Can you include a `shuffle` method to set the `suit` and `face` properties to represent a random card from the deck? (Hint: Use the `Math.random()` method described in Hour 4.)

Extend JavaScript's `Date` object using the `prototype` keyword to add a new method `getYesterday()`, which returns the name of the previous day to that represented by the `Date` object.

Meet JSON

In the previous hour, you saw how to directly instantiate an object using the `new Object()` syntax. In this hour you learn about JavaScript Object Notation (JSON) which, as its name implies, offers another way to create object instances, and which can also act as a general-purpose data exchange syntax.

What Is JSON?

JSON (pronounced "Jason") is a simple and compact notation for JavaScript objects. Once expressed in JSON, objects can easily be converted to strings to be stored and transmitted (across networks or between applications, for instance).

However, the real beauty of JSON is that an object expressed in JSON is really just expressed in normal JavaScript code. You therefore take advantage of "automatic" parsing in JavaScript; you can just have JavaScript interpret the contents of a JSON string as code, with no extra parsers or converters.

JSON Syntax

JSON data is expressed as a sequence of parameter and value pairs, each pair using a colon character to separate parameter from value. These `"parameter":"value"` pairs are themselves separated by commas:

```
"param1":"value1", "param2":"value2", "param3":"value3"
```

WHAT YOU'LL LEARN IN THIS HOUR

▶ What JSON is
▶ How to simulate associative arrays
▶ About JSON and objects
▶ Accessing JSON data
▶ Data serialization with JSON
▶ How to keep JSON secure

NOTE

The official home of JSON is at http://json.org/, which also has links to a wide variety of JSON resources on the Web.

Finally, the whole sequence is enclosed between curly braces to form a JSON object representing your data:

```
var jsonObject = {
    "param1":"value1",
    "param2":"value2",
    "param3":"value3"
}
```

The object `jsonObject` just defined uses a subset of standard JavaScript notation—it's just a little piece of valid JavaScript code.

Objects written using JSON notation can have properties and methods accessed directly using the usual dot notation:

```
alert(jsonObject.param1); // alerts 'value1'
```

More generally, though, JSON is a general-purpose syntax for exchanging data in a string format. Not only objects, but *any* data that can be expressed as a series of `parameter:value` pairs can be expressed in JSON notation. It is then easy to convert the JSON object into a string by a process known as serialization; serialized data is convenient for storage or transmission around networks. You'll see how to serialize a JSON object later in this hour.

JSON has gathered momentum recently through offering a number of important advantages. JSON is

▶ Easy to read for both people and computers

▶ Simple in concept, a JSON object being nothing more than a series of `parameter:value` pairs enclosed by curly braces

▶ Largely self-documenting

▶ Fast to create and parse

▶ A subset of JavaScript, meaning that no special interpreters or other additional packages are necessary

NOTE

See http://www.flickr.com/ services/api/response.json.html for details of how Flickr supports JSON.

A number of leading online services and APIs including Flickr, Twitter, and several services from Google and Yahoo now offer data encoded using JSON notation.

Accessing JSON Data

To recover the data encoded into the JSON string, you need to somehow convert the string back to JavaScript code. This is usually referred to as *deserializing* the string.

Using `eval()`

Only more recent browsers have native support for JSON syntax (we talk about using native browser support in just a moment). However, because JSON syntax is a subset of JavaScript, the JavaScript function `eval()` can be used to convert a JSON string into a JavaScript object.

The `eval()` function uses the JavaScript interpreter to parse the JSON text and produce a JavaScript object:

```
var myObject = eval ('(' + jsonObjectString + ')');
```

You can then use the JavaScript object in your script:

```
var user = '{"username" : "philb1234","location" : "Spain","height" :
➡1.80}';
var myObject = eval ('(' + user + ')');
alert(myObject.username);
```

Using Native Browser Support

All recent browsers offer native support for JSON, making the use of `eval()` unnecessary.

Browsers with native JSON support create a JavaScript object called `JSON` to manage JSON encoding and decoding. The `JSON` object has two methods, `stringify()` and `parse()`.

JSON.parse()

You can interpret a JSON string using the method `JSON.parse()`, which takes a string containing a JSON-serialized object and breaks it up, creating an object with properties corresponding to the `"parameter":"value"` pairs found in the string:

```
var Mary = '{ "height":1.9, "age":36, "eyeColor":"brown" }';
var myObject = JSON.parse(Mary);
var out = "";
```

NOTE

The JavaScript `eval()` function evaluates or executes whatever is passed as an argument. If the argument is an expression, `eval()` evaluates the expression, for example,

```
var x = eval(4 * 3);
// x=12
```

If the argument comprises one or more JavaScript statements, `eval()` executes those statements:

```
eval("a=1; b=2;
document.write(a+b);"); //
writes 3 to the page
```

CAUTION

The string must be enclosed in parentheses like this to avoid falling foul of an ambiguity in the JavaScript syntax.

NOTE

Browsers natively supporting JSON include

▶ Firefox (Mozilla) 3.5+
▶ Internet Explorer 8+
▶ Google Chrome
▶ Opera 10+
▶ Safari 4+

FIGURE 8.1
Using JSON.parse()

```
for (i in myObject) {
    out += i + " = " + myObject[i] + "\n";
}
alert(out);
```

You can see the result in Figure 8.1

Data Serialization with JSON

In the context of data storage and transmission, *serialization* is the name given to the process of converting data into a format that can be stored or transmitted across a network and recovered later into the same format as the original.

In the case of JSON, a string is the chosen format of the serialized data. To serialize your JSON object (for instance, to send it across a network connection), you need to express it as a string.

In later browsers, those having JSON support, you can simply use the JSON.stringify() method.

JSON.stringify()

You can create a JSON-encoded string of an object using the JSON.stringify() method.

Let's create a simple object and add some properties:

```
var Dan = new Object();
Dan.height = 1.85;
Dan.age = 41;
Dan.eyeColor = "blue";
```

Now you can serialize the object using JSON.stringify:

```
alert( JSON.stringify("Dan") );
```

The serialized object is shown in Figure 8.2.

FIGURE 8.2
Using JSON.stringify()

Javascript Alert

{"height":1.85,"age":41,"eyeColor":"blue"}

OK

Create an HTML file using your editor and enter the code of Listing 8.1.

LISTING 8.1   Parsing a JSON String

```html
<!DOCTYPE html>
<html>
<head>
    <title>Parsing JSON</title>
    <script>
        function jsonParse() {
            var inString = prompt("Enter JSON object");
            var out = "";
            myObject = JSON.parse(inString);
            for (i in myObject) {
                out += "Property: " + i + " = " + myObject[i] + '\n';
            }
            alert(out);
        }
    </script>
</head>
<body onload="jsonParse()">
</body>
</html>
```

The function `jsonParse()` is called when the page finishes loading, by using the `onload` event handler of the `window` object attached to the `<body>` element of the page, as we discussed in Hour 6, "Scripts That Do More."

The first line of code inside the function invites you to enter a string corresponding to a JSON object.

```
var inString = prompt("Enter JSON object");
```

Type it carefully, remembering to enclose any strings in quotation marks, as in Figure 8.3.

The script then declares an empty string variable `out`, which later holds the output message.

```
var out = "";
```

The `JSON.parse()` method is then used to create an object based on the input string:

```
myObject = JSON.parse(inString);
```

FIGURE 8.3
Entering a JSON string

▼ TRY IT YOURSELF
Parsing a JSON String
continued

You can now build your output message string by looping around the object methods:

```
for (i in myObject) {
    out += "Property: " + i + " = " + myObject[i] + '\n';
}
```

Finally, display the result:

```
alert(out);
```

The output message should look like the one in Figure 8.4

FIGURE 8.4
The object created by parsing a JSON string

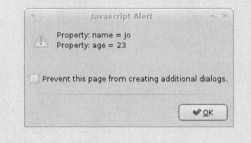

Reload the page and retry the script with a different number of `"parameter":"value"` pairs.

JSON Data Types

The parameter part of each `parameter:value` pair must follow a few simple grammatical rules:

▶ It must not be a JavaScript reserved keyword.

▶ It must not start with a number.

▶ It must not include any special characters except the underscore or dollar sign.

The values in JSON objects can contain any of the following data types:

▶ Number

▶ String

▶ Boolean

▶ Array

▶ Object

▶ null (empty)

CAUTION

JavaScript syntax has several data types that are not included in the JSON standard, including Date, Error, Math, and Function. These data types must be represented as some other data format, with the encoding and decoding programs following the same encoding and decoding rules.

Simulating Associative Arrays

In Hour 5, "Different Types of Data," we discussed the JavaScript array object and looked at its various properties and methods.

You may recall that the elements in JavaScript arrays have unique numeric identifiers:

```
var myArray = [];
myArray[0] = 'Monday';
myArray[1] = 'Tuesday';
myArray[2] = 'Wednesday';
```

In many other programming languages, you can use textual keys to make the arrays more descriptive:

```
myArray["startDay"] = "Monday";
```

Unfortunately, JavaScript does not directly support such so-called *associative* arrays.

However, using objects it is easy to go some way toward simulating their behavior. Using JSON notation makes the code easy to read and understand:

```
var conference = { "startDay" : "Monday",
    "nextDay"  : "Tuesday",
    "endDay"   : "Wednesday"
}
```

You can now access the object properties as if the object were an associative array:

```
alert(conference["startDay"]);   // outputs "Monday"
```

Creating Objects with JSON

You might recall from Hour 5 that one convenient way to express an array is with square brackets:

```
var categories = ["news", "sport", "films", "music", "comedy"];
```

JSON provides us with a somewhat similar shorthand for defining JavaScript objects.

TIP

This works because the two syntaxes

`object["property"]`

and

`object.property`

are equivalent in JavaScript.

CAUTION

Remember that this is not really an associative array, although it looks like one. If you loop through the object you will get, as well as these three properties, any methods that have been assigned to the object.

TIP

Although it was developed for describing JavaScript objects, JSON is independent of any language or platform. JSON libraries and tools exist for many programming languages including Java, PHP, C, and others.

You may recall that using the statement

```
var myObject = new Object();
```

creates an "empty" instance of an object with no properties or methods. The equivalent in JSON notation, unsurprisingly, is

```
var myObject = {};
```

While adding methods in this manner works fine in a JavaScript context, it is not permitted when using JSON as a general-purpose data interchange format. Functions declared this way will not be parsed correctly in a browser using native JSON parsing, though eval() will work. However, if you simply need to instantiate objects for use within your own script, you can add methods this way.

See the following section on JSON security.

Properties

As you've already seen, to express an object in JSON notation, you enclose the object in curly braces, rather than square ones, and list object properties as `"property":"value"` pairs:

```
var user = {
    "username" : "philb1234",
    "location" : "Spain",
    "height" : 1.80
}
```

The object properties are immediately available to access in the usual fashion:

```
var name = user.username; //  variable 'name' contains 'philb1234'
```

Methods

You can add methods this way too, by using anonymous functions within the object definition:

```
var user = {
    "username" : "philb1234",
    "location" : "Spain",
    "height" : 1.80,
    "setName":function(newName){
        this.username=newName;
    }
}
```

Then you can call the setName method in the usual way:

```
var newname = prompt("Enter a new username:");
user.setName(newname);
```

Arrays

Property values themselves can be JavaScript arrays:

```
var bookListObject = {
    "booklist": ["Foundation",
            "Dune",
            "Eon",
            "2001 A Space Odyssey",
            "Stranger In A Strange Land"]
}
```

In the preceding example, the object has a property `booklist`, the value of which is an array. You can access the individual items in the array by passing the required array key (remember that the array keys begin at zero):

```
var book = bookListObject.booklist[2]; // variable book has value "Eon"
```

The preceding line of code assigns to variable `book` the second item in the `booklist` array object, which is a property of the object named `bookListObject`.

Objects

The JSON object can even incorporate other *objects*. By making the array elements themselves JSON encoded objects, you can access them using dot notation.

In the following example code, the value associated with the property `booklist` is an array of JSON objects. Each JSON object has two `"parameter":"value"` pairs, holding the title and author respectively of the book in question.

After retrieving the array of books, as in the previous example, it is easy to then access the `title` and `author` properties:

```
var bookListObject = {
    "booklist": [{"title":"Foundation", "author":"Isaac Asimov"},
        {"title":"Dune", "author":"Frank Herbert"},
        {"title":"Eon", "author":"Greg Bear"},
        {"title":"2001 A Space Odyssey", "author":"Arthur C. Clarke"},
        {"title":"Stranger In A Strange Land", "author":"Robert A.
➥Heinlein"}]
    }
    //show the author of the third book
    alert(bookListObject.booklist[2].author); // displays "Greg Bear"
```

TRY IT YOURSELF ▼

Manipulating JSON Objects

Let's take the previous JSON object `bookListObject` and construct a user message that lists the books and authors in an easily-read format. Create an HTML file and enter the code from Listing 8.2. Your JSON object is identical to the one in the previous example, but this time you're going to access the array of books, and step through it with a loop, building a message string by appending the books and authors as you go. Finally you'll display the book information to the user.

▼ TRY IT YOURSELF

Manipulating JSON Objects
continued

LISTING 8.2   Handling JSON Multilevel Objects

```html
<!DOCTYPE html>
<html>
<head>
    <title>Understanding JSON</title>
    <script>
    var booklistObject = {
        "booklist": [{"title":"Foundation", "author":"Isaac Asimov"},
            {"title":"Dune", "author":"Frank Herbert"},
            {"title":"Eon", "author":"Greg Bear"},
            {"title":"2001 A Space Odyssey", "author":"Arthur C.
➥Clarke"},
            {"title":"Stranger In A Strange Land", "author":"Robert A.
➥Heinlein"}]
    }

        // a variable to hold our user message
        var out = "";

        // get the array
        var books = booklistObject.booklist;

        //Loop through array, getting the books one by one
        for(var i =0; i<books.length;i++) {
            var booknumber = i+1;
            out += "Book "  + booknumber +
                " is: '" + books[i].title +
                "' by " + books[i].author +
                "\n";
        }
    </script>
</head>
<body onload="alert(out)">
</body>
</html>
```

After designing the JSON object, you declare a variable and assign an empty string. This variable will hold the output message as you build it:

```
var out = "";
```

Now you extract the array of books, assigning this array to a new variable books, to avoid a lot of long-winded typing later:

```
var books = booklistString.booklist;
```

Afterwards you simply need to loop through the books array, reading the title and author properties of each book object and constructing a string to append to your output message:

```
for(var i =0; i<books.length;i++) {
    var booknumber = i+1; // array keys start at zero!
    out += "Book " + booknumber +
        " is: '" + books[i].title +
        "' by " + books[i].author +
        "\n";
}
```

TRY IT YOURSELF ▼

Manipulating JSON Objects

continued

Finally, show your message to the user:

```
alert(out);
```

The result of running this script is shown in Figure 8.5

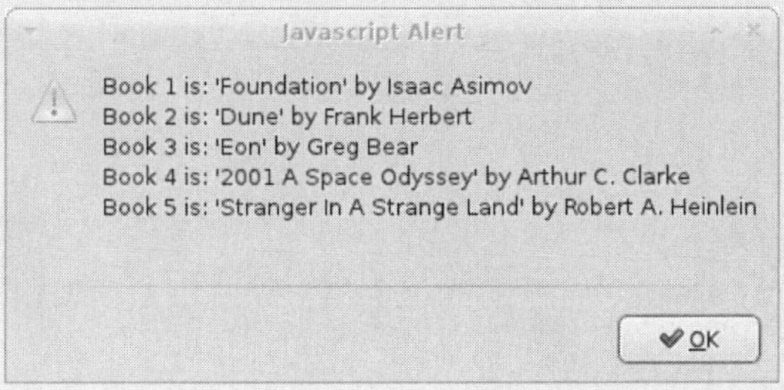

FIGURE 8.5
Your book information is displayed to the user.

JSON Security

Using JavaScript's eval() function can execute any JavaScript command. This could represent a potential security problem, especially when working with JSON data from untrusted sources.

It is safer to use a browser with a native JSON parser to convert a JSON string into a JavaScript object. A JSON parser will recognize only JSON text and will not execute script commands. Native JSON parsers are generally faster than using eval(), too.

Native JSON support is implemented in the newer browsers and in the latest ECMAScript (JavaScript) standard.

Summary

In this hour you learned about JSON notation, a simple data interchange syntax that can also be used to create instances of JavaScript objects.

You learned how to use the native JSON support of modern browsers to serialize objects into JSON strings and parse JSON strings into JavaScript objects.

Q&A

Q. **Where can I read the official JSON documentation?**

A. The JSON syntax is formally described in RFC 4627. You can read it at http://www.ietf.org/rfc/rfc4627. There is also a good deal of information at the official home of JSON, http://json.org/.

Q. **How can I find out whether my browser supports JSON natively?**

A. You can check for the existence of the JSON object using the `typeof` operator, as described in Hour 7, "Object Oriented Programming."

```
if(typeof JSON == 'object') {
    // you have JSON support, go ahead!
} else {
    // find another way to work, e.g. using eval()
}
```

Of course, you must be sure that your script hasn't defined its own object called JSON, or this won't work as expected.

Workshop

Try to answer all the questions before reading the subsequent "Answers" section.

Quiz

1. JSON is an acronym standing for

    a. JavaScript Object Notation

    b. Java String Object Notation

    c. JavaScript Serial Object Notation

2. Which of these can you do with JSON?

    a. Create a constructor function.

    b. Parse XML data.

    c. Directly instantiate an object.

3. What character is normally used to enclose the series of parameter:value pairs in a JSON object?

    a. Curly braces {}

    b. Square braces []

    c. Parentheses ()

Answers

1. a. JavaScript Object Notation

2. c. Directly instantiate an object

3. a. Curly braces {}

Exercises

Load your file containing Listing 8.1 back into your browser. Try entering some JSON strings using arrays as property values, for example:

```
{"days":["Mon","Tue","Wed"] }
```

How does the program react? Is its behavior as you would expect?

Instantiate an object using the new `Object()` syntax you learned in Hour 7 and add some properties with values of type array. Use the `stringify()` method to turn the object into a JSON string and display it.

HOUR 9
Responding to Events

In this hour you learn what event handling is about and how to write proper cross-browser event handlers for your scripts.

Understanding Event Handlers

To a scripting language seeking to add interactivity to web pages, events are fundamental; the user does something (causes some event to fire), and the page reacts to that event. Therefore JavaScript needs a way of detecting user actions so that it knows how to react appropriately.

There are also some events that aren't caused directly by user interaction, for example, the `window.onload` event introduced in Hour 6, "Scripts That Do More," which fires when a page finishes loading.

JavaScript can detect many of these events whenever they happen. Normally the event passes by unnoticed, unless there is some default action the browser has to take—for instance, following a link that has been clicked.

However, by writing an event handler to capture and react to a particular event, you can force something to happen. You can write your own code for handling the event, which will be executed whenever the event takes place. To enable your code to be executed when the associated event fires, you call it from an *event handler* for a specific event associated with a specific HTML element.

WHAT YOU'LL LEARN IN THIS HOUR

▶ More on JavaScript's built-in event handlers
▶ Adding and removing your own event handlers
▶ Using event handling for form validation

Examples of Events

In previous hours you created various event handlers to work with events such as click, mouseover, mouseout, and the body element's load event. Table 9.1 lists the common event handlers.

TABLE 9.1   Common Event Handlers

Event Handler	Event That It Handles
onBlur	User has left the field.
onChange	User has changed the value, then tried to leave.
onClick	User clicked.
onDblClick	User double-clicked.
onFocus	User arrived at field (clicked on it/tabbed to it).
onKeydown	A key was pressed over an element.
onKeyup	A key was released over an element.
onKeypress	A key was pressed over an element then released.
onLoad	The object has loaded.
onMousedown	The mouse was clicked over the object.
onMouseup	The mouse was released.
onMouseover	The cursor moved over the object.
onMousemove	The cursor moved while hovering over an object.
onMouseout	The cursor moved off the object.
onReset	User has reset a form.
onSelect	User selected some contents of the object.
onSubmit	User submitted a form.
onUnload	User closes the browser window.

Adding Event Handlers

You saw in Part I, "First Steps with JavaScript," how to add *inline* event handlers:

```
<input type="button" onclick="myFunction()" />
```

NOTE

In Hour 13, "JavaScript and CSS," we discuss good coding practice and why separating HTML from JavaScript is generally a good thing.

This technique dates from the early days of JavaScript. It is reliable and easy to remember but has some serious flaws. Above all, it mixes up your JavaScript with your HTML. The more you can keep these apart, the better.

There is a rather more elegant and flexible way to add event handlers. Suppose you have a function `buttonAlert()` that you want to call from the `onclick` event handler of a button on your HTML page.

```
function buttonAlert() {
    alert ("You clicked the button");
}
```

Instead of typing

```
<input type="button" id="myButton" onclick="buttonAlert()" />
```

you can instead access the button element within your JavaScript code by using the `document.getElementById()` method and assign your function to the `onClick` method of the element:

```
document.getElementById("myButton").onclick = buttonAlert;
```

This gives you more flexibility in your code; for instance you can now conditionally turn the event handler on or off, apply it to a different page element, or change its operation, all of which would have been much more difficult with an inline event handler.

Alternatively, if you don't need the function `buttonAlert()` to be available for use elsewhere, you can conveniently add the event handler by using an anonymous function instead:

```
document.getElementById("myButton").onclick = function() {
    alert ("You clicked the button");
}
```

Of course, there is no reason why you need to limit yourself to carrying out only one JavaScript statement in the function passed to the `onClick` event handler:

```
document.getElementById("myButton").onclick = function() {
    alert ("You clicked the button");
    counter++;
    document.getElementById("someId").innerHTML = "foo";
}
```

Removing an Event Handler

To remove an event handler, you can simply assign a `null` value:

```
document.getElementById("myButton").onclick = null;
```

The new value of `null` overwrites whatever was previously assigned, effectively removing the event handler.

CAUTION

Note that when registering an event handler you do not use parentheses with the function name. If you write

```
document.getElementById
("myButton").onclick =
myFunction();
```

the function `myFunction()` would first be executed, and its *return value* passed to the element's `onclick` event handler.

Default Actions

Generally the event handler for any specified HTML element is executed *before* the default action of that element. For example, assigning a function to the onClick event handler of a link:

```
<a href="target.html" id="myLink">Link text</a>
<script>
    document.getElementById("myLink").onclick = function() {
        // code statements go here
    }
</script>
```

The default action of the link element, when clicked by the user, would be to follow the link to target.html. Because the onClick event handler is executed before this default action, you can use it to change the default action of the element to something else.

Let's suppose you want to change the target of the link.

```
<a href="target.html" id="myLink">Link text</a>
<script>
    document.getElementById("myLink").onclick = function() {
        this.href = "http://www.google.com";
    }
</script>
```

Because the code of the onClick event handler executes first, by the time the link is followed, its href property has been modified to www.google.com instead of the original link target.

Preventing Default Action

You can also use the fact that event handler code executes first to *prevent* the default action of an HTML element from taking place.

If the event handler returns a value of Boolean false to the HTML element, the default action will not happen.

```
<a href="target.html" id="myLink">Link text</a>
<script>
    document.getElementById("myLink").onclick = function() {
        this.href = "http://www.google.com";
        return false;
    }
</script>
```

With a little effort, you can let the code in the event handler itself decide
whether the default behavior is allowed to happen:

```
<a href="target.html" id="myLink">Link text</a>
<script>
    document.getElementById("myLink").onclick = function() {
        this.href = "http://www.google.com";
        return confirm("I'm going to send you to Google instead. OK?");
    }
</script>
```

The value returned by the function will now depend on the user's
response to the confirm() dialog. If OK is clicked, the function will return
Boolean true, and the link will be followed to its new target URL. If the
user clicks Cancel in the dialog, the function will return false, and the
link's default behavior will not occur—the link simply won't work.

TRY IT YOURSELF ▼

**Preventing the
onSubmit Default
Action**

Every HTML form element has a handy event handler called onSubmit, which
is fired when a call is made to submit the form. You can attach a function to
this event handler that can prevent form submission by simply returning a
Boolean value of false to the form element.

Create an HTML document using the code in Listing 9.1.

LISTING 9.1   Canceling onSubmit Default Behavior

```
<!DOCTYPE html>
<html>
<head>
    <title>Canceling Default Behavior</title>
    <script>
        function checkform() {
            document.getElementById("form1").onsubmit = function() {
                var allowSubmit = true;
                if(document.getElementById("user").value == "") {
                    alert("Name field cannot be blank");
                    allowSubmit = false;
                }
                if(allowSubmit) alert("Data OK - submitting form");
                return allowSubmit;
            }
        }
        window.onload = checkform;
    </script>
</head>
```

▼ TRY IT YOURSELF

**Preventing the
onSubmit Default
Action**
continued

```
<body>
    <form id="form1">
        Name: <input type="text" value="" name="username" id="user" />
➥[Required field]<br/>
        Phone: <input type="text" value="" name="telephone" id="phone" />
➥[Optional field]<br/>
        <input type="submit" />
    </form>
</body>
</html>
```

In the head of the HTML page you define the function checkform(). This function is executed when the page has completed loading by employing the window.onload event handler. You have seen this event handler in use in previous hours, but this time the event handler has been added in JavaScript, rather than in the <body> tag of the page:

```
window.onload = checkform;
```

Let's take a closer look at the function checkform(). The first thing that happens inside the function definition is that the page's <form> element is identified using getElementById(), and an anonymous function is added to the form element's onSubmit event handler. This function will be executed when an attempt is made to submit the form; you want the function to return a value of true to allow submission or false to prevent submission.

First you define a variable to hold this return value and set its default value to true:

```
var allowSubmit = true;
```

Now for the nitty-gritty of the test condition:

```
if(document.getElementById("user").value == "") {
    alert("Name field cannot be blank");
    allowSubmit = false;
}
```

NOTE

In this example, the only check made on the form is that the user has entered something in the username field. In a real-world form, you'll almost certainly want to test many more conditions, and with much more rigor.

Such testing is usually referred to as *form validation*, and is a common use for JavaScript.

You can access the input element you wish to test by passing its id to the getElementById() method, as usual. In this case, you're interested in what (if anything) the user has entered into the input field—this is accessed via the value property of the element. The if() statement tests for the field being empty, which is the condition you want to prevent. If this condition is detected, you output a message to the user explaining the problem and change the value of your variable allowSubmit from true to false.

Finally, the value of `allowSubmit` is returned by the function; but because the form in our example doesn't actually do anything useful, I've first added a success message that is displayed only if the variable `allowSubmit` is still set to `true` as the function prepares to return:

```
if(allowSubmit) alert("Data OK - submitting form");
return allowSubmit;
```

Load the page into your browser, and try submitting the form with and without data in the Name field. Trying to submit the form with the Name field empty should produce a result as shown in Figure 9.1 and prevent the form from submitting.

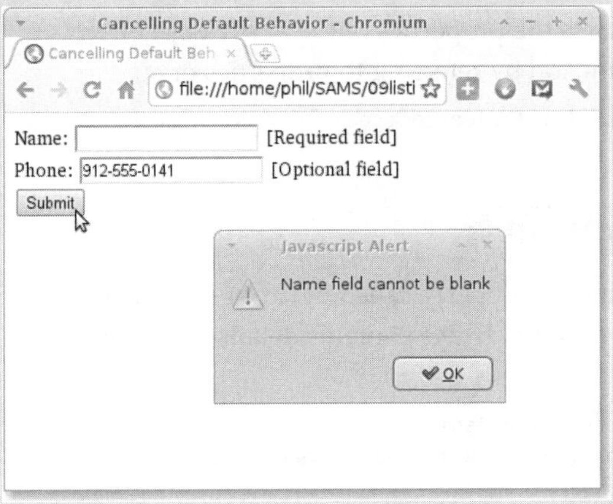

TRY IT YOURSELF ▼

Preventing the onSubmit Default Action
continued

FIGURE 9.1
Preventing form submission

The event Object

It's interesting and useful to know that an event has happened, but sometimes you want to know more about the event itself. *Which* key on the keyboard was pressed? *Where* was the mouse when the event was fired?

To access this information you have to use the `event` object. The `event` object is automatically generated by the browser and contains properties detailing various aspects of the event that has been fired.

How events are handled has suffered from browser incompatibilities perhaps more than any other part of JavaScript. To fully understand how to write good cross-browser code, you need to understand about the different approaches taken by (on the one hand) W3C compliant browsers and (on the other) Microsoft's Internet Explorer range of browsers.

The W3C Approach

In browsers such as Firefox that have more closely followed the W3C recommendations, the event object is automatically passed to an event handler function as an argument whenever the event is fired. To be able to access the properties of the event object, you need to give it a name, which you declare as an argument to the event handler, for example:

```
myElement = document.getElementById("someID");
myElement.onclick = function (e) { ... }
```

In this example, you can access the properties of the event object from within the event handler function by referring to properties of e:

```
myElement.onclick = function (e) { alert(e.type); }
```

The Microsoft Approach

Microsoft, in contrast, invented a property called event of the window object. The window.event property always contains details of the latest event to have been fired:

```
myElement = document.getElementById("someID");
myElement.onclick = function (e) { alert(window.event.type); }
```

Cross-Browser Event Handlers

Thankfully, there's an easy solution to make sure you always have a valid event object to examine.

The trick is to test for the presence of the event object within your event handler function. If it's there, all well and good; this is what would happen in a W3C compliant browser. If not, your user is probably using a browser with Microsoft-style event handling. In this case, you get the window.event property and assign it to a new object e:

```
myElement.onclick = function (e) {
    if (!e) var e = window.event;
    // e gives access to the event in all browsers
    ... more statements ...
}
```

So now we're good in all browsers? Unfortunately, no, not quite.

Although you now have an `event` object regardless of which browser we're using, the W3C and Microsoft differ on what to call many of the event object properties. Table 9.2 lists those that are the same in both W3C and Microsoft browsers.

TABLE 9.2   Common Event Properties

Property	Description
type	Type of event.
altKey	The Alt key was pressed (boolean).
clientX, clientY	Event coordinates relative to browser window.
ctrlKey	The Ctrl key was pressed (boolean).
keyCode	Keyboard character code.
screenX, screenY	Event coordinates relative to screen.
shiftKey	The Shift key was pressed (boolean).

Unfortunately, there are rather more properties that differ between the two browser types, some of which are shown in Table 9.3.

TABLE 9.3   Some Differing Event Properties

Microsoft	W3C	Description
fromElement	relatedTarget	Object **from** which the pointer moved for mouseover or mouseout
toElement	relatedTarget	Object **to** which the pointer moved for a mouseover or mouseout
offsetX, offsetY	n/a	Horizontal and vertical coordinates of the event within the element
n/a	pageX, pageY	Horizontal and vertical coordinates of the event within the document
x, y	layerX, layerY	Horizontal and vertical coordinates of the event within <body> element
srcElement	target	Object intended to receive the event

In all of these cases, you need to write some code to examine the event and find which method has been defined. Here's an example:

```
if (!e) var e = window.event;
var element = (e.target) ? e.target : e.srcElement;
```

In this code snippet, the existence of e.target is tested. If it exists, that is, if your user is using a W3C-style browser, the variable element is assigned the value of e.target. If e.target doesn't exist, you try to assign the value of e.srcElement instead.

▼ TRY IT YOURSELF

Listing onClick Event Properties

We can easily write a small program to list the properties and values associated with an event. In this case we take the onClick event of a button element and capture the properties of the event, posting them to the screen. Create an HTML document containing the code from Listing 9.2.

LISTING 9.2   Capturing onClick Event Properties

```
<!DOCTYPE html>
<html>
<head>
    <title>The event object</title>
    <script>
        function showEvent() {
            var out = "";
            document.getElementById("myButton").onclick = function (e) {
                if (!e) var e = window.event;
                for(i in e) {
                    out += i + " = " + e[i] + "<br/>";
                }
                document.getElementById("output").innerHTML = out;
            }
        }
        window.onload = showEvent;
    </script>
</head>
<body>
    <input id="myButton" type="button" value="Show Event Properties" />
    <div id="output"></div>
</body>
</html>
```

The body of your HTML document contains just two elements: a button to receive the onClick event and a <div> element to receive output from the script.

```
<input id="myButton" type="button" value="Show Event Properties" />
<div id="output"></div>
```

TRY IT YOURSELF ▼

Listing onClick **Event Properties**

continued

The function attached to the button's onClick event handler simply captures the object created by the click event and then loops through the event's properties, appending them to an output string.

Finally the script outputs its findings to the <div> element by assigning its innerHTML property.

```
document.getElementById("myButton").onclick = function (e) {
    if (!e) var e = window.event;
    for(i in e) {
        out += i + " = " + e[i] + "<br/>";
    }
    document.getElementById("output").innerHTML = out;
}
```

The results are shown in Figure 9.2.

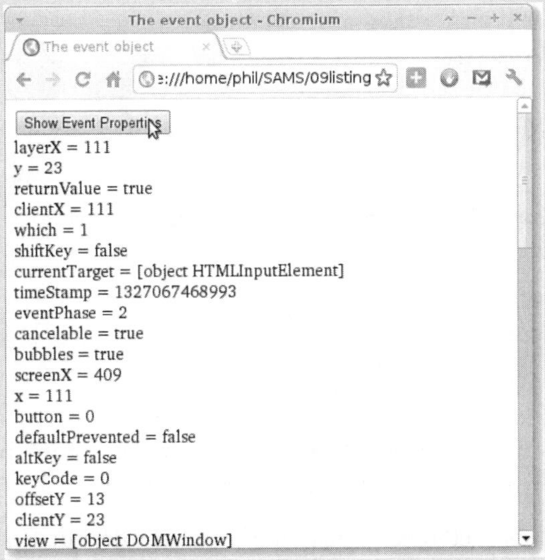

FIGURE 9.2
Capturing onClick event properties

If you have more than one browser available, compare the results of running the script in each one.

Advanced Event Handler Registration

So far we've looked at two ways to add event handlers—inline, that is, added as attributes to the HTML tag and by adding a function directly, such as

```
element.onclick = myFunction;
```

You've seen that adding event handlers inline is messy, mixing HTML and JavaScript in your page and making your code less flexible and harder to maintain.

The second method is better, but it has one major drawback; you can only add *one* event handler function to each property. What if you want to register two event handlers to the `onclick` property? If after writing

```
element.onclick = myFunction;
```

you then add a further line

```
element.onclick = myOtherFunction;
```

the second assignment will overwrite the first, and your call to `myFunction()` will be lost.

You could, of course, wrap both functions into another function that executes both:

```
element.onclick = function() {
    myFunction;
    myOtherFunction;
}
```

However, this isn't as flexible as we would like. What if you later want to remove just one of these two event handlers, or add a third?

Thankfully, there is a further method of registering event handlers that allows you the flexibility you need. Unfortunately, in this too the W3C and Microsoft have differed in how it will be implemented.

The W3C Method

The W3C offers the `addEventListener` and `removeEventListener` methods to let you add and remove as many event handlers as you need:

```
element.addEventListener('click',myFunction,false);
element.addEventListener('click',myOtherFunction,false);
```

The first argument declares which event is to be captured, while the second argument declares which function is to be executed on that event.

The third argument is a Boolean value that affects the order in which events are handled when two nested elements capture the same event; for instance, when a user clicks a <p> element within a <div> element, which of the two elements should execute its onClick handler first? You normally want to leave this argument set to false.

To later remove an event handler, you can simply call it with removeEventListener:

```
element.removeEventListener('click',myFunction,false);
```

The Microsoft Method

Microsoft's approach offers two similar methods, attachEvent and detachEvent:

```
element.attachEvent('onclick',myFunction);
element.detachEvent('onclick',myFunction);
```

No third argument is passed to these functions. Notice that the Microsoft methods prefix the event name with on, so the onClick event is referred to as click in the W3C method, but onclick for Microsoft browsers.

A Cross-Browser Implementation

You can make your event handling work cross-browser quite simply, once again by using feature detection to determine which event handling methods are supported:

```
function addEventHandler(element,eventType,handlerFunction) {
    if (element.addEventListener) {
        element.addEventListener (eventType,handlerFunction,false);
    } else if (element.attachEvent) {
        element.attachEvent ('on'+eventType,handlerFunction);
    }
}
var eventType = 'click';
var myButton = document.getElementById('button01');
addEventHandler(myButton,eventType,myFunction);
```

TIP

The browser manufacturers and the W3C refer to two possible scenarios when the same event is detected in two or more nested elements—*capturing*, in which the outer elements execute their event handlers first, followed by the nested elements, working inward; and *bubbling*, where the innermost event handler executes first, followed by the others working outward. There is a good description of the two approaches at www.quirksmode.org/js/events_order.html.

> **NOTE**
>
> The latest version of Internet Explorer, IE9, implements the W3C methods `addEventListener` and `removeEventListener`.
>
> Once again, though, your cross-browser solution works fine, given we are using feature detection rather than browser sniffing.

Removing events in a cross-browser fashion is just as straightforward:

```
function removeEventHandler(element,eventType,handlerFunction) {
    if (element.removeEventListener) {
        element.removeEventListener(eventType,handlerFunction,false);
    } else if (element.detachEvent) {
        element.detachEvent ('on'+eventType,handlerFunction);
    }
}
removeEventHandler(myButton,eventType,myFunction);
```

▼ TRY IT YOURSELF

Adding and Removing Event Listeners

Let's use these cross-browser methods to demonstrate adding and removing onClick event handlers from some HTML buttons. Create an HTML file containing the code from Listing 9.3.

LISTING 9.3   Adding and Removing Event Handlers

```
<!DOCTYPE html>
<html>
<head>
    <title>Adding and Removing Event Handlers</title>
    <script src="events.js"></script>
</head>
<body>
    <input id="buttonA" type="button" value="Button A" />
    <input id="button-a" type="button" value="Remove onClick Handler from
➥button A" /><br/>
    <input id="buttonB" type="button" value="Button B" />
    <input id="button-b" type="button" value="Remove onClick Handler from
➥button B" /><br/>
    <input id="reset" type="button" value="Reset" />
    <div id="div1" style="border:1px solid
➥black;width:300px;height:200px;" ></div>
</body>
</html>
```

This simple HTML page displays some buttons above a single <div> element. On this occasion, you're going to contain all of your JavaScript code in an external file events.js and link to it from the <head> of the page.

You want your JavaScript program to do the following:

▶ Initially, add event handlers to Button A and Button B. These event handlers should capture the onClick event and output the id of the clicked button to the page's <div> element, which we'll use to display all of the program output.

TRY IT YOURSELF ▼

Adding and Removing Event Listeners
continued

▶ Add event handlers to the buttons labeled Remove onClick Handler to capture the onClick event for these buttons and remove the onClick event handler from Button A or Button B as appropriate.

▶ Add an onCLick event handler to a fifth button that will reset Button A and Button B to their initial conditions, that is, re-add their onClick event handlers.

The source code of events.js is shown in Listing 9.4.

LISTING 9.4 JavaScript Source Code for events.js

```
function addEventHandler(element,eventType,handlerFunction) {
    if (element.addEventListener) {
        element.addEventListener(eventType,handlerFunction,false);
    } else if (element.attachEvent) {
        element.attachEvent ('on'+eventType,handlerFunction);
    }
}
function removeEventHandler(element,eventType,handlerFunction) {
    if (element.removeEventListener) {
        element.removeEventListener(eventType,handlerFunction,false);
    } else if (element.detachEvent) {
        element.detachEvent ('on'+eventType,handlerFunction);
    }
}
function appendText(e) {
    if (!e) var e = window.event;
    var element = (e.target) ? e.target : e.srcElement;
    document.getElementById('div1').innerHTML += element.id + "<br/>";
}
function removeOnClickA() {

    removeEventHandler(document.getElementById('buttonA'),'click',appendText);
}
function removeOnClickB() {

    removeEventHandler(document.getElementById('buttonB'),'click',appendText);
}
function reset() {
    addEventHandler(document.getElementById('buttonA'),'click',appendText);
    addEventHandler(document.getElementById('buttonB'),'click',appendText);
}
window.onload = function() {
    addEventHandler(document.getElementById('button-a'),'click',
removeOnClickA);
    addEventHandler(document.getElementById('button-b'),'click',
removeOnClickB);
    addEventHandler(document.getElementById('reset'),'click',reset);
reset();
}
```

▼ TRY IT YOURSELF

**Adding and Removing
Event Listeners**

continued

This might look a little daunting, but we'll take it step by step.

First, you declare your two functions addEventHandler and removeEventHandler that add and remove event handlers in a cross-browser fashion.

Next you declare a function appendText, which uses the techniques described earlier in the hour to identify the calling element, and then append its id property to the output area of the page<div>:

```
function appendText(e) {
    if (!e) var e = window.event;
    var element = (e.target) ? e.target : e.srcElement;
    document.getElementById('div1').innerHTML += element.id + "<br/>";
}
```

The methods removeOnClickA and removeOnClickB, when called, remove the appendText function from buttons A and B, respectively:

```
function removeOnClickA() {
    removeEventHandler(document.getElementById('buttonA'),'click',
➥appendText);
}
function removeOnClickB() {
    removeEventHandler(document.getElementById('buttonB'),'click',
➥appendText);
}
```

The function reset() calls addEventHandler twice, to add the appendText function as an onClick handler to Buttons A and B, respectively. You can call this function from your Reset button.

```
function reset() {
addEventHandler(document.getElementById('buttonA'),'click',appendText);
addEventHandler(document.getElementById('buttonB'),'click',appendText);
}
```

Finally, you use the window.onload event to set up the initial conditions for your script once the HTML loading has completed.

Next, add onClick event handlers to the Remove... buttons:

```
addEventHandler(document.getElementById('button-
➥a'),'click',removeOnClickA);
addEventHandler(document.getElementById('button-
➥b'),'click',removeOnClickB);
```

And then add the `reset()` function as an event handler to the `onClick` event of the Reset button:

```
addEventHandler(document.getElementById('reset'),'click',reset);
```

Finally, to initialize the page, call `reset()` to add the `onClick` handlers for Button A and Button B:

```
reset();
```

The operation of the page is depicted in Figure 9.3. Clicking Buttons A and B will, on each occasion, write the `id` of the clicked button into the output area. Clicking either of the Remove... buttons will remove the event handler from the relevant button (A or B), rendering it inoperative until the Reset button is clicked.

Load the completed page into your browser and check its operation.

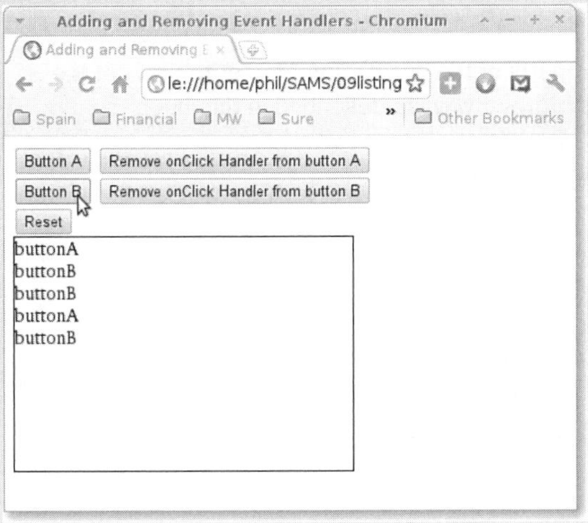

TRY IT YOURSELF ▼

Adding and Removing Event Listeners
continued

FIGURE 9.3
Adding and removing event handlers

Summary

In this hour you learned a good deal about how JavaScript can be used to handle events, including adding inline event handlers, adding event handlers via JavaScript code statements, and finally a cross-browser method of adding event handlers using the `addEventListener` and `attachEvent` methods.

Q&A

Q. My programs don't work correctly in Internet Explorer when I'm detecting mouse clicks. What am I doing wrong?

A. This is another area where Microsoft and the W3C have slightly different solutions. They both employ the button property of the event, but the integer values returned are different in each case.

In W3C browsers, the left button returns 0, the middle button 1, and the right button 2.

In Microsoft browsers, the left button returns 1, the right button 2, and the middle button 4. At first that seems a little crazy, but it disguises a neat trick; because the values are all powers of 2, they can be combined to reveal which buttons have been pressed in combination. A value of 3, for example, would indicate that the left and right buttons had been pressed together.

Q. How can I tell in a cross-browser way which keyboard key has been pressed?

A. Detect the `keyCode` property of the event. Don't forget to first get the event object in a cross-browser way, as described in this hour.

```
document.onkeydown = function(e) {
    if (!e) var e = window.event;
    alert(e.keyCode + " is the code for " +
String.fromCharCode(e.keyCode));
}
```

Workshop

Try to answer all the questions before reading the subsequent "Answers" section.

Quiz

1. How can you prevent the default behavior of an HTML element from occurring after its `onClick` event handler is executed?

    a. Return a value of `cancel` from the event handler.

    b. Return a value of Boolean `false` from the event handler.

    c. The default behavior cannot be prevented.

2. When does the `window.onload` event fire?

   a. When the page is fully loaded in the browser

   b. When the page starts to load in the browser

   c. When the page <head> has loaded

3. The object intended to receive an event is called `target` in:

   a. All browsers

   b. W3C browsers

   c. Microsoft browsers

Answers

1. b. Return Boolean `false` to prevent default behavior.

2. a. The `onload` event fires when the page is fully loaded in the browser.

3. b. W3C browsers use `target`; Microsoft browsers use `srcElement`.

Exercises

Modify the code of Listing 9.1 to also validate that the phone field of the form is not blank. Have the program produce only one alert message, saying which field(s) require attention.

In the exercise involving Listing 9.3 and Listing 9.4, modify the code such that the <div> element is cleared of content when it is double-clicked.

[Hint: Add an extra event handler in the page initialization that registers a new event handler to the `dblclick` event of the output <div>. This should call a function that sets `innerHTML` of the <div> to the empty string.]

JavaScript and Cookies

Something that the JavaScript techniques that you have seen so far can't do is transfer information from one page to another. Cookies provide a convenient way to give your web pages the means to store and retrieve small pieces of information on a user's own computer, allowing your website to save details such as a user's preferences or dates of his or her prior visits to your site.

In this hour you learn how to create, save, retrieve, and delete cookies using JavaScript.

What Are Cookies?

The HTTP protocol that you use to load web pages into your browser is a so-called *stateless* protocol. This means that once the server has delivered the requested page to your browser, it considers the transaction complete and retains no memory of it. This makes it difficult to maintain certain sorts of continuity during a browsing session (or between one session and the next) such as keeping track of which information the visitor has already read or downloaded, or of his or her login status to a private area of the site.

Cookies are a way to get around this problem; you could, for example, use cookies to remember a user's last visit, save a list of that user's preferences, or keep track of shopping cart items while he or she continues to shop. Correctly used, cookies can help improve the experience perceived by the user while using your site.

WHAT YOU'LL LEARN IN THIS HOUR

▶ What cookies are
▶ All about cookie attributes
▶ How to set and retrieve cookies
▶ About cookie expiration dates
▶ How to save multiple data items in a single cookie
▶ Deleting cookies
▶ Escaping and unescaping data
▶ Limitations of cookies

The cookies themselves are small strings of information that can be stored on a user's computer by the web pages he or she visits, to be later read by any other web pages from within the correct domain and path. Cookies are set to expire after a specified length of time.

Limitations of Cookies

Your browser may have a limit to how many cookies it can store, normally a few hundred cookies or more. Usually 20 cookies per domain name are permitted. A total of 4KB of cookie information can be stored for an individual domain.

In addition to the potential problems created by these size limitations, cookies can also vanish from a hard disk for various reasons, such as the cookie's expiry date being reached or the user clearing cookie information or switching browsers. Cookies should therefore never be used to store critical data, and your code should always be written to cope with situations where an expected cookie cannot be retrieved.

The `document.cookie` Property

Cookies in JavaScript are stored and retrieved by using the `cookie` property of the `document` object.

Each cookie is essentially a text string consisting of a name and a value pair, like this:

```
username=sam
```

When a web page is loaded into your browser, the browser marshals all of the cookies available to that page into a single stringlike property, which is available as `document.cookie`. Within `document.cookie`, the individual cookies are separated by semicolons:

```
username=sam;location=USA;status=fullmember;
```

Escaping and Unescaping Data

Cookie values may not include certain characters. Those disallowed include semicolons, commas, and whitespace characters such as space and tab. Before storing data to a cookie, you need to encode the data in such a way that it will be stored correctly.

You can use the JavaScript `escape()` function to encode a value before storing it, and the corresponding `unescape()` function to later recover the original cookie value.

The `escape()` function converts any non-ASCII character in the string to its equivalent two- or four-digit hexadecimal format—so a blank space is converted into %20, and the ampersand character & to %26.

For example, the following code snippet writes out the original string saved in variable `str` followed by its value after applying the `escape()` function:

```
var str = 'Here is a (short) piece of text.';
document.write(str + '<br />' + escape(str));
```

The output to the screen would be

```
Here is a (short) piece of text.
Here%20is%20a%20%28short%29%20piece%20of%20text.
```

Notice that the spaces have been replaced by %20, the opening parenthesis by %28, and the closing parenthesis by %29.

All special characters with the exception of: `*@-_+./` are encoded.

Cookie Ingredients

The cookie information in `document.cookie` may look like a simple string of name and value pairs, each in the form of

```
name=value;
```

but really each cookie has certain other pieces of information associated with it, as outlined in the following sections.

cookieName **and** cookieValue

These are the name and value visible in each `name=value` pair in the cookie string.

domain

The `domain` attribute tells the browser to which domain the cookie belongs. This attribute is optional, and when not specified its value defaults to the domain of the page setting the cookie.

NOTE

The definitive specification for cookies was published in 2011 as RFC6265. You can read it at http://tools.ietf.org/html/rfc6265.

The purpose of the domain attribute is to control cookie operation across subdomains. If the domain is set to www.example.com, then pages on a subdomain such as code.example.com cannot read the cookie. If, however, domain is set to example.com, then pages in code.example.com will be able to access it.

You cannot set the `domain` attribute to any domain outside the one containing your page.

path

The `path` attribute lets you specify a directory where the cookie is available. If you want the cookie to be only set for pages in directory `documents`, set the path to `/documents`. The path attribute is optional, the usual default path being `/`, in which case the cookie is valid for the whole domain.

secure

The optional and rarely used `secure` flag indicates that the browser should use SSL security when sending the cookie to the server.

expires

Each cookie has an `expires` date after which the cookie is automatically deleted. The `expires` date should be in UTC time (Greenwich Mean Time or GMT). If no value is set for `expires`, the cookie will only last as long as the current browser session and will be automatically deleted when the browser is closed.

Writing a Cookie

To write a new cookie, you simply assign a value to `document.cookie` containing the attributes required:

```
document.cookie = "username=sam;expires=15/06/2013 00:00:00";
```

To avoid having to set the date format manually, we could do the same thing using JavaScript's `Date` object:

```
var cookieDate = new Date ( 2013, 05, 15 );
document.cookie = "username=sam;expires=" + cookieDate.toUTCString();
```

This produces a result identical to the previous example.

TIP

Note the use of
`cookieDate.toUTCString();`

instead of
`cookieDate.toString();`

because cookie dates always need to be set in UTC time.

In practice, you should use `escape()` to ensure that no disallowed charac-ters find their way into the cookie values:

```
var cookieDate = new Date ( 2013, 05, 15 );
var user = "Sam Jones";
document.cookie = "username=" + escape(user) + ";expires=" +
➥cookieDate.toUTCString();
```

A Function to Write a Cookie

It's fairly straightforward to write a function to write your cookie for you, leaving all the escaping and the wrangling of optional attributes to the function. The code for such a function appears in Listing 10.1.

LISTING 10.1   Function to Write a Cookie

```
function createCookie(name, value, days, path, domain, secure) {
    if (days) {
        var date = new Date();
        date.setTime(date.getTime() + (days*24*60*60*1000));
        var expires = date.toGMTString();
    }
    else var expires = "";
    cookieString = name + "=" + escape (value);
    if (expires) cookieString += "; expires=" + expires;
    if (path) cookieString += "; path=" + escape (path);
    if (domain) cookieString += "; domain=" + escape (domain);
    if (secure) cookieString += "; secure";
    document.cookie = cookieString;
}
```

The operation of the function is straightforward. The `name` and `value` argu-ments are assembled into a `name=value` string, after escaping the `value` part to avoid errors with any disallowed characters.

Instead of specifying a date string to the function, we are asked to pass the number of days required before expiry. The function then handles the con-version into a suitable date string.

The remaining attributes are all optional and are appended to the string only if they exist as arguments.

CAUTION

Your browser security may pre-vent you from trying out the examples in this hour if you try simply loading the files from your local machine into your browser. To see the examples working, you may need to upload the files to a web server on the Internet or elsewhere on your local network.

Let's use this function to set the values of some cookies. The code for our simple page is shown in Listing 10.2. Create a new file testcookie.html and enter the code as listed. Feel free to use different values for the name and value pairs that you store in your cookies.

LISTING 10.2   Writing Cookies

```
<!DOCTYPE html>
<html>
<head>
<title>Using Cookies</title>
<script>
    function createCookie(name, value, days, path, domain, secure) {
    if (days) {
            var date = new Date();
            date.setTime(date.getTime() + (days*24*60*60*1000));
            var expires = date.toGMTString();
        }
        else var expires = "";
        cookieString = name + "=" + escape (value);
        if (expires) cookieString += "; expires=" + expires;
        if (path) cookieString += "; path=" + escape (path);
        if (domain) cookieString += "; domain=" + escape (domain);
        if (secure) cookieString += "; secure";
        document.cookie = cookieString;
    }
    createCookie("username","Sam Jones", 5);
    createCookie("location","USA", 5);
    createCookie("status","fullmember", 5);
</script>
</head>
<body>
Check the cookies for this domain using your browser tools.
</body>
</html>
```

Upload this HTML file to an Internet host or a web server on your local area network, if you have one. The loaded page displays nothing but a single line of text:

```
Check the cookies for this domain using your browser tools.
```

In the Chromium browser, I can open Developer Tools using Shift+Ctrl+I—if you are using a different browser, check the documentation for how to view cookie information.

TRY IT YOURSELF ▼

My result is shown in Figure 10.1.

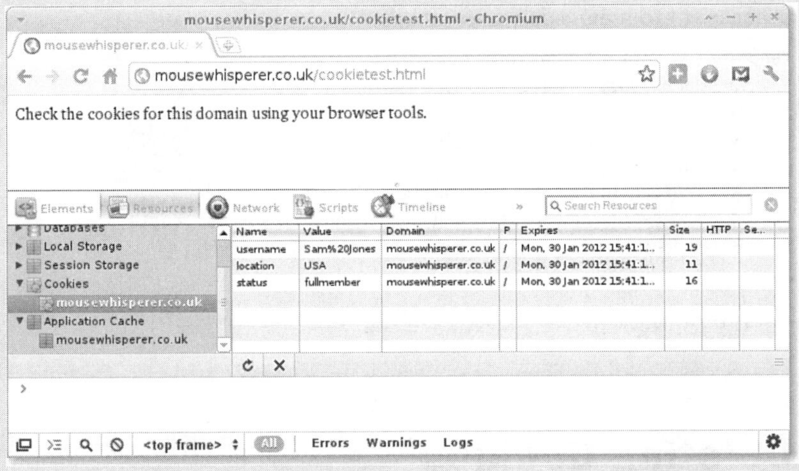

Writing Cookies
continued

FIGURE 10.1
Displaying our cookies

Reading a Cookie

The function to read the value of a cookie relies heavily on JavaScript's `split()` string method that you learned about in Hour 5, "Different Types of Data." You may recall that `split()` takes a string and splits it into an array of items, using a specified character to determine where the string should be divided:

```
myString = "John#Paul#George#Ringo";
var myArray = myString.split('#');
```

The preceding statement would divide string `myString` into a series of separate parts, cutting the string at each occurrence of the hash (#) character; `myArray[0]` would contain "John," `myArray[1]` would contain "Paul," and so forth.

Because in `document.cookie` the individual cookies are divided by the semicolon character, this character is initially used this to break up the string returned by `document.cookie`:

```
var crumbs = document.cookie.split(';');
```

You want to search for a cookie of a specific name, so the resulting array crumbs is next searched for any items having the appropriate name= part.

The indexOf() and substring() methods are combined to return the value part of the cookie, which is then returned by the function after using unescape() to remove any encoding:

```
function getCookie(name) {
    var nameEquals = name + "=";
    var crumbs = document.cookie.split(';');
    for (var i = 0; i < crumbs.length; i++) {
        var crumb = crumbs[i];
        if (crumb.indexOf(nameEquals) == 0) {
            return unescape(crumb.substring(nameEquals.length,
➥crumb.length));
        }
    }
    return null;
}
```

CAUTION

Some versions of some browsers maintain the cookie until you restart your browser even if you have deleted it in the script. If your program depends on the deletion definitely having happened, do another getCookie test on the deleted cookie to make sure it has really gone.

Deleting Cookies

To delete a cookie, all that is required is to set it with an expiry date before the current day. The browser infers that the cookie has already expired and deletes it.

```
function deleteCookie(name) {
    createCookie(name,"",-1);
}
```

▼ TRY IT YOURSELF

Using Cookies

Let's put together all you've learned so far about cookies by building some pages to test cookie operation.

First, collect the functions createCookie(), getCookie(), and deleteCookie() into a single JavaScript file and save it as cookie.js, using the code in Listing 10.3.

LISTING 10.3   cookies.js

```
function createCookie(name, value, days, path, domain, secure) {
    if (days) {
        var date = new Date();
        date.setTime( date.getTime() + (days*24*60*60*1000));
        var expires = date.toGMTString();
    }
    else var expires = "";
    cookieString = name + "=" + escape (value);
```

```
        if (expires) cookieString +=    "; expires=" + expires;
        if (path) cookieString += "; path=" + escape (path);
        if (domain) cookieString += "; domain=" + escape (domain);
        if (secure) cookieString += "; secure";
        document.cookie = cookieString;
}

function getCookie(name) {
    var nameEquals = name + "=";
    var crumbs = document.cookie.split(';');
    for (var i = 0; i < crumbs.length; i++) {
        var crumb = crumbs[i];
        if (crumb.indexOf(nameEquals) == 0) {
            return unescape(crumb.substring(nameEquals.length,
➡crumb.length));
        }
    }
    return null;
}

function deleteCookie(name) {
    createCookie(name,"",-1);
}
```

This file will be included in the <head> of your test pages so that the three functions are available for use by your code.

The code for the first test page, cookietest.html, is listed in Listing 10.4, and that for a second test page, cookietest2.html, in Listing 10.5. Create both of these pages in your text editor.

LISTING 10.4   cookietest.html

```
<!DOCTYPE html>
<html>
<head>
    <title>Cookie Testing</title>
    <script src="cookies.js"></script>
    <script>
        window.onload = function() {
            var cookievalue = prompt("Cookie Value:");
            createCookie("myCookieData", cookievalue);
        }
    </script>
</head>
<body>
    <a href="cookietest2.html">Go to Cookie Test Page 2</a>
</body>
</html>
```

▼ TRY IT YOURSELF

Using Cookies
continued

LISTING 10.5   cookietest2.html

```
<!DOCTYPE html>
<html>
<head>
    <title>Cookie Testing</title>
    <script src="cookies.js"></script>
    <script>
        window.onload = function() {
            document.getElementById("output").innerHTML = "Your cookie
value: " + getCookie("myCookieData");
        }
    </script>
</head>
<body>
    <a href="cookietest.html">Back to Cookie Test Page 1</a><br/>
    <div id="output"></div>
</body>
</html>
```

The only visible page content in cookietest.html is a link to the second page cookietest2.html. However, the `window.onload` event is captured by the code on the page and used to execute a function that launches a `prompt()` dialog as soon as the page has finished loading. The dialog asks you for a value to be saved to your cookie and then calls `createCookie()` to set a cookie of name myCookieData with the value that you just entered.

The page cookietest.html is shown working in Figure 10.2.

FIGURE 10.2
Enter a value for your cookie.

After setting your cookie, use the link to navigate to cookietest2.html.

When this page loads, the `window.onload` event handler executes a function that retrieves the stored cookie value using `getCookie()` and writes it to the page, as shown in Figure 10.3.

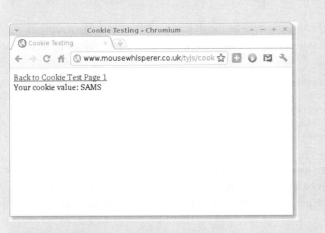

TRY IT YOURSELF ▼

Using Cookies
continued

FIGURE 10.3
Retrieving the value of your cookie

To try it out for yourself, you need to upload the files cookietest.html, cookietest2.html, and cookies.js to a web server on the Internet (or one on your local network, if you have one) as browser security will probably prevent you from setting cookies when using the `file://` protocol to view a file on your own computer.

Setting Multiple Values in a Single Cookie

Each cookie contains one `name=value` pair, so if you need to store several separate pieces of data such as a user's name, age, and membership number, you need three different cookies.

However, with a little ingenuity you can make your cookie store all three values by concatenating the required values into a single string, which becomes the value stored by your cookie.

This way, instead of having three separate cookies for name, age, and membership number, you could have just one, perhaps named `user`, containing all three pieces of data. To separate the details later, you place in your value string a special character called a *delimiter* to separate the different pieces of data:

```
var userdata = "Sandy|26|A23679";
createCookie("user", userdata);
```

Here the | (pipe) character acts as the delimiter. When you later retrieve the cookie value, you can split it into its separate variable values by using the | delimiter:

```
var myUser = getCookie("user");
var myUserArray = myUser.split('|');
var name = myUserArray[0];
var age = myUserArray[1];
var memNo = myUserArray[2];
```

NOTE

This is a further example of serialization, which you learned
about in Hour 8, "Meet JSON."

Cookies that store multiple values use up fewer of the allowed 20 cookies per domain allowed by some browsers, but remember that your use of cookies is still subject to the 4KB overall limit for cookie information.

Summary

In this hour you learned about cookies and how to set, retrieve, and delete them using JavaScript. You also learned how to concatenate multiple values into a single cookie.

Q&A

Q. When concatenating multiple values into a single cookie, can you use any character as a delimiter?

A. You can't use any character that might appear in your escaped data (except as the delimiter character), nor can you use equals (=) or the semicolon (;) as these are used to assemble and concatenate the name=value pairs in `document.cookie`. Additionally, cookies may not include whitespace or commas, so naturally they cannot be used as delimiters either.

Q. Are cookies safe?

A. Questions are often raised over the security of cookies, but such fears are largely unfounded. Cookies *can* help website owners and advertisers track your browsing habits, and they can (and do) use such information to select advertisements and promotions to show on web pages that you visit. They can't, however, find out personal information about you or access other items on your hard disk simply through the use of cookies.

Workshop

Try to answer all the questions before reading the subsequent "Answers" section.

Quiz

1. Cookies are small pieces of text information stored

    a. On a user's hard disk

    b. On the server

    c. At the user's Internet service provider

2. Encoding a string to store it safely in a cookie can be carried out by using

    a. `escape()`

    b. `unescape()`

    c. `split()`

3. A character used to separate multiple values in a single cookie is known as

    a. An escape sequence

    b. A delimiter

    c. A semicolon

Answers

1. a. Cookies are stored on a user's hard disk.

2. a. You can use `escape()` to safely encode string values for storage in a cookie.

3. b. Multiple values are separated by a character called a delimiter.

Exercises

Find out how to view cookie information in your favorite browser. Use the browser tools to examine the cookie set by the code of Listing 10.4.

Rewrite the code for cookietest.html and cookietest2.html to write multiple values to the same cookie and separate them on retrieval, displaying the values on separate lines. Use the hash character # as your delimiter.

Add a button to cookietest2.html to delete the cookie set in cookietest.html and check that it works as requested. [Hint: Use the button to call `deleteCookie()`.]

PART III
Working with the Document Object Model (DOM)

Navigating the DOM

You've already learned about the W3C DOM and, in the worked examples of previous hours, you used various DOM objects, properties, and methods.

In this hour you begin exploring how JavaScript can directly interact with the DOM. In particular, you learn some new ways to navigate around the DOM, selecting particular DOM objects that represent parts of the page's HTML contents.

DOM Nodes

In Part I, "First Steps with JavaScript," you were introduced to the W3C Document Object Model (DOM) as a hierarchical tree of parent-child relationships that together form a model of the current web page. By using appropriate methods, you can navigate to any part of the DOM and retrieve details about it.

You probably recall that the top-level object in the DOM hierarchy is the window object, and that one of its children is the document object. In this hour and the next we mainly deal with the document object and its properties and methods.

Take a look at the simple web page of Listing 11.1.

LISTING 11.1   A Simple Web Page

```
<!DOCTYPE html>
<html>
<head>
    <title>To-Do List</title>
</head>
```

WHAT YOU'LL LEARN IN THIS HOUR

- ▶ The concept of nodes
- ▶ The different types of node
- ▶ Using nodeName, nodeType, and nodeValue
- ▶ Using the childNodes collection
- ▶ Selecting elements with getElementsByTagName()
- ▶ How to use Mozilla's DOM Inspector

LISTING 11.1   Continued

```
<body>
    <h1>Things To Do</h1>
    <ol id="toDoList">
        <li>Mow the lawn</li>
        <li>Clean the windows</li>
        <li>Answer your email</li>
    </ol>
    <p id="toDoNotes">Make sure all these are completed by 8pm so you can
➥watch the game on TV!</p>
</body>
</html>
```

Figure 11.1 shows the page displayed in Mozilla Firefox.

FIGURE 11.1
Our simple web page displayed in Firefox

CAUTION

Remember, the DOM is not available until the page has finished loading. Don't try to execute any statements that use the DOM until then, or your script is likely to produce errors.

When page loading has completed, the browser has a full, hierarchical DOM representation of this page available for us to examine. Figure 11.2 shows a simplified version of how part of that representation might look.

Look at how the tree diagram of Figure 11.2 relates to the code in Listing 11.1.

The <html> element contains all the other markup of the page. It is the *parent* element to two immediate *child* elements, the <head> and <body> elements. These two elements are *siblings*, as they share a parent. They are also parents themselves; the <head> element has one child element <title>, and the <body> element three children, the <h1> heading, the ordered list <ol>, and a paragraph <p>. Of these three siblings, only <ol> has children, those being three <li> line item elements. Various of these elements of the tree contain text, shown represented in the gray boxes in Figure 11.2.

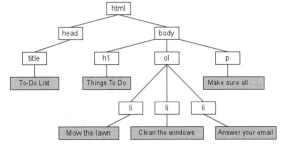

FIGURE 11.2
The DOM's tree model of our page

The DOM is constructed as a hierarchy of such relationships. The boxes that make up the junctions and terminating points of the tree diagram are known as *nodes*.

Types of Nodes

Figure 11.2 shows various *element nodes*, each of which represents an HTML element such as a paragraph element <p>, along with some *text nodes*, representing the text content of such page elements.

There are a number of other node types, representing such information as each element's attributes, HTML comments, and other information relevant to the page. Many node types can, of course, contain other nodes as children.

Each different type of node has an associated number known as its nodeType property. The nodeType properties for the various types of nodes are listed in Table 11.1.

TABLE 11.1   nodeType Values

nodeType	Type of Node
1	element
2	attribute
3	text (including whitespace)
4	CDATA section
5	entity reference
6	entity
7	processing instruction
8	HTML comment

TIP

Where they exist, text nodes are always contained within element nodes. However, not every element node contains a text node.

TIP

You'll likely do most of your work using node types 1, 2, and 3 as you manipulate page elements, their attributes, and the text that those elements contain.

TABLE 11.1   Continued

nodeType	Type of Node
9	document
10	document type (DTD)
11	document fragment
12	notation

The `childNodes` Property

A useful DOM property for each node is a collection of its immediate children. This array-like list is called `childNodes` and allows you access to information about the children of any DOM node.

The `childNodes` collection is a so-called *NodeList*, in which the items are numerically indexed. A collection looks and (for the most part) behaves like an array—you can refer to its members like those of an array, and you can iterate through them like you would for an array. However, there are a few array methods you can't use like `push()` and `pop()`. For all the examples here, you can treat the collection like you would a regular array.

A node list is a live collection, which means that any changes to the collection to which it refers are immediately reflected in the list; you don't have to fetch it again when changes occur.

▼ TRY IT YOURSELF

Using the `childNodes` Property

You can use the collection returned by the `childNodes` property to examine the ordered list element `<ol>` that appears in Listing 11.1. You're going to write a small function to read the child nodes of the `<ol>` element and return the total number present in the list.

First, you can retrieve the `<ol>` element via its id.

```
var olElement = document.getElementById("toDoList");
```

The child nodes of the `<ol>` element will now be contained in the object

```
olElement.childNodes
```

You only want to select the `<li>` elements in the list, so you now want to step through the `childNodes` collection, counting just those nodes for which `nodeType==1` (i.e., those corresponding to HTML elements), ignoring anything else contained in the ordered list element such as comments and white-space. Remember, you can treat the collection pretty much like an array; here you use the length property as you would for an array:

```
var count = 0;
for (var i=0; i < olElement.childNodes.length; i++) {
    if(olElement.childNodes[i].nodeType == 1) count++;
}
```

Let's cook up a little function to carry out this task when the page has loaded, and output the result with an alert dialog.

```
function countListItems() {
    var olElement = document.getElementById("toDoList");
    var count = 0;
    for (var i=0; i < olElement.childNodes.length; i++) {
        if(olElement.childNodes[i].nodeType == 1) count++;
    }
    alert("The ordered list contains " + count + " items");
}
window.onload = countListItems;
```

Create a new HTML page in your editor and enter the code of Listing 11.1. Incorporate the preceding JavaScript code into a <script> element in the page head and load the page into the browser.

Figure 11.3 shows the result of loading the page in Mozilla Firefox.

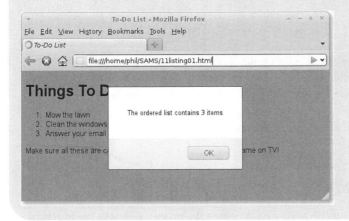

TRY IT YOURSELF ▼

Using the childNodes **Property**
continued

CAUTION

Whitespace (such as the space and tab characters) in HTML code are generally ignored by the browser when rendering the page. However, the presence of whitespace within a page element, for example, within your ordered list element, will in many browsers create a child node of type text (nodeType == 3) within the element. This makes simply using

childNodes.length

a risky business.

FIGURE 11.3
Using the childNodes array

firstChild **and** lastChild

There is a handy shorthand for selecting the first and last elements in the childNodes array.

`firstChild` is, unsurprisingly, the first element in the `childNodes` array. Using `firstChild` is equivalent to using `childNodes[0]`.

To access the last element in the collection you gain a big advantage by using `lastChild`. To access this element you would otherwise have to do something like this:

```
var lastChildNode = myElement.childNodes[myElement.childNodes.length
➡- 1];
```

That's pretty ugly. Instead, you can simply use

```
var lastChildNode = myElement.lastChild;
```

The `parentNode` Property

The `parentNode` property, unsurprisingly, returns the parent node of the node to which it's applied. In the previous example, you used

```
var lastChildNode = myElement.lastChild;
```

Using `parentNode` you can go one step back up the tree. The line

```
var parentElement = lastChildNode.parentNode;
```

would return the parent element of `lastChildNode`, which is of course object `myElement`.

`nextSibling` and `previousSibling`

Sibling nodes are nodes that share a parent node. When applied to a specified parent node, these read-only properties return the next and previous sibling nodes, respectively, or `null` if there is no such node.

```
var olElement = document.getElementById("toDoList");
var firstOne = olElement.firstChild;
var nextOne = firstOne.nextSibling;
```

Node Value

In addition to `nodeType`, the DOM offers the property `nodeValue` to return the value stored in a node. You generally want to use this to return the text stored in a text node.

Let's suppose that instead of counting the list items in the previous example, you wanted to extract the text contained in the <p> element of the page. To do this you need to access the relevant <p> node, find the text node that it contains, and then use `nodeValue` to return the information:

```
var text = '';
var pElement = document.getElementById("toDoNotes");
for (var i=0; i < pElement.childNodes.length; i++) {
    if(pElement.childNodes[i].nodeType == 3) {
        text += pElement.childNodes[i].nodeValue;
    };
}
alert("The paragraph says:\n\n" + text );
```

Node Name

The `nodeName` property returns the name of the specified node as a string value. The values returned by the `nodeName` value are summarized in Table 11.2. The `nodeName` property is read-only—you can't change its value.

Where `nodeName` returns an element name, it does so without the surrounding < and > that you would use in HTML source code:

```
var pElement = document.getElementById("toDoNotes");
alert( pElement.nodeName);  // alerts 'P'
```

TABLE 11.2   Values Returned by the nodeName Property

nodeType	Node Type	nodeName
1	element	element (tag) name
2	attribute	attribute name
3	text	the string "#text"

Selecting Elements with getElementsByTagName()

You already know how to access an individual page element using the document object's `getElementById()` method. Another method of the document object, `getElementsByTagName()`, allows you to build an array populated with all of the occurrences of a particular tag.

Like `getElementById()`, the `getElementsByTagName()` method accepts a single argument. However, in this case it's not the element id but the required tag name that is passed to the method as an argument.

CAUTION

Make careful note of the spelling. *Elements* (plural) is used in `getElementsByTagName()`, whereas *Element* (singular) is used in `getElementById()`.

TIP

Even if there is only one element with the specified tag name, getElementsByTagName() still returns a collection, although it will contain only one item.

As an example, suppose you wanted to work with all of the <div> elements in a particular document. You can populate a variable with an array-like collection called myDivs by using

```
var myDivs = document.getElementsByTagName("div");
```

You don't have to use getElementsByTagName() on the entire document. It can be applied to any individual object and return a collection of elements with the given tag name contained within that object.

▼ TRY IT YOURSELF

Using getElements ByTagName()

Earlier you wrote a function to count the list items <li> inside an ordered list <ol> element:

```
function countListItems() {
    var olElement = document.getElementById("toDoList");
    var count = 0;
    for (var i=0; i < olElement.childNodes.length; i++) {
        if(olElement.childNodes[i].nodeType == 1) count++;
    }
alert("The ordered list contains " + count + " items");
}
```

You used the childNodes array to get all the child nodes and then selected those corresponding to elements by testing for nodeType == 1.

You can easily implement the same function by using getElementsByTagName().

You start the same way by selecting the <ol> element based on its id:

```
var olElement = document.getElementById("toDoList");
```

Now you can create an array listItems and populate it with all if the <li> elements contained in our <ol> object olElement:

```
var listItems = olElement.getElementsByTagName("li");
```

All that remains is to display how many items are in the array:

```
alert("The ordered list contains " + listItems.length + " items");
```

Listing 11.2 contains the complete code for the page, including the revised function countListItems().

LISTING 11.2   Using getElementsByTagName()

```
<!DOCTYPE html>
<html>
<head>
    <title>To-Do List</title>
    <script>
        function countListItems() {
            var olElement = document.getElementById("toDoList");
            var listItems = olElement.getElementsByTagName("li");
            alert("The ordered list contains " + listItems.length + "
➥items");
        }
        window.onload = countListItems;
    </script>
</head>
<body>
    <h1>Things To Do</h1>
    <ol id="toDoList">
        <li>Mow the lawn</li>
        <li>Clean the windows</li>
        <li>Answer your email</li>
    </ol>
    <p id="toDoNotes">Make sure all these are completed by 8pm so you can
➥watch the game on TV!</p>
</body>
</html>
```

Save this listing as an HTML file and load it into your browser. Check that the result is the same as in Figure 11.3.

TRY IT YOURSELF ▼

Using getElements
ByTagName()
continued

NOTE

A further useful method for getting a collection of elements is

document.getElementsBy
ClassName()

As you'll have worked out from the method name, this method returns all the page elements having a particular value of the class attribute. However, this was not supported in Internet Explorer until IE9.

Reading an Element's Attributes

HTML elements often contain a number of attributes with associated values:

```
<div id="id1" title="report">Here is some text.</div>
```

The attributes are always placed within the opening tag, each attribute being of the form attribute=value. The attributes themselves are child nodes of the element node in which they appear, as depicted in Figure 11.4

FIGURE 11.4
Attribute nodes

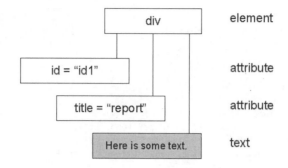

FIGURE 11.4
Attribute nodes

Having navigated to the element node of interest, you can read the value of any of its attributes using the getAttribute() method:

```
var myNode = document.getElementById("id1");
alert(myNode.getAttribute("title"));
```

The previous code snippet would display "report" within the alert dialog. If you try to retrieve the value of a non-existent attribute, getAttribute() will return null. You can use this fact to efficiently test whether an element node has a particular attribute defined:

```
if(myNode.getAttribute("title")) {
  ... do something ...
}
```

The if() condition will only be met if getAttribute() returns a non-null value, given that null is interpreted by JavaScript as a "falsy" value (not Boolean false, but considered as such).

Mozilla's DOM Inspector

One of the easiest ways to view node information is by using the DOM Inspector available for Mozilla Firefox. If you use Firefox, you may find the DOM Inspector already installed, though since Firefox 3 it's been available as a separate add-on. You can download it at https://addons.mozilla.org/en-US/firefox/addon/dom-inspector-6622/.

Once installed, you can open the DOM Inspector for any page you have loaded in the browser by pressing Ctrl+Shft+I. The window that opens is shown in Figure 11.5, displaying the DOM representation of the web page of Listing 11.1.

CAUTION

There also exists a property simply called attributes that contains an array of all of a node's attributes. In theory you can access the attributes as name=value pairs in the order they appear in the HTML code by using a numerical key; so attributes[0].name would be id and attributes[1].value would be 'report'. However, its implementation in Internet Explorer and some versions of Firefox is buggy. It's safer to use getAttribute() instead.

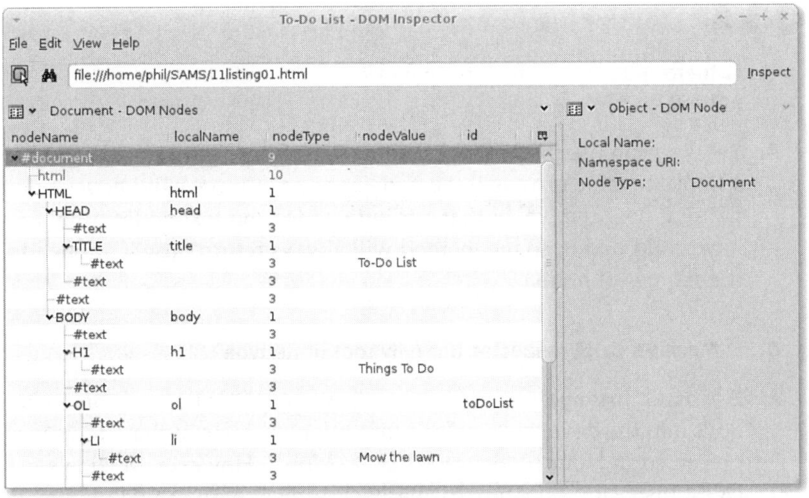

FIGURE 11.5
Mozilla's DOM Inspector

A DOM node is selected from the tree structure in the left-hand display pane, and details about it can be examined in the right-hand pane. As well as the viewer for the DOM tree, other viewers are included for viewing CSS Rules, Style Sheets, Computed Style, JavaScript Objects, and more.

The interface can seem a little daunting at first, but it's well worth exploring the program's capabilities.

Summary

In this hour you learned about nodes and how to navigate the DOM using a variety of node-related methods.

You also learned about using Mozilla's DOM Inspector to examine the DOM of your page.

Q&A

Q. Is there a quick way to determine whether a node has any child nodes?

A. Yes, you can use the `hasChildNodes()` method. This method returns a Boolean value of `true` if the node has one or more child nodes or `false` if not. Remember that attribute nodes and text nodes cannot have child nodes, so the method will always return false if applied to these types of node.

Q. Is Mozilla's DOM Inspector the only tool of its type?

A. Not at all. Just about every browser has some DOM inspection tools built into the developer tools. Information on some of these tools was presented in Hour 6, "Scripts That Do More." However, Mozilla's DOM Inspector gives a particularly clear view of the DOM hierarchy and the parameters of individual nodes; that's why I presented it here.

Workshop

Try to answer all the questions before reading the subsequent "Answers" section.

Quiz

1. Which of the following is *not* a type of node?

    a. Element

    b. Attribute

    c. Array

2. The `getElementsByTagName()` method returns:

    a. An array-like collection of element objects

    b. An array-like collection of `nodeType` values

    c. An array-like collection of tag names

3. In some browsers the whitespace within a page element will cause the creation of

    a. A text node

    b. A JavaScript error

    c. An attribute node

Answers

1. c. An array is not a type of node.

2. a. An array of element objects is returned.

3. a. Whitespace within an element usually creates a text node as a child node of the element.

Exercises

Using the nodeType information listed in Table 11.1, write a function to find all the HTML comments in the body section of a page and concatenate them into a single string. Add some comments to the code listed in Listing 11.2; then introduce and test your new function.

If you have Firefox, download and install the DOM Inspector and familiarize yourself with its interface. Use the program to investigate the DOM of some of your favorite web pages.

Scripting the DOM

In the previous hour, you learned how to navigate the DOM tree to select specific nodes (or collections of nodes) and how to examine their properties.

In addition to reading information from the DOM, you can use DOM methods to alter your page too. If you change the DOM representation of a document, you also change how it's viewed in the browser window.

In this hour, you see how to create new elements, how to add, edit, and remove nodes of the DOM tree, and how to manipulate elements' attributes.

Creating New Nodes

Adding new nodes to the DOM tree is a two-stage process:

First you create a new node. Once created, the node is initially in a kind of "limbo"; it exists, but it's not actually located anywhere in the DOM tree and therefore doesn't appear on the visible page in the browser window.

Next you add the new node to the tree in the desired location. At this point it becomes part of the visible page.

Let's look at some of the methods of the document object that are available for creating nodes.

createElement()

You can call on the createElement() method to create new HTML elements having any of the standard HTML element types—paragraphs, spans, tables, lists and so on.

TIP

When you amend the DOM using the methods described in this hour, you change the way a page appears in the browser. Bear in mind, though, that you're not changing the document itself. If you ask your browser to display the source code of the page, you won't see any changes there.

That's because the browser is actually displaying the current DOM representation of the document. Change that, and you change what appears onscreen.

Let's suppose you've decided to create a new <div> element for your document. To do so, you simply need to pass the relevant nodeName value—in this case "div"—to the createElement method:

```
var newDiv = document.createElement("div");
```

The new <div> element now exists but currently has no contents, no attributes, and no location in the DOM tree. You see how to solve these issues shortly.

createTextNode()

Many of the HTML elements in your page need some content in the form of text. The createTextNode() method takes care of that. It works pretty much like createElement(), except that the argument it accepts is not a nodeName value, but a string containing the desired text content of the element:

```
var newTextNode = document.createTextNode("Here is some text content.");
```

As with createElement(), the newly created node is not yet located in the DOM tree; JavaScript has it stored in the newTextNode variable while it waits for you to place it in its required position.

cloneNode()

There's no point in reinventing the wheel. If you already have a node in your document that's just like the new one you want to create, you can use cloneNode() to do so.

Unlike createElement() and createTextNode(), cloneNode() takes a single argument—a Boolean value of *true* or *false*.

Passing true to the cloneNode() function tells JavaScript that you want to clone not only the node, but all of its child nodes:

```
var myDiv = document.getElementById("id1");
var newDiv = myDiv.cloneNode(true);
```

In this example, I've asked JavaScript to clone the element's child nodes too; for example, any text that myDiv contained (which would be contained in a child text node of the element) will be faithfully reproduced in the new <div> element.

Had I called

```
var newDiv = myDiv.cloneNode(false);
```

then the new <div> element would be identical to the original, except that it would have no child nodes. It would, for instance, have any attributes belonging to the original element (provided that the original node was an element node, of course).

As with new nodes created by `createElement()` and `createTextNode()`, the new node created by `cloneNode()` is initially floating in space; it does not yet have a place in the DOM tree.

You see how to achieve that next.

Manipulating Child Nodes

The new nodes you've created aren't yet of any practical value, as they don't yet appear anywhere in the DOM. A few methods of the `document` object are specifically designed for placing nodes in the DOM tree, and they are described in the following sections.

appendChild()

Perhaps the simplest way of all to attach a new node to the DOM is to append it as a child node to a node that already exists somewhere in the document. Doing so is just a matter of locating the required parent node and calling the `appendChild()` method:

```
var newText = document.createTextNode("Here is some text content.");
var myDiv = document.getElementById("id1");
myDiv.appendChild(newText);
```

In the preceding code snippet, a new text node has been created and added as a child node to the currently existing <div> element having an id of id1.

Of course, `appendChild()` works equally well with all types of nodes, not just text nodes. Suppose you needed to add another <div> element within the parent <div> element:

```
var newDiv = document.createElement("div");
var myDiv = document.getElementById("id1");
myDiv.appendChild(newDiv);
```

Your originally existing <div> element now contains a further <div> element as its last child; if the parent <div> element already contained some text content in the form of a child text node, then the parent div (as represented in the newly modified DOM, not in the source code) would now have the form:

```
<div id="id1">
    Original text contained in text node
    <div></div>
</div>
```

insertBefore()

Whereas appendChild() always adds a child element to the end of the list of children, with insertBefore() you can specify a child element and insert the new node immediately before it.

The method takes two arguments: the new node, and the child before which it should be placed. Let's suppose that your page contains the following HTML snippet:

```
<div id="id1">
    <p id="para1">This paragraph contains some text.</p>
    <p id="para2">Here's some more text.</p>
</div>
```

To insert a new paragraph between the two that are currently in place, first create the new paragraph:

```
var newPara = document.createElement("p");
```

Identify the parent node and the child node before which you want to make the insertion:

```
var myDiv = document.getElementById("id1");
var para2 = document.getElementById("para2");
```

Then pass these two as arguments to insertBefore():

```
myDiv.insertBefore(newPara, para2);
```

replaceChild()

You can use replaceChild() when you want to replace a current child node of a specific parent element with another node. The method takes two arguments—a reference to the new child element followed by a reference to the old one.

Take a look at the code of Listing 12.1.

LISTING 12.1   Replacing Child Elements

```
<!DOCTYPE html>
<html>
<head>
    <title>Replace Page Element</title>
</head>
<body>
    <div id="id1">
        <p id="para1">Welcome to my web page.</p>
        <p id="para2">Please take a look around.</p>
        <input id="btn" value="Replace Element" type="button" />
    </div>
</body>
</html>
```

Suppose that you want to use the DOM to remove the first paragraph in the <div> and replace it instead with an <h2> heading as follows:

<h2>Welcome!</h2>

First create the new node representing the <h2> heading:

```
var newH2 = document.createElement("h2");
```

This new element needs to contain a text node for the heading text. You can either create and add it now or do it later when you've added your new <h2> element to the DOM. Let's do it now:

```
var newH2Text = document.createTextNode("Welcome!");
newH2.appendChild(newH2Text);
```

Now you can swap out the unwanted child node of the <div> element and replace it with the new one:

```
var myDiv = document.getElementById("id1");
var oldP = document.getElementById("para1");
myDiv.replaceChild(newH2, oldP);
```

Finally, you need to add an onclick event handler to the button element so that when the button is clicked, your element replacement function is executed. We do that with an anonymous function assigned to the window.onload method.

```
window.onload = function() {
    document.getElementById("btn").onclick = replaceHeading;
}
```

▼ TRY IT YOURSELF

Replacing Child Elements

continued

Listing 12.2 shows the code for the page with the JavaScript added.

Listing 12.2   The Completed Code to Replace Child Elements

```
<!DOCTYPE html>
<html>
<head>
    <title>Replace Page Element</title>
    <script>
        function replaceHeading() {
            var newH2 = document.createElement("h2");
            var newH2Text = document.createTextNode("Welcome!");
            newH2.appendChild(newH2Text);
            var myDiv = document.getElementById("id1");
            var oldP = document.getElementById("para1");
            myDiv.replaceChild(newH2, oldP);
        }
        window.onload = function() {
            document.getElementById("btn").onclick = replaceHeading;
        }
    </script>
</head>
<body>
    <div id="id1">
        <p id="para1">Welcome to my web page.</p>
        <p id="para2">Please take a look around.</p>
        <input id="btn" value="Replace Element" type="button" />
    </div>
</body>
</html>
```

Create a new HTML file with your editor and insert the code listed in Listing 12.2. On loading the page into your browser, you should see the two single-line paragraphs of text with the button beneath. If all has gone according to plan, clicking the button should swap the first <p> element for your <h2> heading, as depicted in Figure 12.1.

TRY IT YOURSELF ▼

Replacing Child Elements

continued

FIGURE 12.1
The element-replacement script in action

removeChild()

There is a DOM method specifically provided for removing child nodes from the DOM tree.

Referring once more to Listing 12.1, if you wanted to remove the <p> element with id="para2" you can just use:/

```
var myDiv = document.getElementById("id1");
var myPara = document.getElementById("para2");
myDiv.removeChild(myPara);
```

The return value from the removeChild() method contains a reference to the removed node. If you need to, you can use this to further process the child node that has just been removed:

```
var removedItem = myDiv.removeChild(myPara);
alert('Item with id ' + removedItem.getAttribute("id") + ' has been
➥removed.');
```

TIP

If you don't have a handy reference to the element's parent, just use the parentNode property:

```
myPara.parentNode.
removeChild(myPara);
```

Editing Element Attributes

In the previous hour you saw how to read element attributes using the getAttribute() method.

There is a corresponding method setAttribute() to allow you to create attributes for element nodes and assign values to those attributes. The method takes two arguments; unsurprisingly, these are the attribute to be added and the value it should have.

In the following example, the title attribute is added to a <p> element, and assigned the value "Opening Paragraph":

```
var myPara = document.getElementById("para1");
myPara.setAttribute("title", "Opening paragraph");
```

Setting the value of an attribute that already exists effectively overwrites the value of that attribute. You can use that knowledge to effectively edit existing attribute values:

```
var myPara = document.getElementById("para1");
myPara.setAttribute("title", "Opening paragraph"); // set 'title'
➥attribute
myPara.setAttribute("title", "New title");  // overwrite 'title'
➥attribute
```

Dynamically Loading JavaScript Files

On occasion you'll want to load JavaScript code on-the-fly to a page that's already loaded in the browser. You can use createElement() to dynamically create a new <script> element containing the required code and then add this element to the page's DOM.

```
var scr = document.createElement("script");
scr.setAttribute("src", "newScript.js");
document.head.appendChild(scr);
```

Remember that the appendChild() method places the new child node after the last child currently present, so the new <script> element will go right at the end of the <head> section of the page.

Take note, though, that if you dynamically load JavaScript source files using this method, the JavaScript code contained in those files will not be available to your page until the external file has finished loading.

You would be well advised to have your program check that this is so before attempting to use the additional code.

Nearly all modern browsers implement an onload event when the script has downloaded. This works just like the window.onload event you've already met, but instead of firing when the main page has finished loading, it does so when the external resource (in this case a JavaScript source file) is fully downloaded and available for use:

```
src.onload = function() {
    ... things to do when new source code is downloaded ...
}
```

CAUTION

This won't work in older versions of Internet Explorer, but onload has been supported for script elements since IE8. To be sure, you may prefer to use object detection of the

TRY IT YOURSELF ▼

A Dynamically Created Menu

In this exercise you're going to use the techniques learned in this and the previous hour to create page menus on-the-fly.

Our example HTML page has a top-level <h1> heading, followed by a number of short articles each consisting of an <h2> heading followed by some paragraphs of text. This is similar to a format you might see in a blog, a news page, or the output from an RSS reader, among other examples.

What you are going to do is employ DOM methods to automatically generate a menu at the page head, having links that allow the user to jump to any of the articles on the page. The HTML file is shown in Listing 12.3. Create your own HTML file based on this script. Feel free to use your own content for the headings and text, as long as the section titles are contained in <h2> elements.

LISTING 12.3   HTML File for Dynamic Menu Creation

```
<!DOCTYPE html>
<html>
<head>
    <meta charset="utf-8" />
    <title>Scripting the DOM</title>
    <script src="menu.js"></script>
    <script>window.onload = makeMenu;</script>
</head>
<body>
    <h1>The Extremadura Region of Western Spain</h1>
    <h2>Geography Of The Region</h2>
    <p>The autonomous community of Extremadura is in western Spain
alongside the Portuguese border. It borders the Spanish regions of
Castilla y Leon, Castilla La Mancha and Andalucía as well as Portugal (to
the West). Covering over 40,000 square kilometers it has two provinces:
Cáceres in the North and Badajoz in the South.</p>
    <h2>Where To Stay</h2>
    <p>There is a wide range of accommodation throughout Extremadura
including small inns and guest houses ('Hostals') or think about renting
a 'casa rural' (country house) if you are traveling in a group.</p>
    <h2>Climate</h2>
```

▼ TRY IT YOURSELF

**A Dynamically
Created Menu**

continued

     <p>Generally Mediterranean, except for the north, where it is
continental. Generally known for its extremes, including very hot and dry
summers with frequent droughts, and its long and mild winters.</p>
     <h2>What To See</h2>
     <p>Extremadura hosts major events all year round including theater,
music, cinema, literature and folklore. Spectacular venues include
castles, medieval town squares and historic centers. There are special
summer theater festivals in the Mérida, Cáceres, Alcántara and
Alburquerque.</p>
     <h2>Gastronomy</h2>
     <p>The quality of Extremaduran food arises from the fine quality of
the local ingredients. In addition to free-range lamb and beef, fabulous
cheeses, red and white wines, olive oil, honey and paprika, Extremadura
is particularly renowned for Iberian ham. The 'pata negra' (blackfoot)
pigs are fed on acorns in the cork-oak forests, the key to producing the
world's best ham and cured sausages. .</p>
</body>
</html>

The page is shown in Figure 12.2.

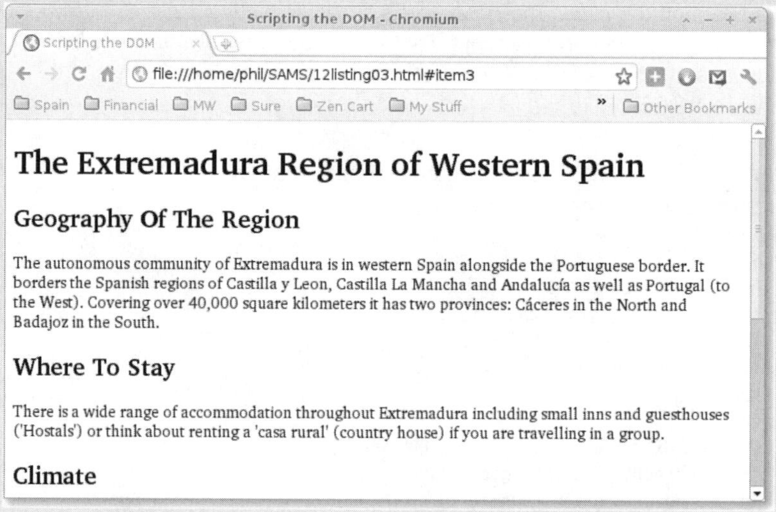

FIGURE 12.2
Page which is to have a dynami-
cally-created menu

The first thing to do is make a collection of all the <h2> elements from the
page. These will form the items in your menu. For each of these headings
make a link to an anchor element that you place right next to the corresponding <h2> element.

The menu links will be arranged as links in an unordered list <ul> element. This list will be placed in a <div> container that you insert at the page head.

First, get the collection of <h2> elements:

```
var h2s = document.getElementsByTagName("h2");
```

You need to create the <div> container to hold your menu; inside that <div>, there'll be a <ul>list element to contain the menu items:

```
var menu = document.createElement("div");
var menuUl = document.createElement("ul");
menu.appendChild(menuUl);
```

Now you can cycle through the collection of <h2> headings.

```
for(var i = 0; i < h2s.length; i++) {
    ... do things for each heading ...
}
```

For each heading you find in the document, you have a number of tasks to perform:

▶ Collect the content of the heading's child text node, which forms the text of the heading:

```
var itemText = h2s[i].childNodes[0].nodeValue;
```

▶ Create a new list item <li> element for the menu:

```
var menuLi = document.createElement("li");
```

▶ Add that <li> element to the menu:

```
menuUl.appendChild(menuLi);
```

▶ Each list item must contain a link to an anchor located next to the heading to which the menu item points:

```
var menuLiA = document.createElement("a");
menuLiA = menuLi.appendChild(menuLiA);
```

▶ Set an appropriate href attribute of the link (remember that variable i increments as you count through the headings in the array). These links will have the form

```
<a href="#itemX">[Title Text]</a>
```

where X is the index number of the menu item:

```
menuLiA.setAttribute("href", "#item" + i);
```

TRY IT YOURSELF ▼

A Dynamically Created Menu

continued

▼ TRY IT YOURSELF

**A Dynamically
Created Menu**

continued

▶ Create a matching anchor element just before each <h2> heading. The anchor elements have the form

```
<a name="itemX">
```

so you need to add the name attribute and locate the link just before the associated heading:

```
var anc = document.createElement("a");
anc.setAttribute("name", "item" + i);
document.body.insertBefore(anc, h2s[i]);
```

When all that has been completed for each <h2> heading, you can add your new menu to the page:

```
document.body.insertBefore(menu, document.body.firstChild);
```

The content of the JavaScript source file menu.js is shown in Listing 12.4. The code has been incorporated into a function makeMenu() that is called by the window.onload event handler, building your menu as soon as the page has loaded and the DOM is therefore available.

LISTING 12.4   JavaScript Code for menu.js

```javascript
function makeMenu() {
    // get all the H2 heading elements
    var h2s = document.getElementsByTagName("h2");
    // create a new page element for the menu
    var menu = document.createElement("div");
    // create a UL element and append to the menu div
    var menuUl = document.createElement("ul");
    menu.appendChild(menuUl);
    // cycle through h2 headings
    for(var i = 0; i < h2s.length; i++) {
        // get text node of h2 element
        var itemText = h2s[i].childNodes[0].nodeValue;
        // add a list item
        var menuLi = document.createElement("li");
        // add it to the menu list
        menuUl.appendChild(menuLi);
        // the list item contains a link
        var menuLiA = document.createElement("a");
        menuLiA = menuLi.appendChild(menuLiA);
        // set the href of the link
        menuLiA.setAttribute("href", "#item" + i);
        // set the text of the link
        var menuText = document.createTextNode(itemText);
        menuLiA.appendChild(menuText);
        // create matching anchor element
```

LISTING 12.4   Continued

```
        var anc = document.createElement("a");
        anc.setAttribute("name", "item" + i);
        // add anchor before the heading
        document.body.insertBefore(anc, h2s[i]);
    }
    // add menu to the top of the page
    document.body.insertBefore(menu, document.body.firstChild);
}
window.onload = makeMenu;
```

Figure 12.3 shows the script in action.

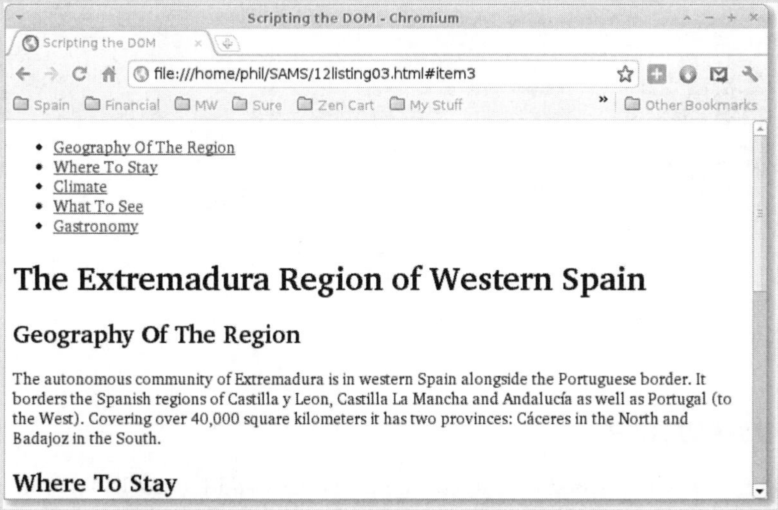

TRY IT YOURSELF ▼

**A Dynamically
Created Menu**

continued

FIGURE 12.3
The automatic menu script in
action

By examining the modified DOM using your browser tools, you can see the
additional DOM elements added to the page to form the menu and the
anchors. Figure 12.4 shows how this is displayed in Google Chromium's
Developer Tools, highlighting the additional elements.

**A Dynamically
Created Menu**
continued

FIGURE 12.4
The additional DOM elements

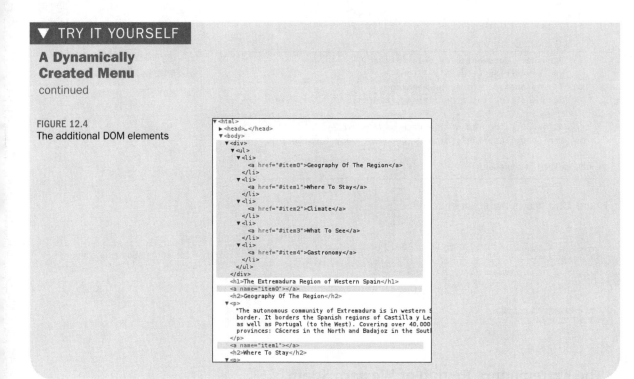

Summary

In this hour you learned how to create new nodes to add to the DOM. You also saw how to add, edit, and remove DOM nodes to edit page content dynamically.

Q&A

Q. Is it better to use the DOM to insert and retrieve HTML or innerHTML?

A. Each has its advantages and disadvantages. To insert a chunk of HTML into a document, using innerHTML is quick and easy. However, it returns no references to the code you've inserted, so you can't carry out operations on that content very easily. DOM methods offer finer-grained control for manipulating page elements.

Wherever you use innerHTML, the same result is achievable using DOM methods, though usually with a little more code.

Remember, too, that innerHTML is not a W3C standard. It is well supported currently, but there's no guarantee that that will always be so.

Q. I've seen references on the Web to DOM Core and HTML DOM. What are these, and what are the differences between them?

A. The DOM Core describes a basic nucleus of DOM methods that are applicable not just to HTML pages, but also pages written in any similar markup language—XML, for example. HTML DOM is a larger collection of additional methods relating specifically to HTML pages. They do offer some shorthand ways of carrying out certain tasks, at the expense of making your code a little less portable to non-HTML applications.

The examples in this book generally use DOM Core methods to be more general. In Listing 12.4, for example, I used the statement

```
menuLiA.setAttribute("href", "#item" + i);
```

I could equally have used the HTML DOM statement

```
menuLiA.href = "#item" + i;
```

which is a little shorter.

Workshop

Try to answer all the questions before reading the subsequent "Answers" section.

Quiz

1. To create a new <span> element you could use

    a. `document.createElement("span");`

    b. `document.createElement(span);`

    c. `document.appendChild("span");`

2. To copy a copy of node including all of its child nodes, you could use

    a. cloneNode(false);

    b. copyNode();

    c. cloneNode(true);

3. To set the alt attribute of an <img> element to "Company Logo" you can use

    a. setAttribute(alt, "Company Logo");

    b. setAttribute("alt", "Company Logo");

    c. setAttribute(alt = "Company Logo");

Answers

1. a. Use document.createElement("span");

2. c. Use cloneNode(true);

3. b. Use setAttribute("alt", "Company Logo");

Exercises

Having used the insertBefore() method, you might reasonably expect that there would be an insertAfter() method available. Unfortunately, that's not so. Can you write an insertAfter() function to do this task? Use similar arguments to insertBefore(), that is, insertAfter(newNode, targetNode). [Hint: Use insertBefore() and the nextSibling property.]

When you click a menu item generated by the code in Listing 12.4, the page scrolls to the relevant item. To return to the menu, you have to manually scroll back up.

Can you modify the script such that, as well as inserting an anchor, it inserts a Back to Top' link before each H2 element? [Hint: You don't need to add a new link, just add an href and some link text to each anchor.]

JavaScript and CSS

In the early days of the World Wide Web, pages were all about their text content. Early browsers had rudimentary support for graphic effects— some didn't even support images. Styling a web page was largely a matter of using the few style-related attributes and tags allowed by the early incarnations of HTML.

Things improved markedly with the introduction of browser support for Cascading Style Sheets (CSS), which allowed the styling of a page to be treated independently from its HTML markup.

In the previous hour, you learned how to edit the structure of your page using JavaScript's DOM methods. However, JavaScript can also be used to access and amend CSS styles for the current page. In this hour you learn how.

A Ten Minute CSS Primer

If you've decided to learn JavaScript, there's a pretty good chance that you're already familiar with CSS styling. Just in case it's managed to pass you by, let's review the basics.

Separating Style from Content

Before CSS came along, most styling in HTML pages was carried out using HTML tags and/or their attributes. To change the font color of a piece of text, for example, you would have used something like this:

```
<p><font color="red">This text is in red!</font></p>
```

This was pretty awful for a number of reasons:

- ▶ Every single piece of text in the page that we wanted to be colored red had to be marked up with these extra tags.

- ▶ The created style could not be carried over to other pages; they too had to be marked up individually with additional HTML.

- ▶ To later change pages' styles, you had to edit each and every page and sift through the HTML, changing every style-related tag and attribute individually.

- ▶ With all this extra markup, the HTML became very hard to read and maintain.

CSS attempts to separate the styling of an HTML element from the markup function of that element. This is done by defining individual *style declarations* and then applying these to HTML elements or collections of elements.

You can use CSS to style the visual properties of a page element, such as color, font, and size, as well as format-related properties such as positioning, margins, padding, and alignment.

Separating style from content in this way brings with it a lot of benefits:

- ▶ Style declarations can be applied to more than one element or even (when using external stylesheets) more than one page.

- ▶ Changes to style declarations affect all associated HTML elements, making updating your site's style more accurate, quick, and efficient.

- ▶ Sharing styles encourages more consistent styling through your site.

- ▶ HTML markup is clearer to read and maintain.

CSS Style Declarations

The syntax of CSS style declarations is not unlike that of JavaScript functions. Suppose you want to declare a style for all paragraph elements in a page, causing the font color inside the paragraphs to be colored red:

```
p {
    color: red
}
```

You can apply more than one style rule to your chosen element or collection of elements, separating them with semicolons:

```
p {
    color: red;
    text-decoration: italic
}
```

Because you have used the selector p, the preceding style declarations
affect every paragraph element on the page. To select just one specific page
element, you can do so by using its id. To do so, the selector you use for
your CSS style declaration is not the name of the HTML element, but the id
value prefixed by a hash character. For instance, the following HTML
element

```
<p id="para1">Here is some text.</p>
```

could be styled by the following style declaration:

```
#para1 {
    font-weight: bold;
    font-size: 12pt;
    color: black;
}
```

To style multiple page elements using the same style declaration, you can
simply separate the selectors with commas. The following style declaration
affects all <div> elements on the page, plus whatever element has the id
value para1:

```
div, #para1 {
    color: yellow;
    background-color: black;
}
```

Alternatively, you can select all elements sharing a particular class attribute, by prefixing the class name with a dot to form your selector:

```
<p class="info">Welcome to my website.</p>
<span class="info">Please log in or register using the form below.</span>
```

We can style these elements with one declaration:

```
.info {
    font-family: arial, verdana, sans-serif;
    color: green;
}
```

Where to Place Style Declarations

Somewhat similarly to JavaScript statements, CSS style declarations can either appear within the page or be saved in an external file and referenced from within the HTML page.

To reference an external stylesheet, normal practice is to add a line to the page <head> like this:

```
<link rel="stylesheet" type="text/css" href="style.css" />
```

Alternatively, you can place style declarations directly in the <head> of your page between <style> and </style> tags:

```
<style>
    p {
        color: black;
        font-family: tahoma
    }
    h1 {
        color: blue;
        font-size: 22pt
    }
</style>
```

TIP

Styles defined in external stylesheets have the advantage that they can easily be applied to multiple pages, whereas styles defined within the page can't.

Finally, it's possible to add style declarations directly into an HTML element by using the style attribute:

```
<p style="color:red; font-size: 12px;">Please see our terms of
➥service.</p>
```

The DOM style Property

You saw in previous hours how the HTML page is represented by the browser as a DOM tree. The DOM *nodes*—individual "leaves and branches" making up the DOM tree—are objects, each having their own properties and methods.

You've seen various methods that allow you to select individual DOM nodes, or collections of nodes, such as document.getElementById().

Each DOM node has a property called style, which is itself an object containing information about the CSS styles pertaining to its parent node. Let's see an example:

```
<div id="id1" style="width:200px;">Welcome back to my site.</div>
<script>
    var myNode = document.getElementById("id1");
    alert(myNode.style.width);
</script>
```

In this case the alert would display the message "200px."

Unfortunately, while this method works fine with *inline* styles, if you applied a style to a page element via a `<style>` element in the head of your page, or in an external stylesheet, the DOM style object won't be able to access it.

The DOM `style` object, though, is not read-only; you can set the values of style properties using the `style` object, and properties you've set this way *will* be returned by the DOM `style` object.

NOTE

CSS contains many properties with names that contain hyphens, such as `background-color`, `font-size`, `text-align`, and so on. Because the hyphen is not allowed in JavaScript property and method names, we need to amend the way these properties are written. To access such a property in JavaScript, remove the hyphen from the property name and capitalize the character that follows, so `font-size` becomes `fontSize`, `text-align` becomes `textAlign`, and so on.

TRY IT YOURSELF ▼

Setting Style Properties

Let's write a function to toggle the background color and font color of a page element between two values, using the DOM `style` object:

```
function toggle() {
    var myElement = document.getElementById("id1");
    if(myElement.style.backgroundColor == 'red') {
        myElement.style.backgroundColor = 'yellow';
        myElement.style.color = 'black';
    } else {
        myElement.style.backgroundColor = 'red';
        myElement.style.color = 'white';
    }
}
```

The function `toggle()` first finds out the current `background-color` CSS property of a page element and then compares that color to `red`.

If the `background-color` property currently has the value of `red`, it sets the style properties of the element to show the text in black on a yellow background; otherwise, it sets the style values to show white text on a red background.

We use this function to toggle the colors of a `<span>` element in an HTML document.

The complete listing is shown in Listing 13.1.

▼ TRY IT YOURSELF

**Setting Style
Properties**

continued

LISTING 13.1   Styling Using the DOM `style` Object

```
<!DOCTYPE html>
<html>
<head>
    <title>Setting the style of page elements</title>
    <style>
        span {
            font-size: 16pt;
            font-family: arial, helvetica, sans-serif;
            padding: 20px;
        }
    </style>
    <script>
        function toggle() {
            var myElement = document.getElementById("id1");
            if(myElement.style.backgroundColor == 'red') {
                myElement.style.backgroundColor = 'yellow';
                myElement.style.color = 'black';
            } else {
                myElement.style.backgroundColor = 'red';
                myElement.style.color = 'white';
            }
        }
        window.onload = function() {
            document.getElementById("btn1").onclick = toggle;
        }
    </script>
</head>
<body>
    <span id="id1">Welcome back to my site.</span>
    <input type="button" id="btn1" value="Toggle" />
</body>
</html>
```

Create the HTML file in your editor and try it out.

You should see that when the page originally loads, the text is in default black and has no background color. That happens because these style properties are initially not set in the <style> instructions in the page head, as an inline style, or via the DOM.

Executing when the button is clicked, the `toggle()` function checks the current background color of the <span> element. On finding that its value is not currently red, `toggle()` sets the background color to red and the text color to white.

The next time the button is clicked, the test condition

```
if(myElement.style.backgroundColor == 'red')
```

returns a value of `true`, causing the colors to be set instead to black on a yellow background.

Figure 13.1 shows the program in action.

TRY IT YOURSELF ▼

Setting Style Properties
continued

FIGURE 13.1
Setting style properties in JavaScript

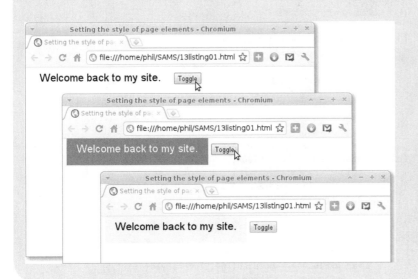

Accessing Classes Using `className`

Earlier in this hour we discussed separating style from content and the benefits that this can bring.

Using JavaScript to edit the properties of the `style` object, as in the previous exercise, works well—but it does carry with it the danger of reducing this separation of style and content. If your JavaScript code routinely changes elements' style declarations, the responsibility for styling your pages is no longer lodged firmly in CSS. If you later decide to change the styles your JavaScript applies, you'll have to go back and edit all of your JavaScript functions.

Thankfully, we have a mechanism by which JavaScript can restyle pages without overwriting individual style declarations. By using the `className` property of the element, we can switch the value of the `class` attribute and with it the associated style declarations for the element. Take a look at the example in Listing 13.2.

LISTING 13.2   Changing Classes Using `className`

```html
<!DOCTYPE html>
<html>
<head>
    <title>Switching classes with JavaScript</title>
    <style>
        .classA {
            width: 180px;
            border: 3px solid black;
            background-color: white;
            color: red;
            font:  normal 24px arial, helvetica, sans-serif;
            padding: 20px;
        }
        .classB {
            width: 180px;
            border: 3px dotted white;
            background-color: black;
            color: yellow;
            font: italic bold 24px "Times New Roman", serif;
            padding: 20px;
        }
    </style>
    <script>
        function toggleClass() {
            var myElement = document.getElementById("id1");
            if(myElement.className == "classA") {
                myElement.className = "classB";
            } else {
                myElement.className = "classA";
            }
        }
        window.onload = function() {
            document.getElementById("btn1").onclick = toggleClass;
        }
    </script>

</head>
<body>
    <div id="id1" class="classA"> An element with a touch of class.</div>
    <input type="button" id="btn1" value="Toggle" />
</body>
</html>
```

The <style> element in the page <head> lists style declarations for two classes, classA and classB. The JavaScript function toggleClass() uses similar logic to the earlier function toggle() of Listing 13.1, except that toggleClass() does not work with the element's style object. Instead, toggleClass() gets the class name associated with the <div> element and switches its value between classA and classB.

Figure 13.2 shows the script in action.

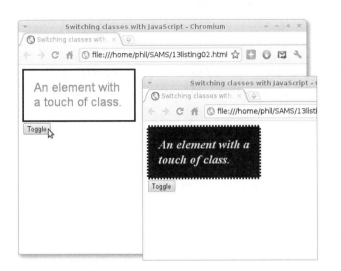

FIGURE 13.2
Switching classes in JavaScript

NOTE

As an alternative to using classNamename, you could try setting the class attribute for an element to value classA by using
`element.setAttribute("class", "classA");`

Unfortunately, various versions of Internet Explorer have trouble when trying to set the class attribute but work fine with className. The statement
`element.className = "classA";`

seems to work in all browsers.

The DOM `styleSheets` Object

The `styleSheets` property of the `document` object contains an array of all the stylesheets on the page, whether they are contained in external files and linked into the page head, or declared between `<style>` and `</style>` tags in the page head. The items in the `styleSheets` array are indexed numerically, starting at zero for the stylesheet appearing first.

TIP

You can access the total number of spreadsheets on your page by using `document.styleSheets.length`.

Enabling, Disabling, and Switching Stylesheets

Each stylesheet in the array has a property `disabled`, containing a value of Boolean `true` or `false`. This is a read/write property, so we are able to effectively switch individual stylesheets on and off in JavaScript:

```
document.styleSheets[0].disabled = true;
document.styleSheets[1].disabled = false;
```

The preceding code snippet "switches on" the second stylesheet in the page (index 1) while "switching off" the first stylesheet (index 0).

Listing 13.3 has a working example. The script on this page first declares a variable `whichSheet`, initializing its value at zero:

```
var whichSheet = 0;
```

This variable keeps track of which of the two stylesheets is currently active. The second line of code initially disables the second of the two stylesheets on the page:

```
document.styleSheets[1].disabled = true;
```

The function `sheet()`, which is attached to the `onClick` event handler to the button on the page when the page loads, carries out three tasks when the button is clicked:

- ▶ Disable the stylesheet whose index is stored in variable `whichSheet`:

  ```
  document.styleSheets[whichSheet].disabled = true;
  ```

- ▶ Toggle variable `whichSheet` between one and zero:

  ```
  whichSheet = (whichSheet == 1) ? 0 : 1;
  ```

- ▶ Enable the stylesheet corresponding to the new value of `whichSheet`:

  ```
  document.styleSheets[whichSheet].disabled = false;
  ```

The combined effect of these activities is to toggle between the two active stylesheets for the page. The script is shown in action in Figure 13.3.

LISTING 13.3   Toggling Between Stylesheets Using the `styleSheets` Property

```
<!DOCTYPE html>
<html>
<head>
    <title>Switching Stylesheets with JavaScript</title>
    <style>
        body {
            background-color: white;
            color: red;
            font:  normal 24px arial, helvetica, sans-serif;
            padding: 20px;
        }
    </style>
    <style>
        body {
            background-color: black;
            color: yellow;
            font: italic bold 24px "Times New Roman", serif;
            padding: 20px;
        }
    </style>
    <script>
        var whichSheet = 0;
        document.styleSheets[1].disabled = true;
```

LISTING 13.3   Continued

```
        function sheet() {
            document.styleSheets[whichSheet].disabled = true;
            whichSheet = (whichSheet == 1) ? 0 : 1;
            document.styleSheets[whichSheet].disabled = false;
        }
        window.onload = function() {
            document.getElementById("btn1").onclick = sheet;
        }
    </script>
</head>
<body>
    Switch my stylesheet with the button below!<br />
    <input type="button" id="btn1" value="Toggle" />
</body>
</html>
```

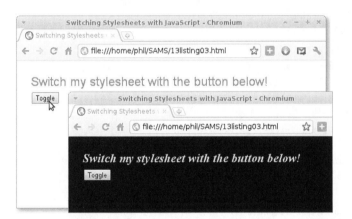

FIGURE 13.3
Switching stylesheets with the
styleSheets property

Having your stylesheets indexed by number doesn't make it easy to select the stylesheet you need. It would be easier if you had a function to allow you to title your stylesheets and select them by their title attributes.

You need your function to respond in a useful manner if you ask for a stylesheet that doesn't exist; you want it to maintain the previous stylesheet and send us a message.

First, declare a couple of variables and initialize their values:

```
var change = false;
var oldSheet = 0;
```

▼ TRY IT YOURSELF

Selecting a Particular Stylesheet

continued

The Boolean variable change keeps track of whether you've found a stylesheet with the requested name; once you do so, you change its value to true, indicating that you intend to change stylesheets.

The integer oldSheet, originally set to zero, will eventually be assigned the number of the currently active sheet; in case you don't find a new stylesheet matching the requested title, you set this back to active before returning from the function.

Now you need to cycle through the styleSheets array:

```
for (var i = 0; i < document.styleSheets.length; i++) {
    ...
}
```

For each stylesheet:

- ▶ If you find that this is the currently active stylesheet, store its index in the variable oldSheet:

    ```
    if(document.styleSheets[i].disabled == false) {
        oldSheet = i;
    }
    ```

- ▶ As you cycle through, make sure all sheets are disabled:

    ```
    document.styleSheets[i].disabled = true;
    ```

- ▶ If the current sheet has the title of the requested sheet, make it enabled by setting its disabled value to false, and immediately set your variable change to true:

    ```
    if(document.styleSheets[i].title == mySheet) {
        document.styleSheets[i].disabled = false;
        change = true;
    }
    ```

When you've cycled through all sheets, you can determine from the state of the variables change and oldSheet whether you are in a position to change the stylesheet. If not, reset the prior stylesheet to be enabled again:

```
if(!change) document.styleSheets[oldSheet].disabled = false;
```

Finally, the function returns the value of variable change—true if the change has been made or false if not.

The code is listed in Listing 13.4. Save this code in an HTML file and load it into your browser.

TRY IT YOURSELF ▼

Selecting a Particular Stylesheet

continued

Listing 13.4   Selecting Stylesheets by Title

```html
<!DOCTYPE html>
<html>
<head>
    <title>Switching stylesheets with JavaScript</title>
    <style title="sheet1">
        body {
            background-color: white;
            color: red;
        }
    </style>
    <style title="sheet2">
        body {
            background-color: black;
            color: yellow;
        }
    </style>
    <style title="sheet3">
        body {
            background-color: pink;
            color: green;
        }
    </style>
    <script>
        function ssEnable(mySheet) {
            var change = false;
            var oldSheet = 0;
            for (var i = 0; i < document.styleSheets.length; i++) {
                if(document.styleSheets[i].disabled == false) {
                    oldSheet = i;
                }
                document.styleSheets[i].disabled = true;
                if(document.styleSheets[i].title == mySheet) {
                    document.styleSheets[i].disabled = false;
                    change = true;
                }
            }
            if(!change) document.styleSheets[oldSheet].disabled = false;
            return change;
        }
        function sheet() {
            var sheetName = prompt("Stylesheet Name?");
            if(!ssEnable(sheetName)) alert("Not found - original
stylesheet retained.");
        }
        window.onload = function() {
            document.getElementById("btn1").onclick = sheet;
        }
    </script>
```

▼ TRY IT YOURSELF

Selecting a Particular Stylesheet

continued

```
</head>
<body>
    Switch my stylesheet with the button below!<br />
    <input type="button" id="btn1" value="Change Sheet" />
</body>
</html>
```

The small function sheet() is added to the button's onClick event handler when the page loads. Each time the button is clicked, sheet() prompts the user for the name of a stylesheet

```
var sheetName = prompt("Stylesheet Name?");
```

then calls the ssEnable() function, passing the requested name as an argument.

If the function returns false, indicating that no change of stylesheet has taken place, you alert the user with a message:

```
if(!ssEnable(sheetName)) alert("Not found - original stylesheet
retained.");
```

The script is shown operating in Figure 13.4.

FIGURE 13.4
Switching stylesheets with the styleSheets property

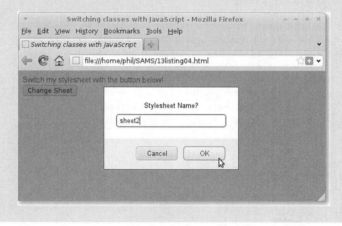

Summary

In this hour you learned a number of ways in which JavaScript can be put to work on the CSS styles of your page. You learned how to use the style property of page elements, how to work with CSS classes, and how to manipulate entire stylesheets.

Q&A

Q. Is it possible for JavaScript to work with individual CSS style rules?

A. Yes it is, but at the time of writing this does not work very well cross-browser. Mozilla browsers support the `cssRules` array, while Internet Explorer calls the equivalent array `Rules`. There is also considerable difference among browsers in how the notion of a "rule" is interpreted. It's to be hoped that future browser versions will resolve these differences.

Q. Is it possible to alter the mouse cursor in JavaScript?

A. Yes, it is. The `style` object has a property `cursor` that can take various values. Popular cursors include the following:

- ▸ **Crosshair**—Pointer renders as a pair of crossed lines like a gun sight.

- ▸ **Pointer**—Usually a pointing finger.

- ▸ **Text**—Text entry caret.

- ▸ **Wait**—The program is busy.

Workshop

Try to answer all the questions before reading the subsequent "Answers" section.

Quiz

1. To set the `font-family` property for element `myElement` to Verdana, you would use

    a. `myElement.style.font-family = "verdana";`

    b. `myElement.style.fontFamily = "verdana";`

    c. `myElement.style.font-family("verdana");`

2. The property `className` can be used

    a. To access the value of the `class` attribute of an element

    b. To access the value of the `name` attribute of an element

    c. To add an attribute `classname` to an element

3. How can you enable the stylesheet with index n in the `styleSheets` array?

    a. `document.styleSheets[n].active = true;`

    b. `document.styleSheets[n].enabled = true;`

    c. `document.styleSheets[n].disabled = false;`

Answers

1. b. `myElement.style.fontFamily = "verdana";`

2. a. To access the value of the `class` attribute of an element.

3. c. `document.styleSheets[n].disabled = false;`

Exercises

Edit the program of Listing 13.1 to change other style properties such as font face and decoration, element borders, padding, and margins.

Change the program of Listing 13.4 so that some of the stylesheets are externally linked, rather than situated between `<style>` and `</style>` tags in the page `<head>`. Does everything work the same?

Good Coding Practice

JavaScript has gained an unfortunate reputation in certain circles. Because its main goal as a scripting language was to add functionality to web page designs, accessibility for first-time programmers has always been an important aspect of the language. Unfortunately, that has often led to poorly written code being allowed into web pages, leading to frustration for more software-savvy users.

Throughout the book so far I've made reference to aspects of coding that are good and bad. In this hour we pull all that together to form some general guidelines for good coding practice.

Don't Overuse JavaScript

How much JavaScript do you need? There's often a temptation to include JavaScript code and enhanced interaction where it's not strictly necessary or advisable.

▶ It's important to remember that your users are likely to spend most of their Internet time on sites other than yours. Experienced Internet users become accustomed to popular interface components such as menus, breadcrumb trails, and tabbed browsing. These elements are popular, in general, because they work well, can be made to look good, and don't require the user to read a manual first. Is familiarity with a site's operation likely to increase a user's productivity more than the potential benefits of your all-new whizz-bang design?

▶ Many of the visual effects that once needed to be coded in JavaScript can now be achieved perfectly well using CSS. Where both approaches are possible (image rollovers and some types of menus come immediately to mind), CSS is usually preferable. It's well supported across browsers (despite a few variations) and isn't as commonly turned off by the user. In the rare case that CSS isn't supported, the page is rendered as standard HTML, usually leaving a page that's at least perfectly functional, even if it's not so pretty.

▶ Users in many areas of the world are still using outdated, underpowered, hand-me-down computers and may also have slow and/or unreliable Internet access. The CPU cycles taken up by your unnecessary code may be precious to them.

▶ In some cases you may cost yourself a degree of search engine page rank because their spiders don't always correctly index content that's been generated by JavaScript or designs that require it for navigation.

Used carefully and with forethought, JavaScript can be a great tool, but sometimes you can have too much of a good thing.

Writing Readable and Maintainable Code

There is no way of knowing who will one day need to read and understand your code. Even if that person is you, several years and many projects may have intervened; the code that is so familiar to you at the time of writing can seem mystifying further down the line. If others have to interpret your code, they may not share your coding style, naming conventions, or areas of expertise, and you may not be available to help them out.

Use Comments Sensibly

Well-chosen comments at critical places in your code can make all the difference in such situations. Comments are your notes and pointers for those who come later. The trick is in deciding what comments are likely to be helpful. The subject has often raised debate, and opinions vary widely, so what follows is largely my own opinion.

It's perhaps reasonable to assume that the person who ends up reading your code has an understanding of JavaScript, so a commentary on the way the language itself works is going too far; JavaScript developers may vary widely in their styles and abilities, but the one thing we do all share is the language syntax!

Harder to interpret when reading code are the thought processes and algorithms that lie behind the code's operation. Personally, when reading code written by others I find it helpful to see

▶ A prologue to any object or function containing more than a few lines of simple code.

```
function calculateGroundAngle(x1, y1, z1, x2, y2, z2) {
    /**
    * Calculates the angle in radians at which
    * a line between two points intersects the
    * ground plane.
    * @author Phil Ballard phil@www.example.com
    */
    if(x1 > 0) {
        .... more statements
```

▶ Inline comments wherever the code would otherwise be confusing or prone to misinterpretation.

```
// need to use our custom sort method for performance reasons
var finalArray = rapidSort(allNodes, byAngle) {
    .... more statements
```

▶ A comment wherever the original author can pass on specialist knowledge that the reader is unlikely to know.

```
// workaround for image onload bug in browser X version Y
if(!loaded(image1)) {
    .... more statements
```

▶ Instructions for commonly used code modifications.

```
// You can change the following dimensions to your preference:
var height = 400px;
var width = 600px;
```

TIP

There are various schemes that use code comments to help you generate documentation for your software. See for example http://code.google.com/p/jsdoc-toolkit/.

Choose Helpful File, Property, and Method Names

The amount of comments required in your source code can be greatly reduced by making the code as self-commenting as possible. You can go some way toward this by choosing meaningful human-readable names for methods and properties.

JavaScript has rules about the characters allowed in the names of methods (or functions) and properties (or variables), but there's still plenty of scope to be creative and concise.

A popular convention is to put the names of constants into all uppercase:

```
MONTHS_PER_YEAR = 12;
```

For regular function, method, and variable names, so-called CamelCase is a popular option; names constructed from multiple words are concatenated with each word except the first initialized. The first letter can be upper- or lowercase:

```
var memberSurname = "Smith";
var lastGroupProcessed = 16;
```

It's recommended that constructor functions for instantiating objects have the first character capitalized:

```
function Car(make, model, color) {
    .... statements
}
```

The capitalization provides a reminder that the new keyword needs to be used:

```
var herbie = new Car('VW', 'Beetle', 'white');
```

Reuse Code Where You Can

Generally, the more you can modularize your code, the better. Take a look at this function:

```
function getElementArea() {
    var high = document.getElementById("id1").style.height;
    var wide = document.getElementById("id1").style.width;
    return high * wide;
}
```

The function attempts to return the area of screen covered by a particular HTML element. Unfortunately it can only ever work with an element having id = "id1", which is really not very helpful at all.

Collecting your code into modules such as functions and objects that you can use and reuse throughout your code is a process known as *abstraction*. We can give the function *a higher level of abstraction* to make its use more general by passing as an argument the id of the element to which the operation should be applied:

```
function getElementArea(elementId) {
    var elem = document.getElementById(elementId);
    var high = elem.style.height;
```

```
    var wide = elem.style.width;
    return parseInt(high) * parseInt(wide);
}
```

You could now call your function into action for any element having an id:

```
var area1 = getElementArea("id1");
var area2 = getElementArea("id2");
```

Don't Assume

What happens in the previous function when we pass a value for
elementId that doesn't correspond to any element on the page? The function causes an error, and code execution halts.

The error is to assume that an allowable value for elementId will be
passed. Let's edit the function getElementArea() to carry out a check that
the page element does indeed exist and also that it has a numeric area:

```
function getElementArea(elementId) {
    if(document.getElementById(elementId)) {
        var elem = document.getElementById(elementId);
        var high = elem.style.height;
        var wide = elem.style.width;
        var area = parseInt(high) * parseInt(wide);
        if(!isNaN(area)) {
            return area;
        } else {
            return false;
        }
    } else {
        return false;
    }
}
```

That's an improvement. Now the function will return false if it cannot
return a numeric area, either because the relevant page element couldn't be
found or because the id corresponded to a page element without accessible
width and height properties .

Graceful Degradation

Among the earliest web browsers were some that didn't even support the
inclusion of images in HTML. When the <img> element was introduced, a
way was needed to allow those text-only browsers to present something
helpful to the user whenever such a nonsupported tag was encountered.

In the case of the `<img>` tag, that facility was provided by the `alt` (alternative text) attribute. Web designers could assign a string of text to `alt`, and text-only browsers would display this text to the user instead of showing the image. At the whim of the page designer, the `alt` text might be simply a title for the image, a description of what the picture would have displayed, or a suggestion for an alternative source of the information that would have been carried in the graphic.

This was an early example of *graceful degradation*, the process by which a user whose browser lacks the required technical features to make full use of a web page's design—or has those features disabled—can still benefit as fully as possible from the site's content.

Let's take JavaScript itself as another example. Virtually every browser supports JavaScript, and few users turn it off. So do you really need to worry about visitors who don't have JavaScript enabled? The answer is probably yes. One type of frequent visitor to your site will no doubt be the spider program from one of the search engines, busy indexing the pages of the Web. The spider will attempt to follow all the navigation links on your pages to build a full index of your site's content; if such navigation requires the services of JavaScript, you may find some parts of your site not being indexed. Your search ranking will probably suffer as a result.

Another important example lies in the realm of accessibility. No matter how capable a browser program is, there are some users who suffer with other limitations, such as perhaps the inability to use a mouse, or the necessity to use screen-reading software. If your site does not cater to these users, they're unlikely to return.

Progressive Enhancement

When we talk about graceful degradation, it's easy to imagine a fully functional web page with all the bells and whistles providing charitable assistance to users whose browsers have lesser capabilities.

Supporters of *progressive enhancement* tend to look at the problem from the opposite direction. They favor the building of a stable, accessible, and fully functional website, the content of which can be accessed by just about any imaginable user and browser, to which they can later add extra layers of additional usability for those who can take advantage of them.

This ensures that the site will work for even the most basic browser setup, with more advanced browsers simply gaining some additional enhancements.

Separate Style, Content, and Code

The key resource of a web page employing progressive enhancement techniques is the content. HTML provides markup facilities to allow you to describe your content semantically; the markup tags themselves identify page elements as being headings, tables, paragraphs, and so on. We might refer to this as the *semantic layer*.

What this semantic layer should ideally *not* contain is any information about how the page should appear. You can add this additional information afterwards using CSS techniques to form the *presentation layer*. By linking external CSS stylesheets into the document, you avoid any appearance-related information from appearing in the HTML markup itself. Even a browser having no understanding of CSS, however, can still access and display all of the page's information, even though it might not look so pretty.

When you now add JavaScript into the mix, you do so as yet another notional layer—you might think of it as the *behavior layer*. Users without JavaScript still have access to the page content via the semantic markup; if their browser understands CSS, they'll also benefit from the enhanced appearance of the presentation layer. If the JavaScript of the behavior layer is applied correctly, it will offer more functionality to those who can use it, without prejudicing the abilities of the preceding layers.

To achieve that, you need to write JavaScript that is *unobtrusive*.

Unobtrusive JavaScript

There is no formal definition of unobtrusive JavaScript, but the concepts upon which it's built all involve maintaining the separation between the behavior layer and the content and presentation layers.

Leave That HTML Alone

The first and perhaps most important consideration is the removal of JavaScript code from the page markup. Early applications of JavaScript clutter the HTML with inline event handlers such as the `onClick` event handler in this example:

```
<input type="button" style="border: 1px solid blue;color: white"
➥onclick="doSomething()" />
```

Inline style attributes, such as the one in the preceding example, can make the situation even worse.

Thankfully you can effectively remove the style information to the style layer, for example, by adding a `class` attribute to the HTML tag referring to an associated style declaration in an external CSS file:

```
<input type="button" class="blueButtons" onclick="doSomething()" />
```

And in the associated CSS definitions:

```
.blueButtons {
    border: 1px solid blue;
    color: white;
}
```

To make your JavaScript unobtrusive you can employ a similar technique to the one we just used for CSS. By adding an `id` attribute to a page element within the HTML markup, you can attach the required `onClick` event listener from within your external JavaScript code, keeping it out of the HTML markup altogether. Here's the revised HTML element:

```
<input type="button" class="blueButtons" id="btn1" />
```

The `onClick` event handler is attached from within your JavaScript code:

```
function doSomething() {
    .... statements ....
}
document.getElementById("btn1").onclick = doSomething;
```

Use JavaScript Only as an Enhancement

In the spirit of progressive enhancement, you want your page to work even if JavaScript is turned off. Any improvements in the usability of the page that JavaScript may add should be seen as a bonus for those users whose browser setup permits them.

Let's imagine you want to write some form validation code—a popular use for JavaScript. Here's a little HTML search form:

```
<form action="process.php">
<input id="searchTerm" name="term" type="text" /><br />
<input type="button" id="btn1" value="Search" />
</form>
```

You want to write a routine to prevent the form from being submitted if the search field is blank. You might write this function checkform(), which will be attached to the onClick handler of the search button:

```
function checkform() {
    if(document.forms[0].term.value == "") {
        alert("Please enter a search term.");
        return false;
    } else {
        document.forms[0].submit();
    }
}
window.onload = function() {
    document.getElementById("btn1").onclick = checkform;
}
```

That should work just fine. But what happens when JavaScript is switched off? The button now does nothing at all, and the form can't be submitted by the user. Your users would surely prefer that the form could be used, albeit without the *enhancement* of input checking.

Let's change the form slightly to use an input button of type="submit" rather than type="button" and edit the checkform() function.

```
<form action="process.php">
    <input id="searchTerm" name="term" type="text" /><br />
    <input type="submit" id="btn1" value="Search" />
</form>
```

Here's the modified checkform() function:

```
function checkform() {
    if(document.forms[0].term.value == "") {
        alert("Please enter a search term.");
        return false;
    } else {
        return true;
    }
}
window.onload = function() {
    document.getElementById("btn1").onclick = checkform;
}
```

If JavaScript is active, returning a value of `false` to the submit button will prevent the default operation of the button, preventing form submission. Without JavaScript, however, the form will still submit when the button is clicked.

Feature Detection

Where possible, try to directly detect the presence or absence of browser features and have your code use those features only where available.

As an example, let's look at the `clipboardData` object, which at the time of writing is only supported in Internet Explorer. Before using this object in your code, it's a good idea to perform a couple of tests:

> ► Does JavaScript recognize the object's existence?

> ► If so, does the object support the method I want to use?

The following function `setClipboard()` attempts to write a particular piece of text directly to the clipboard using the `clipboardData` object.

```
function setClipboard(myText){
    if((typeof clipboardData != 'undefined') && (clipboardData.setData)){
        clipboardData.setData("text", myText);
    } else {
        document.getElementById("copytext").innerHTML = myText;
        alert("Please copy the text from the 'Copy Text' field to your
➥clipboard");
    }
}
```

NOTE

The `typeof` operator returns one of the following, depending on the type of the operand:

"undefined", "object", "function", "boolean", "string", or "number".

First it tests for the object's existence using `typeof`:

```
if((typeof clipboardData != 'undefined') ....
```

Additionally, the function insists that the `setData()` method must be available :

```
... && (clipboardData.setData)){
```

If either test fails, the user is offered an alternative, if less elegant, method of getting the text to the clipboard; it is written to a page element, and the user is invited to copy it:

```
document.getElementById("copytext").innerHTML = myText;
alert("Please copy the text from the 'copyt ext' field to your
➥clipboard");
```

At no point does the code try to explicitly detect that the user's browser is Internet Explorer (or any other browser); should some other browser one day implement this functionality, the code should detect it correctly .

Handling Errors Well

When your JavaScript program encounters an error of some sort, a warning or error will be created inside the JavaScript interpreter. Whether and how this is displayed to the user depends on the browser in use and the user's settings; the user may see some form of error message, or the failed program may simply remain silent but inactive.

Neither situation is good for the user; he or she is likely to have no idea what has gone wrong or what to do about it.

As you try to write your code to handle a wide range of browsers and circumstances, it's possible to foresee some areas in which errors might be generated. Examples include

▶ The uncertainty over whether a browser fully supports a certain object and whether that support is standards-compliant

▶ Whether an independent procedure has yet completed its execution, such as an external file being loaded

Using `try` and `catch`

A useful way to try to intercept potential errors and deal with them cleanly is by using the `try` and `catch` statements.

The `try` statement allows you to attempt to run a piece of code. If the code runs without errors, all is well; however, should an error occur you can use the `catch` statement to intervene before an error message is sent to the user, and determine what the program should then do about the error.

```
try {
    doSomething();
}
catch(err) {
    doSomethingElse();
}
```

Note the syntax:

```
catch(identifier)
```

NOTE

You'll encounter the use of `try` and `catch` in Hour 16, "Introducing Ajax," as you learn a cross-browser way to create an object required for Ajax programs.

Here `identifier` is an object created when an error is caught. It contains information about the error; for instance, if you wanted to alert the user to the nature of a JavaScript runtime error, you could use a code construct like this:

```
catch(err) {
    alert(err.description);
}
```

to open a dialog containing details of the error.

▼ TRY IT YOURSELF

Converting Code into Unobtrusive Code

From time to time you may find yourself in the position of having to modernize code to make it less obtrusive. Let's do that with some code we wrote way back in Hour 4, "DOM Objects and Built-In Objects," presented once again here in Listing 14.1.

LISTING 14.1   An Obtrusive Script

```
<!DOCTYPE html>
<html>
<head>
    <title>Current Date and Time</title>
    <style>
        p {font: 14px normal arial, verdana, helvetica;}
    </style>
    <script>
        function telltime() {
            var out = "";
            var now = new Date();
            out += "<br />Date: " + now.getDate();
            out += "<br />Month: " + now.getMonth();
            out += "<br />Year: " + now.getFullYear();
            out += "<br />Hours: " + now.getHours();
            out += "<br />Minutes: " + now.getMinutes();
<!DOCTYPE html>
<html>
<head>
    <title>Current Date and Time</title>
    <style>
        p {font: 14px normal arial, verdana, helvetica;}
    </style>
    <script>
        function telltime() {
            var out = "";
            var now = new Date();
            out += "<br />Date: " + now.getDate();
            out += "<br />Month: " + now.getMonth();
```

```
                out += "<br />Year: " + now.getFullYear();
                out += "<br />Hours: " + now.getHours();
                out += "<br />Minutes: " + now.getMinutes();
                out += "<br />Seconds: " + now.getSeconds();
                document.getElementById("div1").innerHTML = out;
            }
        </script>
    </head>
    <body>
        The current date and time are:<br/>
        <div id="div1"></div>
        <script>
            telltime();
        </script>
        <input type="button" onclick="location.reload()" value="Refresh" />
    </body>
</html>
```

As it stands, this script has a number of areas of potential improvement.

▶ The JavaScript statements are placed between `<script>` and `</script>` tags on the page; they would be better in a separate file.

▶ The button has an inline event handler.

▶ A user without JavaScript would simply see a page with a nonfunction-ing button.

First, let's move all the JavaScript to a separate file and remove the inline event handler. We also give the button an id value, so we can identify it in JavaScript to add the required event handler via our code.

Next, we need to address the issue of users without JavaScript enabled. We use the `<noscript>` page element so that users without JavaScript enabled will see, instead of the button, a short message with a link to an alternative source of time information:

```
<noscript>
    Your browser does not support JavaScript<br />
    Please consult your computer's operating system for local date and
time information or click <a href="clock.php" target="_blank">HERE</a> to
read the server time.
</noscript>
```

TRY IT YOURSELF ▼

Converting Code into Unobtrusive Code
continued

TIP

The `<noscript>` element pro-vides additional page content for users with disabled scripts or with a browser that can't support client-side scripting. Any of the elements that you can put in the `<body>` ele-ment of an HTML page can go inside the `<noscript>` ele-ment and will automatically be displayed if scripts cannot be run in the user's browser.

▼ TRY IT YOURSELF

**Converting Code into
Unobtrusive Code**

continued

The HTML file after modification is listed in Listing 14.2.

LISTING 14.2   The Modified HTML Page

```
<!DOCTYPE html>
<html>
<head>
    <title>Current Date and Time</title>
    <style>
        p {font: 14px normal arial, verdana, helvetica;}
    </style>
    <script src="datetime.js"></script>
</head>
<body>
    The current date and time are:<br/>
    <div id="div1"></div>
    <input id="btn1" type="button" value="Refresh" />
    <noscript>
        <p>Your browser does not support JavaScript.</p>
        <p>Please consult your computer's operating system for local date
and time information or click <a href="clock.php"
target="_blank">HERE</a> to read the server time.</p>
    </noscript>
</body>
</html>
```

Within our JavaScript source file telltime.js, we use window.onload to add
the event listener for the button. Finally we call telltime() to generate the
date and time information to display on the page. The JavaScript code is
shown in Listing 14.3.

LISTING 14.3   datetime.js

```
function telltime() {
    var out = "";
    var now = new Date();
    out += "<br />Date: " + now.getDate();
    out += "<br />Month: " + now.getMonth();
    out += "<br />Year: " + now.getFullYear();
    out += "<br />Hours: " + now.getHours();
    out += "<br />Minutes: " + now.getMinutes();
    out += "<br />Seconds: " + now.getSeconds();
    document.getElementById("div1").innerHTML = out;
}

window.onload = function() {
    document.getElementById("btn1").onclick= function()
{location.reload();}
    telltime();
}
```

With JavaScript enabled, the script works just as it did in Hour 4. However, with JavaScript disabled, the user now sees the page as shown in Figure 14.1.

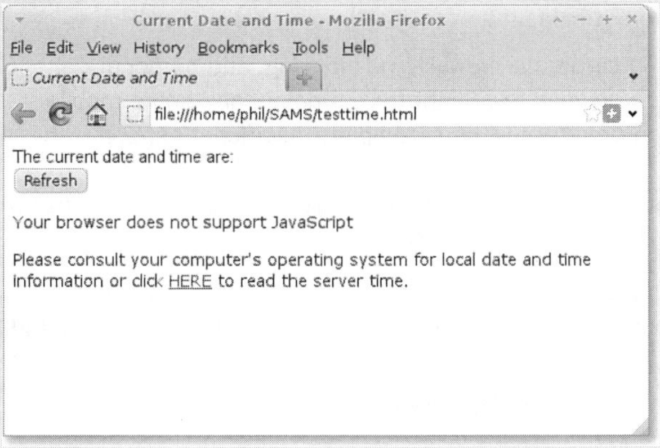

TRY IT YOURSELF ▼

Converting Code into Unobtrusive Code

continued

FIGURE 14.1
Extra information for users without JavaScript

```
┌──────────────────────────────────────────────────────────┐
│  ▼         Current Date and Time - Mozilla Firefox    ^  –  +  ×│
│ File  Edit  View  History  Bookmarks  Tools  Help              │
│ ☐ Current Date and Time              ☐                       ▼│
│ ← C ⌂ | ☐ file:///home/phil/SAMS/testtime.html    ☆ ☐ ▼│
│                                                              │
│ The current date and time are:                               │
│ ┌─────────┐                                                  │
│ │ Refresh │                                                  │
│ └─────────┘                                                  │
│ Your browser does not support JavaScript                     │
│                                                              │
│ Please consult your computer's operating system for local date and time│
│ information or click HERE to read the server time.           │
│                                                              │
└──────────────────────────────────────────────────────────┘
```

Summary

In this hour we rounded up and presented various examples of good practice in writing JavaScript. Used together they should help you deliver your code projects more quickly, with higher quality and much easier maintenance.

Q&A

Q. **Why would a user turn off JavaScript?**

A. Remember that the browser might have been set up by the service provider or employer with JavaScript turned off by default in an effort to improve security. This is particularly likely in environments such as a school or an Internet cafe.

Additionally, some corporate firewalls, ad-blocking, and personal antivirus software prevent JavaScript from running, and some mobile devices have web browsers without complete JavaScript support.

Q. **Are there any other options besides** `<noscript>` **for dealing with users who don't have JavaScript enabled?**

A. An alternative that avoids `<noscript>` is to send users who *do* have JavaScript support to an alternative page containing JavaScript-powered enhancements:

```
<script>window.location="enhancedPage.html";</script>
```

If JavaScript is available and activated, the script redirects the user to the enhanced page. If the browser doesn't have JavaScript support, the script won't be executed, and the user is left viewing the more basic version.

Workshop

Try to answer all the questions before reading the subsequent "Answers" section.

Quiz

1. The modularization of code into reusable blocks for more general use is called:

    a. Abstraction

    b. Inheritance

    c. Unobtrusive JavaScript

2. The CSS for your page should be confined as much as possible to the:

    a. Semantic layer

    b. Presentation layer

    c. Behavior layer

3. Unobtrusive JavaScript code should, wherever possible, be placed

    a. In an external file

    b. Between `<script>` and `</script>` tags in the page `<head>`

    c. Inline

Answers

1. a. Abstraction

2. b. Where possible, all CSS goes in the presentation layer

3. a. User external JavaScript files where it's feasible to do so

Exercises

Pick some Try It Yourself sections from earlier in the book and see what you can do to make the code more unobtrusive without adversely affecting the script's operation.

Can you work out how to further modify the code of Listing 14.2 and Listing 14.3 to ensure that users without JavaScript enabled see just the content of the `<noscript>` tag, without the additional text and button being present? [Hint: Write these items to the page with innerHTML or via DOM methods.]

Graphics and Animation

Since the earliest days of JavaScript, one of its most frequent uses has been to add interest to pages by using graphics effects and animation. In this hour you learn how to do it.

Preloading Images

Various examples earlier in the book have carried out changes to images on the page by changing the value of the image's src attribute.

When src is given a new value, if the browser doesn't already have the newly requested image file in its cache it attempts to download it.

In many instances this works fine, especially for small images on the local server and with a fast connection to the Internet. Problems can occur, though, when image files are larger, served from slow servers, or have to be downloaded across a slow connection. A noticeable delay in retrieving image data can disrupt the smooth operation of your page and frustrate users.

This is where *preloading* images can greatly improve a user's experience of your site. The idea is to retrieve from the server all of the image data that is likely to be required for the page before the user needs it. When images are preloaded this way, the visitor perceives faster image loading and smoother site operation. The technique is especially beneficial for photo galleries and other sites making heavy use of images.

Preloading an image is easily achieved by instantiating a new image object in JavaScript and passing it the URL of the image you want to preload:

```
var img1 = new Image();
img1.src="http://www.example.com/image0.gif";
```

Often you will need to preload more than just one image. A simple way to achieve that is to store the image URLs in an array, then loop through the array, assigning each image URL to the image object, thereby saving them in the browser's cache. Here is the code to do that, wrapped into a function attached to the `window.onload` event; this way the image data will be put into cache when the page first loads:

```
window.onload = function() {
    var img1 = new Image();
    var img_urls = new Array();
    img_urls[0] = "http://www.example.com/image0.gif";
    img_urls[1] = "http://www.example.com/image1.gif";
    img_urls[2] = "http://www.example.com/image2.gif";
    for(i=0; i < img_urls.length; i++) {
        img1.src=img_urls[i];
    }
}
```

Animating Page Elements

We've all seen plenty of examples of animation, ranging from cartoons to video games. In all of these examples, individual visible items have their appearance and/or position changed incrementally over a period of time.

If the increments are sufficiently small, and the time intervals between them suitably short, the motion appears to the viewer as continuous.

Animation in JavaScript is similar in concept. One or more DOM elements are moved around on the page following a pattern determined by program logic.

To achieve the illusion of smooth motion, these DOM elements must be moved with a set frequency—in video this would be referred to as the frame rate, and measured in frames per second (fps).

The simplest way to achieve this in program code is to set up a loop with a preset delay, moving the animated elements once per loop execution.

NOTE

`setTimeout()` and `clearTimeout()` are both methods of the HTML DOM `window` object.

To help you, JavaScript provides two useful methods, `setTimeout()` and
`setInterval()`.

setTimeout()

The `setTimeout(action, delay)` method calls the function (or evaluates
the expression) passed in its first argument after the number of milliseconds specified in its second argument. You can use it, for example, to display an element in a given configuration for a fixed period of time.

```
<div id="id1">I'm about to disappear!</div>
```

Let's suppose your page contains the above <div> element. If you put the
following code into a <script> element in the page <head> section:

```
function hide(elementId) {
    document.getElementById(elementId).style.display = 'none';
}
window.onload = function() {
    setTimeout("hide('id1')", 3000);
}
```

the function `hide()` will be executed 3 seconds after the page finishes loading, making the <div> element invisible.

The `setTimeout()` method returns a value. If later you want to cancel the
timer function, you can refer to it by passing that returned value to the
`clearTimeout()` method.

```
var timer1 = setTimeout("hide('id1')", 3000);
clearTimeout(timer1);
```

setInterval()

The `setInterval(action, delay)` method works similarly to
`setTimeout()`, but instead of imposing a single delay before executing the
statement passed to it as its first argument, it executes it repeatedly, with a
delay between executions corresponding to the number of
milliseconds specified in the second argument.

Like `setTimeout()`, `setInterval()` returns a value that you can later pass
to the `clearInterval()` method to stop the timer:

```
var timer1 = setInterval("updateClock()", 1000);
clearInterval(timer1);
```

NOTE

You saw an example of how to
use `setInterval()` in Hour 6,
"Scripts That Do More."

Animating Transparency

Fading page between transparency and opacity is a popular method of improving how a page appears. To implement fades you need to manipulate the opacity of particular page elements; gradually lowering the opacity of an element (making it more transparent) allows the background page elements to become steadily more visible, making the foreground element appear to be fading away.

CSS opacity has been around for a few years now, but it's been rather frustrating to implement in a cross-browser way. Finally the different browsers are close to agreeing on syntax, and while there is still no universal method to make opacity work on all currently used browsers, things have improved recently. For Firefox, Safari, Chrome/Chromium, Opera, and Internet Explorer 9, you need to set the `opacity` property of the `style` object to a value between 0 and 1.

When `opacity` is set to 0, the element is fully transparent, and when it is set to 1 it the element is fully opaque.

For opacity in Internet Explorer, you have to modify the `filter` property of the `style` object.

The values you set for this property are different, and require a different syntax; `"alpha(opacity=0)"` is the value to set an element to be transparent, and `"alpha(opacity=100)"` to set it to be opaque.

You can rely on feature detection to make sure that the correct property is set for your code to work in a cross-browser manner:

```
function setOpacity(opac) {
    elem.style.opacity = opac/100;
    elem.style.filter = 'alpha(opacity=' + opac + ')';
}
```

The function takes as an argument an opacity value `opac` in the range 1 to 100, and performs the necessary scaling to calculate the equivalent value for `style.opacity`. Whichever opacity statement is understood by the browser will be implemented; the other ignored.

You can then employ `setTimout()` to write a function to perform your fade:

```
var opac = 0;
var timer1;
function fadeIn(opac) {
    if(opac < 100) {
```

```
        opac++;
        setOpacity(opac);
        timer1 = window.setTimeout("fadeIn(" + opac + ")", 50);
    } else {
        clearTimeout(timer1);
    }
}
```

The variable opac stores the current opacity level of the element in a range 1 to 100. This function is recursive; for all values of opac less than 100, the function increments opac by 1, sets the opacity of the target element elem to the incremented value, and then calls itself after a delay of 50 milliseconds.

Once we're done, the clearTimeout() method is called to cancel the timer.

CSS3 Transitions, Transformations, and Animations

You can use JavaScript for all sorts of effects, but it often requires a lot of code to produce an effect that should be straightforward.

It would be better if there were easy ways to add simple effects to elements on the page. In some browsers these already exist in the forms of CSS transitions, transformations, and animations. These are currently being introduced in CSS Level 3, but already have support to varying degrees in some browsers.

Unfortunately the implementations of these effects currently require browser-specific prefixes, creating an awful lot of repetition.

In the following simple example, we add a transition effect (in those browsers that support it) to the change of background color on link hover. As the background color changes, a transition effect will smooth out the transformation.

Currently this effect is only possible in a truly cross-browser way by using JavaScript (or other outside technologies such as Flash), but will one day possible with a few extra lines of CSS.

Here's the code for our example link:

```
<a href="somepage.html" class="trans">Show Me</a>
```

NOTE

You can find comprehensive information about CSS3 transitions, transformations, and animations at http://css3.bradshawenterprises.com/all/.

Below are the CSS declarations showing the original and hover background colors, and the declarations to carry out the transition effect in the various different browsers. Note the range of different prefixes required. The last declaration, without a prefix, will be the one required once the technology moves from an experimental to a finished status.

```
a.trans {
    background: #669999;
    -webkit-transition: background 0.5s ease;
    -moz-transition: background 0.5s ease;
    -o-transition: background 0.5s ease;
    transition: background 0.5s ease;
}
a.trans:hover {
    background: #999966;
}
```

Scripting DOM Positioning

Similar techniques to those you used to animate transparency can just as easily be employed to manipulate the screen location of DOM objects. To move an element from left to right on the screen you can modify the value of the element's `style.left` property with a recursive timing function:

```
function moveItRight() {
    el.style.left = parseInt(el.style.left) + 2 + 'px';
    timer1 = setTimeout(moveItRight, 25);
}
```

The code of Listing 15.1 uses a slightly modified version of the preceding `moveItRight()` function to animate a `<div>` element, moving it across the screen from left to right.

LISTING 15.1   Animating a DOM Element

```
<!DOCTYPE html>
<html>
<head>
    <title>Animating a DOM Element</title>
    <style>
        #div1 {
            position:absolute;
            border:1px solid black;
            width: 50px;
            height: 50px;
            left: 0px;
```

LISTING 15.1   Continued

```
            top: 100px;
            }
    </style>
    <script>
        var timer1 = null;
        var el = null;
        function moveItRight() {
            if(parseInt(el.style.left) > (screen.width - 50))
el.style.left = 0;
            el.style.left = parseInt(el.style.left) + 2 + 'px';
            timer1 = setTimeout(moveItRight, 25);
        }
        window.onload = function() {
            el = document.getElementById("div1");
            el.style.left = '50px';
            moveItRight();
        }
    </script>
</head>
<body>
    <div id="div1">Move It!</div>
</body>
</html>
```

Take a look at the modified version of the function moveItRight():

```
function moveItRight() {
    if(parseInt(el.style.left) > (screen.width - 50)) el.style.left = 0;
    el.style.left = parseInt(el.style.left) + 2 + 'px';
    timer1 = setTimeout(moveItRight, 25);
}
```

The function uses setTimeout() to call itself recursively every 25ms, each time moving the chosen element 2px to the right.

The first line of the function

```
if(parseInt(el.style.left) > (screen.width - 50)) el.style.left = 0;
```

moves the object back to the left-hand side of the screen when it detects that it has reached the right-hand edge.

We can just as easily manipulate the horizontal position of a screen object by using the top property:

```
el.style.top = parseInt(el.style.top) + 2 + 'px';
```

TIP

Remember that the right property is measured from the left-hand side of the element's container, and the top property is measured downwards from the top of the element's container.

In the example of Listing 15.1 the container is simply the <body> element of the page.

Optimizing Performance

There are a few things you can do to make your JavaScript animations as smooth as possible.

Use a Single Timer

Using multiple timers rapidly increases CPU usage. When you want to run several animations at once, try to work out how to control them using a single timer.

Each timer causes the browser to redraw one or more screen elements, and this can happen more quickly and efficiently if there is just one redraw for all animated elements.

Don't Animate Elements Deep in the DOM

The deeper the animated element is in the DOM, the more other elements depend on its size and position, causing the browser to perform more complex calculations. Where possible, attach the animated element directly to the <body> element or to some other high-level container element before starting the animation.

Use the Lowest Frame Rate You Can

Your animations probably don't need to be of movie quality. Extend the timer delays as far as you can before the quality of the animation degrades too much to be acceptable.

▼ TRY IT YOURSELF

A Simple Animated Game

Let's build on the animation routine in Listing 15.1 to make a JavaScript game. You're going to animate a page element as a target, and invite the user to try to "shoot" it by clicking the mouse on the moving element.

The code for the game is in Listing 15.2.

LISTING 15.2   Animated Shooting Game

```
<!DOCTYPE html>
<html>
<head>
    <title>Space Shooter</title>
    <style>
        #range {
```

TRY IT YOURSELF ▼

A Simple Animated Game

continued

LISTING 15.2   Continued

```
            position:absolute;
            top: 0px;
            left: 0px;
            background: url(space.jpg);
            cursor: crosshair;
            width: 100%;
            height: 300px;
        }
        #img1 {
            position:absolute;
            border:none;
            left: 0px;
            top: 100px;
            padding: 10px;
            }
        #score {
            font: 16px normal arial, verdana, sans-serif;
            color: white;
            padding: 10px;
        }
    </style>
    <script>
        var timer1 = null;
        var el = null;
        var score = 0; // number of 'hits'
        var shots = 0; // total 'shots'
        function moveIt() {
            // animate the image
            if(parseInt(el.style.left) > (screen.width - 50))
➥el.style.left = 0;
            el.style.left = parseInt(el.style.left) + 6 + 'px';
            el.style.top = 100 + (80 *
➥Math.sin(parseInt(el.style.left)/50)) + 'px';
            // set the timer
            timer1 = setTimeout(moveIt, 25);
        }
        function scoreUp() {
            // increment the player's score
            score++;
        }
        function scoreboard() {
            // display the scoreboard
            document.getElementById("score").innerHTML = "Shots: " +
➥shots + " Score: " + score;
        }
        window.onload = function() {
            el = document.getElementById("img1");
            // onClick handler calls scoreUp()
            // when the image is clicked
```

LISTING 15.2   Continued

```
            el.onclick = scoreUp;
            // update total number of shots
            // for every click within play field
            document.getElementById("range").onclick = function() {
                shots++;
                // update scoreboard
                scoreboard();
                }
            // initialize game
            scoreboard();
            el.style.left = '50px';
            moveIt();
        }
    </script>
</head>
<body>
    <div id="range">
        <div id="score"></div>
        <img alt="Fire!" id="img1" src="ufo.gif" />
    </div>
</body>
</html>
```

The animation is carried out in the function moveIt():

```
function moveIt() {
    if(parseInt(el.style.left) > (screen.width - 50)) el.style.left = 0;
    el.style.left = parseInt(el.style.left) + 6 + 'px';
    el.style.top = 100 + (80 * Math.sin(parseInt(el.style.left)/50)) +
➥'px';
    timer1 = setTimeout(moveIt, 25);
}
```

The left to right motion is achieved in exactly the same way as in Listing 15.1. However, we have now superimposed an oscillating vertical motion:

```
el.style.top = 100 + (80 * Math.sin(parseInt(el.style.left)/50)) + 'px';
```

The resulting position of the animated element (in this case an image of a UFO) has a top property ranging from 100 - 80 = 20px to 100 + 80 = 180px as the element traverses the screen.

Shooting at the UFO is done with a mouse click. The cursor of the mouse is changed to a more gun-sight-like crosshair while within the <div> element of id="range" that forms the container for the game.

A function scoreUp() is called whenever a mouse click occurs within the animated image, incrementing the player's score, while another function scoreboard() displays the total number of "shots" alongside the number of "hits."

The game is shown in action in Figure 15.1.

TRY IT YOURSELF ▼

A Simple Animated Game

continued

FIGURE 15.1
Playing the animated game

Create an HTML file using the code of Listing 15.2. Feel free to use any images you have on hand for the background and the animated element. When you load the file into your browser, the game should begin with the UFO (or whatever image you used instead) traversing the screen with an undulating motion.

Adjust the calculations within the moveIt() function and see how the motion is affected. Try "hitting" the image by clicking the mouse, and watch the scoreboard update the "shots" and "score."

Summary

In this hour you learned a variety of techniques for animating page elements using JavaScript.

Q&A

Q. What browsers currently support CSS3 transitions, transforms, and animations?

A. At the time of writing, 2D transforms are available in all popular current browsers, while 3D transforms are supported in Safari, Chrome/Chromium, and Firefox. Transitions and 3D transforms will be added in IE10. Most of these effects degrade sensibly, so a user having a browser without support will still be OK, but will see the page elements without animation.

Q. How accurate are the delays programmed into `setTimeout()` and `setInterval()`?

A. Not very accurate. JavaScript interpreters only have what is called a single thread, meaning that asynchronous events like timers sometimes have to wait until the interpreter can execute them. If a timer is unable to execute when scheduled it will be delayed until execution is possible, extending the programmed delay time.

Workshop

Try to answer all the questions before reading the subsequent "Answers" section.

Quiz

1. Preloading images improves a page's apparent speed by:

    a. Compressing images on the page before they are downloaded.

    b. Downloading images on the page before they are needed.

    c. Resizing images to the optimum size.

2. You can animate the vertical location of a page element el by altering:

    a. `el.style.top`

    b. `el.top`

    c. `el.vertical`

3. What is the CSS style property that determines how transparent a page element appears?

   a. Transparency

   b. Alpha

   c. Opacity

Answers

1. b. Images are downloaded before they are needed.

2. a. `el.style.top`

3. c. opacity is the CSS style property.

Exercises

Rewrite the code in Listing 15.2 so the spaceship oscillates in both vertical and horizontal directions, instead of panning left-to-right. At the same time, make the code more unobtrusive by extracting JavaScript and CSS into external files.

Can you further modify the code to include a second spaceship with different motion characteristics?

PART IV
Ajax

Introducing Ajax

JavaScript is a client-side scripting language, and all of the examples you've used so far have been limited entirely to client-side coding. Ajax (also known as remote scripting) allows you to access server-side programs and use their capabilities in your client-side scripts.

Here in Part IV, "Ajax," you learn how to create and deploy Ajax applications.

The Anatomy of Ajax

So far we've discussed only the traditional page-based model of a website user interface.

When you interact with such a website, individual pages containing text, images, data entry forms, and so forth are presented to you one at a time. Each page must be dealt with individually before navigating to the next.

For instance, you may complete the data entry fields of a form, editing and re-editing your entries as much as you want, knowing that the data will not be sent to the server until the form is finally submitted.

This interaction is summarized in Figure 16.1.

After you submit a form or follow a navigation link, you then must wait while the browser screen refreshes to display the new or revised page that has been delivered by the server.

Unfortunately, interfaces built using this model have quite a few drawbacks. First, there is a significant delay while each new or revised page is loaded. This interrupts what we, as users, perceive as the "flow" of the application.

WHAT YOU'LL LEARN IN THIS HOUR

▶ The anatomy of an Ajax application
▶ About the components of an Ajax application
▶ What the XMLHttpRequest object does
▶ Sending messages to the server
▶ Dealing with the server response

FIGURE 16.1
Traditional client–server
interaction

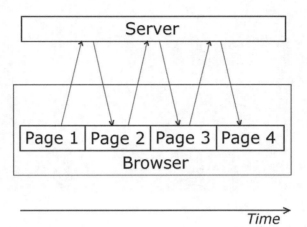

Furthermore, a *whole* page must be loaded on each occasion, even when most of its content is identical to that of the previous page. Items common to many pages on a website, such as header, footer, and navigation sections, can amount to a significant proportion of the data contained in the page.

This unnecessary download of data wastes bandwidth and further exacerbates the delay in loading each new page.

The combined effect of the issues just described is to offer a much inferior user experience compared to that provided by the vast majority of desktop applications. On the desktop, you expect the display contents of your programs to remain visible, and the interface elements to continue responding to your commands, while the computing processes occur quietly in the background.

Introducing Ajax

Ajax allows you to add to your web application interfaces some of this functionality more commonly seen in desktop applications. To achieve this, Ajax builds an extra "layer" of processing between the web page and the server.

This layer, often referred to as an Ajax Engine or Ajax Framework, intercepts requests from the user and in the background handles server communications quietly, unobtrusively, and *asynchronously*. By this you mean that server requests and responses no longer need to coincide with particular user actions but may happen at any time convenient to the user and to the correct operation of the application. The browser does not freeze and await the completion by the server of the last request, but instead lets you carry on scrolling, clicking, and typing in the current page.

The updating of page elements to reflect the revised information received from the server is also looked after by Ajax, happening dynamically while the page continues to be used.

Figure 16.2 represents how these interactions take place.

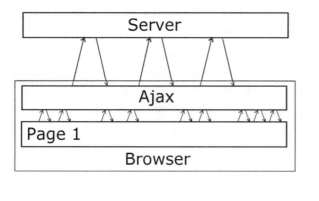

FIGURE 16.2
Ajax client-server interaction

The XMLHttpRequest Object

When you click on a hyperlink or submit an HTML form, you send an HTTP request to the server, which responds by serving to you a new or revised page. For your web application to work asynchronously, however, you must have a means to send HTTP requests to the server *without* an associated request to display a new page.

We can do so by means of the XMLHttpRequest object. This JavaScript object is capable of making a connection to the server and issuing an HTTP request without the necessity of an associated page load.

Later in the hour you see how to create an instance of the XMLHttpRequest object and use it to send server requests.

TIP

As a security measure, the XMLHttpRequest object can generally only make calls to URLs within the same domain as the calling page and cannot directly call a remote server.

Talking with the Server

In the traditional style of web page, when you issue a server request via a hyperlink or a form submission, the server accepts that request, carries out any server-side processing required, and subsequently serves to you a new page with content appropriate to the action you've taken.

While this processing takes place, your user interface is effectively frozen. You are made aware when the server has completed its task by the appearance in the browser of the new or revised page.

With asynchronous server requests, however, such communications occur in the background, and the completion of such a request does not necessarily coincide with a screen refresh or a new page being loaded. You must therefore make other arrangements to find out what progress the server has made in dealing with your request.

The XMLHttpRequest object possesses a convenient property to report on the progress of the server request. You can examine this property using JavaScript routines to determine the point at which the server has completed its task and the results are available for you to use.

Our Ajax armory must therefore include a routine to monitor the status of your request and act accordingly. We look at this in more detail later in the hour.

What Happens at the Server?

So far as the server-side script is concerned, the communication from your XMLHttpRequest object is just another HTTP request. Ajax applications care little about what languages or operating environments exist at the server; provided that the client-side Ajax layer receives a timely and correctly formatted HTTP response from the server, everything will work just fine.

Dealing with the Server Response

Once notified that an asynchronous request has been successfully completed, you may then use the information returned by the server.

Ajax allows for this information to be returned to you in a number of formats, including ASCII text and XML data.

Depending on the nature of the application, you may then translate, display, or otherwise process this information within your current page.

Putting It All Together

Suppose you want to design a new Ajax application or update a legacy web application to include Ajax techniques. How can you go about it?

First you need to decide what page events and user actions will be responsible for causing the sending of an asynchronous HTTP request. You may decide, for example, that the onMouseOver event of an image will result in a request being sent to the server to retrieve further information about the subject of the picture; or that the onClick event belonging to a button will generate a server request for information with which to populate the fields on a form.

You've already learned how JavaScript may be used to execute instructions on occurrences such as these by employing event handlers. In your Ajax applications, such methods will be responsible for initiating asynchronous HTTP requests via XMLHttpRequest.

Having made the request, you need to write routines to monitor the progress of that request until you hear from the server that the request has been successfully completed.

Finally, having received notification that the server has completed its task, you need a routine to retrieve the information returned from the server and apply it in your application.

The flow diagram of all this is shown in Figure 16.3.

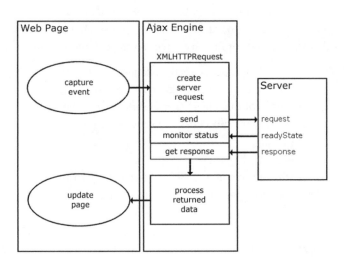

FIGURE 16.3
How the components of an Ajax application work together

The XMLHttpRequest Object

XMLHttpRequest is supported by virtually all modern browsers.

The purpose of the object is to allow JavaScript to formulate HTTP requests and submit them to the server. Using XMLHttpRequest you can have your page make such calls *asynchronously* in the background, allowing you to continue using the page without the interruption of a browser refresh and the loading of a new or revised page.

This capability underpins all Ajax applications, making the XMLHttpRequest object the key to Ajax programming.

TIP

Although the object's name begins with "XML..." in fact any type of document may be returned from the server; ASCII text, HTML, and XML are all popular choices.

Creating Instances of XMLHttpRequest

You can't make use of XMLHttpRequest until you've created an instance of it. As you've seen a number of times in previous hours, creating an instance of an object in JavaScript is usually just a matter of making a call to a method known as the object's constructor. In the case of XMLHttpRequest, however, you must change this routine a little to cater for the peculiarities of different browsers, as you see in the following section.

Different Rules for Different Browsers

Because you don't know in advance which browser, version, or operating system your users have, you must have your code adapt its behavior on-the-fly to ensure that the instance of the object will be created successfully.

For the majority of browsers that support XMLHttpRequest as a native object (Firefox, Opera, and the rest, as well as later versions of Internet Explorer), creating an instance of this object is straightforward. The following line creates an XMLHttpRequest object called request:

```
var request = new XMLHttpRequest();
```

To achieve the equivalent result in some earlier versions of Microsoft Internet Explorer, you need to create an ActiveX object. Here's an example:

```
var request = new ActiveXObject("Microsoft.XMLHTTP");
```

Once again, this assigns the name request to your new object.

To complicate matters a little more, some versions of Internet Explorer have a different version of the Microsoft XML parser installed; in those cases you need to use the instruction

```
var request = new ActiveXObject("Msxml2.XMLHTTP");
```

A Solution for All Browsers

To correctly create an instance of an XMLHttpRequest object regardless of which browser you are using, you can use feature detection to have your script try in turn each method of creating an instance of the object until one such method succeeds. Have a look at Listing 16.1, in which such a strategy is used.

LISTING 16.1   A Cross-Browser XMLHttpRequest Object

```
function getXMLHttpRequest() {
    try {
        try {
            return new ActiveXObject("Microsoft.XMLHTTP");
        }
        catch(e) {
            return new ActiveXObject("Msxml2.XMLHTTP");
        }
    }
    catch(e) {
        return new XMLHttpRequest();
    }
}
```

In this example we used the tests

```
new ActiveXObject("Microsoft.XMLHTTP")
```

and, if that fails,

```
new ActiveXObject("Msxml2.XMLHTTP");
```

to determine whether we need to use the ActiveX method to create our XMLHttpRequest object. If both fail, then XMLHttpRequest is a native object of the browser in use, and you use the constructor method

```
new XMLHttpRequest();
```

to create an instance of the XMLHttpRequest object.

Now to create an instance of the XMLHttpRequest object, you can call this function like this:

```
var myRequest = getXMLHttpRequest();
```

Methods and Properties

Now that you have created an instance of your XMLHttpRequest object, let's look at some of the object's properties and methods by referring to Table 16.1.

TABLE 16.1   XMLHttpRequest Objects and Methods

Properties	Description
onreadystatechange	Determines which event handler will be called when the object's readyState property changes
readyState	Integer reporting the status of the request:
	0 = uninitialized
	1 = loading
	2 = loaded
	3 = interactive
	4 = completed
responseText	Data returned by the server in text string form
responseXML	Data returned by the server expressed as a document object
status	HTTP status code returned by server
statusText	HTTP reason phrase returned by server

Methods	Description
abort()	Stop the current request
getAllResponseHeaders()	Returns all headers as a string
getResponseHeader(x)	Returns the value of header x as a string
open('method','URL','a')	Specifies the HTTP method (e.g., GET or POST), the target URL, and whether the request should be handled asynchronously (if yes, a='true' (default), if no a='false')
send(content)	Sends the request, optionally with POST data
setRequestHeader('x','y')	Sets a parameter and value pair x=y and assigns it to the header to be sent with the request

Over the next few lessons we examine how these methods and properties are used to create the functions that form the building blocks of your Ajax applications.

For now, let's examine just a few of these methods.

The open() Method

The open() method prepares your XMLHttpRequest object to communicate with the server. You need to supply at least the two mandatory arguments to this method:

▶ First, you need to specify which HTTP method you intend to use, usually GET or POST.

▶ Next, the destination URL of the request is included as the second argument. If making a GET request, this URL needs to be suitably encoded with any parameters and their values as part of the URL.

For security reasons, the XMLHttpRequest object is only allowed to communicate with URLs within its own domain. An attempt to connect to a remote domain results in a "permission denied" error message.

Optionally you may include a third argument to the send request, a Boolean value to declare whether the request is being sent in asynchronous mode. If set to false, the request will not be sent in asynchronous mode, and the page will be effectively locked until the request is completed. The default value of true will be assumed if the parameter is omitted, and requests will then be sent asynchronously.

CAUTION

A common mistake is to reference your domain as example.com in a call made from www.example.com. The two will be regarded as different by the JavaScript interpreter, and connection will not be allowed.

The send() Method

Having prepared your XMLHttpRequest using the open() method, you can send the request using the send() method. One argument is accepted by the send() function.

If your request is a GET request, the request information will be encoded into the destination URL, and you can then simply invoke the send() method using the argument null:

```
objectname.send(null);
```

However, if you are making a POST request, the content of the request (suitably encoded) will be passed as the argument.

```
objectname.setRequestHeader('Content-Type', 'application/
➥x-www-form-urlencoded');
objectname.send(var1=value1&var2=value2);
```

In this case you use the setRequestHeader method to indicate what type of content you are including.

Sending the Server Request

We're going to jump right in and write a JavaScript function called callAjax() to send an asynchronous request to the server using an XMLHttpRequest object:

```
function callAjax() {
    // declare a variable to hold some information to pass to the server
    var lastname = 'Smith';
    // build the URL of the server script we wish to call
    var url = "myserverscript.php?surname=" + lastname;
    // ask our XMLHttpRequest object to open a server connection
    myRequest.open("GET", url, true);
    // prepare a function responseAjax() to run when the response has
➥arrived
    myRequest.onreadystatechange = responseAjax;
    // and finally send the request
    myRequest.send(null);
}
```

The first line is fairly trivial, simply declaring a variable and assigning a value to it:

```
var lastname = 'Smith';
```

This is the piece of data that our function intends to send to the server, as the value of a variable called surname that is required by our server-side script. In reality, of course, the value of such data would usually be obtained dynamically by handling a page event such as a mouse click or a keyboard entry, but for now this will serve as a simple example.

The server request we intend to make is a GET request, so we must construct a suitable target URL having our parameter and value pairs suitably coded on the end; the next line carries this out:

```
var url = "myserverscript.php?surname=" + lastname;
```

We dealt briefly with the `open()` method in Hour 15, "Graphics and Animation." We use it in the next line to prepare our server request:

```
myRequest.open("GET", url, true);
```

This line specifies that we are preparing a `GET` request and passes to it the destination URL complete with the appended content of the `GET` request.

The third parameter `true` indicates that we want our request to be handled asynchronously. In this case it could have been omitted, as the default value of `true` is assumed in such cases. However, it does no harm to include it for clarity.

Next, we need to tell our `XMLHttpRequest` object `myRequest` what it should do with the progress reports that it receives from the server. The `XMLHttpRequest` object has a property `onreadystatechange` that contains information about what JavaScript function should be called whenever the server status changes, and in the next line

```
myRequest.onreadystatechange = responseAjax;
```

we assign the function `responseAjax()` to do this job. We write this function later in the hour.

Dealing with the Browser Cache

All browsers maintain a so-called *cache* of visited web pages, a local record of page contents stored on the hard disk of the browser's computer. When we request a particular web page, the browser first tries to load the page from its cache, rather than submitting a new HTTP request.

Although this can sometimes be advantageous in terms of page load times, it creates a difficulty when trying to write Ajax applications. Ajax is all about talking to the server, not reloading information from cache; so when we make an asynchronous request to the server, we require a new HTTP request to be generated every time.

A commonly used trick to work around this problem involves the adding of a parameter with a random and meaningless value to the request data. In the case of a `GET` request, this necessitates adding a further parameter and value pair to the end of the URL.

If the random part of the URL is different each time, this effectively fools the browser into believing that it is to send the asynchronous request to an address not previously visited. This results in the generation of a new HTTP request being sent on every occasion.

Let's see how we might achieve this. In JavaScript, we can generate random numbers using the `Math.random()` method of the native `Math` object. Listing 16.2 contains a couple of changes to our `callAjax()` function.

LISTING 16.2   Using a Random Number to Defeat the Cache

```
function getXMLHttpRequest() {
    try {
        try {
            return new ActiveXObject("Microsoft.XMLHTTP");
        }
        catch(e) {
            return new ActiveXObject("Msxml2.XMLHTTP");
        }
    }
    catch(e) {
        return new XMLHttpRequest();
    }
}

var myRequest = getXMLHttpRequest();

function callAjax() {
    // declare a variable to hold some information to pass to the server
    var lastname = 'Smith';
    // build the URL of the server script we wish to call
    var url = "myserverscript.php?surname=" + lastname;
    // generate a random number
    var myRandom=parseInt(Math.random()*99999999);
    // ask our XMLHttpRequest object to open a server connection
    myRequest. open("GET", url + "&rand=" + myRandom, true);
    // prepare a function responseAjax() to run when the response has
➥arrived
    myRequest.onreadystatechange = responseAjax;
    // and finally send the request
    myRequest.send(null);
}
```

NOTE

Some programmers prefer to add the current timestamp rather than a random number. This is a string of characters derived from the current date and time. In the following example, the JavaScript `Date()` and `getTime()` methods of the native `Date()` object are used:

` ... + "&myRand =" + new Date().getTime();`

You can see from Listing 16.2 that our script now generates a destination URL for your Ajax request that looks something like this:

`myserverscript.php?surname=Smith&rand=XXXX`

where XXXX will be some random number, thereby preventing the page from being returned from cache, and forcing a new HTTP request to be sent to the server.

Monitoring Server Status

When your Ajax request has been sent to the server, you need to monitor its progress. In particular, you want to know when processing of the request is *complete* and whether that processing completed *successfully*.

The XMLHttpRequest object provides some means to provide this information.

The `readyState` Property

The `readyState` property of your `XMLHttpRequest` object gives you information from the server about the current state of a request you've made. This property is monitored by the `onreadystatechange` property, and changes in the value of `readyState` cause `onreadystatechange` to become `true` and therefore cause the appropriate function (`responseAjax()` in our example) to be executed.

Let's look at the different values that `readyState` can take:

> 0 = uninitialized
>
> 1 = loading
>
> 2 = loaded
>
> 3 = interactive
>
> 4 = completed

When a server request is first made, the value of `readyState` is set to zero, meaning *uninitialized*.

As the server request progresses, data begins to be loaded by the server into the `XMLHttpRequest` object, and the value of the `readyState` property changes accordingly, moving to 1 and then 2.

An object `readyState` value of 3, *interactive*, indicates that the object is sufficiently progressed that certain interactivity with it is possible, though it is not fully complete.

When the server request has completed fully and the object is available for further processing, the value of `readyState` changes finally to 4.

In most practical cases, you'll be looking for the `readyState` property to achieve a value of 4, at which point you can be assured that the server has finished its task and the `XMLHttpRequest` object is ready for use.

TIP

The function called on completion of the server request is normally referred to as the *callback function*.

TIP

Not all of the possible values may exist for any given object. The object may "skip" certain states if they bear no relevance to the object's content type.

Server Response Status Codes

In addition to the `readyState` property, we have a further means to check that our asynchronous request has executed correctly: the HTTP server response status code. An HTTP response status code of 200 corresponds to an "OK" message from the server. You see how to test for this as we further develop our callback function.

Callback Functions

By now, then, we have learned how to create an instance of an `XMLHttpRequest` object, declare the identity of a callback function, and prepare and send our asynchronous server request. We also know which property will tell us when the server response is available for us to use.

Let's look at our callback function, `responseAjax()`.

First, note that this function is called every time there is a change in the value of the `onreadystatechange` property. Most times that this function is called we require it to do absolutely nothing, as the value of the `readyState` property has not yet reached 4 and we therefore know that the server request has not completed its processing:

```
function responseAjax() {
    // we are only interested in readyState of 4, i.e. "completed"
    if(myRequest.readyState == 4) {
        … program execution statements …
    }
}
```

However, for added peace of mind we would also like to check the HTTP response status code to ensure that it is equal to 200, indicating a successful response to our asynchronous HTTP request.

Referring quickly back to Table 16.1, we can see that our `XMLHttpRequest` object `myRequest` has two properties that report the HTTP status response. These are

```
myRequest.status
```

which contains the status response code, and

```
myRequest.statusText
```

containing the reason phrase.

We can employ these properties by using a further loop:

```
function responseAjax() {
    // we are only interested in readyState of 4, i.e. "loaded"
    if(myRequest.readyState == 4) {
        // if server HTTP response is "OK"
        if(myRequest.status == 200) {
            … program execution statements …
        } else {
            // issue an error message for any other HTTP response
            alert("An error has occurred: " + myRequest.statusText);
        }
    }
}
```

Any server status response other than 200 will cause the contents of this
else clause to be executed, opening an alert dialog containing the text of
the reason phrase returned from the server.

responseText and responseXML Properties

Table 16.1 listed two properties of the XMLHttpRequest object that we have
yet to describe. These are the responseText and responseXML properties.

By the time our server request has completed, as detected by the condition

myRequest.readyState == 4

then the two properties responseText and responseXML will respectively
contain text and XML representations of the data returned by the server.

Later in the hour we see how to access that information and apply it in our
Ajax application.

The responseText Property

The responseText property tries to represent the information returned by
the server as a text string.

Let's add a program statement to the "success" branch of the if statement,
as follows in Listing 16.3.

TIP
If the XMLHttpRequest call fails
with an error or has not yet been
sent, responseText will have a
value null.

LISTING 16.3   Reporting the Value of the `responseText` Property

```
function responseAjax() {
    // we are only interested in readyState of 4, i.e. "loaded"
    if(myRequest.readyState == 4) {
        // if server HTTP response is "OK"
        if(myRequest.status == 200) {
            alert("The server said: " + myRequest.responseText);
        } else {
            // issue an error message for any other HTTP response
            alert("An error has occurred: " + myRequest.statusText);
        }
    }
}
```

In this simple example, our script opens an alert dialog to display the text returned by the server.

Let's look at an example using a simple PHP file on the server:

```
<?php echo "Hello Ajax caller!"; ?>
```

A successful `XMLHttpRequest` call to this file would result in the `responseText` property containing the string "Hello Ajax caller!", causing the callback function to produce the dialog of Figure 16.4.

FIGURE 16.4
Output generated by Listing 16.3

Because the `responseText` contains a simple text string, we may manipulate it using any of JavaScript's methods relating to strings.

The `responseXML` Property

Let's now suppose that the PHP script we used on the server in the previous example instead looked like Listing 16.4.

LISTING 16.4   An Alternative Server-Side Script

```
<?php
header('Content-Type: text/xml');
echo "<?xml version=\"1.0\" ?><greeting>Hello Ajax caller!</greeting>";
?>
```

The PHP script outputs this simple, but complete, XML document:

```
<?xml version="1.0" ?>
<greeting>
    Hello Ajax caller!
</greeting>
```

When the server call is completed, we find this XML document loaded into the responseXML property of our object. It is important to note that the responseXML property does not contain just a string that forms a text representation of the XML document, as was the case with the responseText property; instead, the entire data and hierarchical structure of the XML document has been stored.

Let's write a small Ajax application that displays the time as reported by the server compared with the time using the computer's own clock.

We're going to use the simplest of PHP scripts to get the server time; the file clock.php simply contains the line

```
<?php echo date('H:i:s'); ?>
```

which returns the server time in the format hours:minutes:seconds, for example, 12:35:44.

We compare that to the local time in the same format retrieved from the computer's local clock by JavaScript:

```
var localTime = now.getHours() + ":" + now.getMinutes() + ":" +
➡now.getSeconds();
```

Listing 16.5 shows the code for the JavaScript file. This will be rather familiar to you from Listing 16.2 except that the target of the Ajax call is now clock.php with no additional parameters except the random number to defeat the cache.

LISTING 16.5   ajax.js

```
function getXMLHttpRequest() {
    try {
        try {
            return new ActiveXObject("Microsoft.XMLHTTP");
        }
        catch(e) {
            return new ActiveXObject("Msxml2.XMLHTTP");
        }
    }
    catch(e) {
        return new XMLHttpRequest();
    }
}
function callAjax() {
    var url = "clock.php";
    var myRandom = parseInt(Math.random()*99999999);
```

LISTING 16.5   Continued

```
        myRequest. open("GET", url + "?rand=" + myRandom, true);
        myRequest.onreadystatechange = responseAjax;
        myRequest.send(null);
}
function responseAjax() {
    if(myRequest.readyState == 4) {
        if(myRequest.status == 200) {
            var now = new Date();
            var localTime = now.getHours() + ":" + now.getMinutes() + ":"
➥+ now.getSeconds();
            var serverTime = myRequest.responseText;
            document.getElementById("clock").innerHTML = "Server: " +
➥serverTime + "<br />Local: " + localTime;
        } else {
            alert("An error has occurred: " + myRequest.statusText);
        }
    }
}
var myRequest = getXMLHttpRequest();
```

The HTML for the clock is shown in Listing 16.6. The only JavaScript contained in this page is used to attach the callAjax() function to the onClick handler of the button on the page.

LISTING 16.6   The HTML for Our Ajax Clock

```
<!DOCTYPE html>
<html>
<head>
    <title>Ajax Clock</title>
    <style>
        #clock { font: 32px normal verdana, helvetica, sans-serif; }
    </style>
    <script src="ajax.js"></script>
    <script>
        window.onload = function() {
            document.getElementById("btn1").onclick = callAjax;
        }
    </script>
</head>
<body>
    <input id="btn1" type="button" value="Get Time" /><br />
    <div id="clock"></div>
</body>
</html>
```

TRY IT YOURSELF ▼
An Ajax Clock
continued

After a successful call, the callback function `responseAjax()` constructs a little piece of HTML code containing the local and server times and places it in the `<div>` having `id="clock"` using the `innerHTML` method.

The resulting program is shown running in Figure 16.5.

Each time the button is clicked, a new Ajax request is made and the current server time returned. You'll see that when I ran the program, my local time was an hour ahead of server time, as I'm currently in Spain and my server is in the UK.

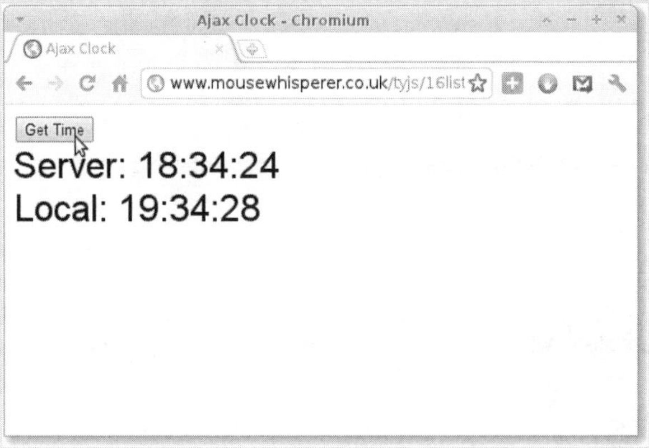

FIGURE 16.5
The Ajax clock

Summary

In this hour you learned the basics of Ajax, a useful method to retrieve information from the server without having to reload the page.

In the next hour you build on this knowledge to build a reusable Ajax library.

Q&A

Q. Can I cancel an Ajax call once it's been sent?

A. Yes, just use the `abort()` method of the `XMLHttpRequest` object:

```
var myRequest = getXMLHttpRequest();
myRequest.abort();
```

Q. When should I make a GET request, and when should I use POST?

A. GET requests are limited to 255 characters. If you need to send a larger amount of data, use POST.

Workshop

Try to answer all the questions before reading the subsequent "Answers" section.

Quiz

1. An Ajax call is complete when the `readyState` property has value:

    a. 0

    b. true

    c. 4

2. Data returned by the server in text string form is found in which property of the `XMLHttpRequest` object?

    a. `responseText`

    b. `statusText`

    c. `responseXML`

3. Your `XMLHttpRequest` object can make Ajax calls directly to

    a. Any domain on the Internet

    b. Only addresses within its own domain

    c. Only PHP pages

Answers

1. c. A `readyState` of 4 shows that an Ajax call has completed.

2. a. The `responseText` property.

3. b. Only addresses within its own domain.

Exercises

Use what you learned in this and the previous hour to change the code of the clock project such that the clock automatically updates at regular intervals, instead of when the button is clicked. [Hint: Use a timer such as `setInterval()` or `setTimeout()`.]

Can you change the clock script to display the difference between the server and local times?

Creating a Simple Ajax Library

In this hour you learn how to encapsulate some of the techniques you learned in Hour 16, "Introducing Ajax," into a small JavaScript library that you can use in your applications.

An Ajax Library

Through the code examples you studied in Hour 16, you learned a number of JavaScript code techniques for implementing the various parts of an Ajax application. Among those methods are

- A method for generating an instance of the XMLHttpRequest object, which works across the range of currently popular browsers

- Routines for building and sending GET and POST requests via the XMLHttpRequest object

- Techniques for avoiding unwanted caching of GET requests

- A style of callback function that checks for correct completion of the Ajax call prior to carrying out its task

- Techniques for dealing with text data returned in the responseText property

In this hour, you employ these ideas to build a JavaScript library that allows Ajax facilities to be added simply to an HTML page with minimal additional code.

Of necessity, our Ajax library will not be as complex or comprehensive as the open source libraries described later in the book; however, it will be complete enough to use in the construction of functional Ajax applications.

WHAT YOU'LL LEARN IN THIS HOUR

- How to build a simple, reusable Ajax library
- Including the library in your application
- Returning text data
- Using XML

What We Want from the Library

In Hour 16 you learned how to construct the basic building blocks of an Ajax application:

- ▶ Creating an instance of XMLHttpRequest
- ▶ Monitoring the server response to determine when a call has completed
- ▶ Using a callback function

Let's consider what we might like to include in the capabilities of our library:

- ▶ The examples in Hour 16 only included GET requests. It would be useful to be able to support HTTP POST requests too.
- ▶ The examples given so far only deal with text information returned via the XMLHttpRequest object's responseText property; our library should also be able to deal with XML data returned via responseXML.

Implementing the Library

Having identified what needs to be done, let's get started constructing the library.

Creating XMLHttpRequest Instances

To create an instance of the XMLHttpRequest object, we use the same function as in Hour 16:

```
function getXMLHttpRequest() {
    try {
        try {
            return new ActiveXObject("Microsoft.XMLHTTP");
        }
        catch(e) {
            return new ActiveXObject("Msxml2.XMLHTTP");
        }
    }
    catch(e) {
        return new XMLHttpRequest();
    }
}
```

Creating an object instance is then simply a matter of calling the function:

```
var req = getXMLHttpRequest();
```

HTTP GET and POST Requests

We start with the GET request, having used this type of request in Hour 16.

```
function requestGET(url, query, req) {
    var myRandom = parseInt(Math.random()*99999999);
    if(query == '') {
        var callUrl = url + '?rand=' + myRandom;
    } else {
        var callUrl = url + '?' + query + '&rand=' + myRandom;
    }
    req.open("GET", callUrl, true);
    req.send(null);
}
```

The requestGET() function takes three arguments:

▶ The URL to which the request will be sent.

▶ The query string to be appended to this URL. This contains all the parameters required by the server-side application, encoded as name=value pairs.

▶ The XMLHttpRequest object that is to make the call.

The function does a little work to make sure that the query string is formatted correctly; in calls having no appended query, the random number must be appended to the URL after a question mark:

```
www.example.com?rand=57483947
```

For calls where the query string is not empty, however, it must be appended after an ampersand (&) character:

```
www.example.com?page=6&user=admin&rand=57483947
```

Next, the POST function.

```
function requestPOST(url, query, req) {
    req.open("POST", url, true);
    req.setRequestHeader('Content-Type', 'application/x-www-form-
➥urlencoded');
    req.send(query);
}
```

CAUTION

The value passed as the query argument must be suitably encoded prior to calling the requestGET() function, though the cache-busting random element is added by the function.

HTTP POST requests are not susceptible to the caching issues that can trouble GET requests, so the addition of a random element to the query string is not required here.

Instead of being appended to the URL, in a POST request the parameter information is passed as an argument to the send() method of the XMLHttpRequest object. You also need to set an HTTP header to tell the server-side application what sort of data you are sending:

```
req.setRequestHeader('Content-Type', 'application/x-www-form-
➡urlencoded');
```

The Callback Function

To make the library as general purpose as possible, you want the user to be able to decide what callback function is to be used, passing the callback function name as an argument when calling the Ajax library routines.

You need JavaScript to take that function name and execute it as a function, passing to it as an argument the data returned from the Ajax call; for this you can use JavaScript's eval() method.

```
eval(callback + '(data)');
```

Making the Ajax Call

Let's look at how these functions might interact to make an Ajax call:

```
function doAjax(url, query, callback, reqtype, getxml) {
    var myreq = getXMLHttpRequest();
    myreq.onreadystatechange = function() {
        if(myreq.readyState == 4) {
            if(myreq.status == 200) {
                var item = myreq.responseText;
                if(getxml == 1) item = myreq.responseXML;
                eval(callback + '(item)');
            }
        }
    }
    if(reqtype.toUpperCase() == "POST") {
        requestPOST(url, query, myreq);
    } else {
        requestGET(url, query, myreq);
    }
}
```

Our function doAjax() takes five arguments:

- **url**—The target URL

- **query**—The encoded query string

- **callback**—The name of the callback function

- **reqtype**—POST or GET

- **getxml**—1 to retrieve XML data, 0 for text

Listing 17.1 shows the complete JavaScript source code for myAjaxLib.js.

LISTING 17.1   Source Code for myAjaxLib.js

```javascript
function getXMLHttpRequest() {
    try {
        try {
            return new ActiveXObject("Microsoft.XMLHTTP");
        }
        catch(e) {
            return new ActiveXObject("Msxml2.XMLHTTP");
        }
    }
    catch(e) {
        return new XMLHttpRequest();
    }
}

function doAjax(url, query, callback, reqtype, getxml) {
    var myreq = getXMLHttpRequest();
    myreq.onreadystatechange = function() {
        if(myreq.readyState == 4) {
            if(myreq.status == 200) {
                var item = myreq.responseText;
                if(getxml == 1) item = myreq.responseXML;
                eval(callback + '(item)');
            }
        }
    }
    if(reqtype.toUpperCase() == "POST") {
        requestPOST(url, query, myreq);
    } else {
        requestGET(url, query, myreq);
    }
}

function requestGET(url, query, req) {
    var myRandom = parseInt(Math.random()*99999999);
    if(query == '') {
        var callUrl = url + '?rand=' + myRandom;
```

LISTING 17.1   Continued

```
    } else {
        var callUrl = url + '?' + query + '&rand=' + myRandom;
    }
    req.open("GET", callUrl, true);
    req.send(null);
}

function requestPOST(url, query, req) {
    req.open("POST", url, true);
    req.setRequestHeader('Content-Type', 'application/x-www-form-
urlencoded');
    req.send(query);
}
```

Using the Library

To demonstrate the use of the library, we start with another simple HTML page, the code for which is shown here:

```
<!DOCTYPE html>
<html>
<head>
    <title>Ajax Test</title>
</head>
<body>
    <input type="button" id="btn1" value="Make call" />
</body>
</html>
```

This simple page displays only a button labeled "Make Call." All the functionality will be created in JavaScript, using our new Ajax library.

The steps required to "Ajaxify" the application are

1. Include the Ajax library myAjaxLib.js in the <head> area of the page.

2. Write a callback function to deal with the returned information.

3. Add an event handler to the button on the page to invoke the server call.

We begin by demonstrating a GET request and using the information returned in the responseText property.

Including the Ajax library is straightforward:

```
<script src="myAjaxLib.js"></script>
```

Next, you need to write the pieces of JavaScript you need that are not part of the library; first, the callback function. For this example simply display the text returned via an `alert()` dialog:

```
function cback(text) {
    alert(text);
}
```

Finally, add an `onClick` event handler to the button:

```
window.onload = function(){
    document.getElementById("btn1").onclick = function(){
        doAjax("libtest.php", "param=hello", "cback", "GET", 0);
    }
}
```

The server-side script `libtest.php` simply echoes back the parameter sent as the query variable called `param`:

```
<?php
echo "Parameter value was: ".$_GET['param'];
?>
```

The remaining arguments of the call to `doAjax()` declare that the callback function is called `cback`, that you want to send an HTTP `GET` request, and that you expect the returned data to be in `responseText`.

Listing 17.2 shows the complete code of our revised HTML page:

LISTING 17.2   HTML Page Rewritten to Call myAjaxLib.js

```
<!DOCTYPE html>
<html>
<head>
    <title>Ajax Test</title>
    <script src="myAjaxLib.js"></script>
    <script>
        function cback(text) {
            alert(text);
            }
        window.onload = function(){
            document.getElementById("btn1").onclick = function(){
                doAjax("libtest.php", "param=hello", "cback", "GET", 0);
            }
        }
    </script>
</head>
<body>
    <input type="button" id="btn1" value="Make call" />
</body>
</html>
```

FIGURE 17.1
Returned text from HTTP GET request

NOTE

This is simply an XML version of the server program `clock.php` used in Hour 16.

Figure 17.1 shows the result of running the program.

To demonstrate the use of the same library to retrieve XML data, we use a small server-side program to return the time as a small XML document:

```php
<?php
header('Content-Type: text/xml');
echo "<?xml version=\"1.0\" ?><clock1><timenow>"
➥.date('H:i:s')."</timenow></clock1>";
?>
```

Your callback function must be modified because you now need to return the parsed XML. Let's use some DOM methods that you may recall from Part III, "Working with the Document Object Model (DOM)," of this book.

```javascript
function cback(text) {
    var servertime =
text.getElementsByTagName("timenow")[0].childNodes[0].nodeValue;
    alert('Server time is ' + servertime);
}
```

The only other thing you need to change is the call to the `doAjax()` function:

```javascript
window.onload = function(){
    document.getElementById("btn1").onclick = function(){
        doAjax("telltimeXML.php", "", "cback", "POST", 1);
    }
}
```

FIGURE 17.2
Server time returned in XML via HTTP POST

Here we have decided to make a POST request. The server script telltimeXML.php does not require a query string, so in this case the second argument is left blank. The final parameter has been set to 1, indicating that you expect to retrieve XML from the property `responseXML`.

Figure 17.2 shows the dialog opened by the program.

▼ TRY IT YOURSELF

Returning Keyword META Information from Remote Sites

You're going to put the myAjaxLib.js library to use in an application that grabs the "keywords" metatag information from a user-entered URL.

NOTE

Metatags are optional HTML container elements in the <head> section of an HTML page. They contain data about the web page that is useful to search engines and indexes in deciding how the page's content should be classified. The "keywords" metatag, where present, typically contains a comma-separated list of words with meanings relevant to the site content.

An example of a "keywords" metatag for an Ajax developer's website might look like this:

```
<meta name="keywords" content="programming, design, development,
Ajax, JavaScript, XMLHttpRequest, script" />
```

TRY IT YOURSELF ▼

Returning Keyword META Information from Remote Sites

continued

Because of the security limitations imposed on JavaScript, the XMLHttpRequest object cannot send server requests to URLs in domains other than its own. If you want to get information from a remote site, as in this example, you have to rely on a server script to do that for you.

In this example, you use another little PHP script, this time called metatags.php, as follows:

```
<?php
$tags = @get_meta_tags('http://'.$_REQUEST['url']);
$result = $tags['keywords'];
if(strlen($result) > 0) {
    echo $result;
} else {
    echo "No keywords metatag is available.";
}
?>
```

This script uses the PHP function get_meta_tags(), which is specifically designed to parse the metatag information from HTML pages in the form of an array. The script then checks for the existence of the "keywords" metatag information and, if it exists, returns the content.

The HTML for the page is straightforward:

```
<!DOCTYPE html>
<html>
<head>
    <title>Keywords Grabber</title>
</head>
<body>
    http://<input type="text" id="txt1" value="" />
    <input type="button" id="btn1" value="Get Keywords" />
    <h3>Keywords Received:</h3>
    <div id="displaydiv"></div>
</body>
</html>
```

For this example, you're going to write out the keywords information into a page element, a <div> with an id value of "displaydiv." The callback function should look familiar:

```
function display(content) {
    document.getElementById("displaydiv").innerHTML = content;
}
```

▼ TRY IT YOURSELF

Returning Keyword META Information from Remote Sites

continued

When the page loads, you need to attach an `onClick` event handler to the button. The code executed when the button is clicked gets the user-entered URL from the input field and then makes the Ajax call to metatags.php:

```
window.onload = function(){
    document.getElementById("btn1").onclick = function(){
        var url = document.getElementById("txt1").value;
        doAjax("metatags.php", "url=" + escape(url), "display", "post",
➥0);
    }
}
```

The complete code for the modified HTML page metatags.html is shown in Listing 17.3.

LISTING 17.3   HTML Page metatags.html

```
<!DOCTYPE html>
<html>
<head>
    <title>Keywords Grabber</title>
    <script src="myAjaxLib.js"></script>
    <script>
        function display(content) {
            document.getElementById("displaydiv").innerHTML = content;
        }
        window.onload = function(){
            document.getElementById("btn1").onclick = function(){
                var url = document.getElementById("txt1").value;
                doAjax("metatags.php", "url=" + url, "display", "post",
➥0);
            }
        }
    </script>
</head>
<body>
    http://<input type="text" id="txt1" value="" />
    <input type="button" id="btn1" value="Get Keywords" />
    <h3>Keywords Received:</h3>
    <div id="displaydiv"></div>
</body>
</html>
```

TIP

If you don't have easy access to a PHP-enabled web server, you can always install your own on your own computer or on another computer on your network, if you have one.

Several free packaged solutions are available to make this easy, XAMPP being one example:

http://www.apachefriends.org/en/xampp.html.

Create the page in your editor and load it along with metatags.php and the Ajax library myAjaxLib.js to a PHP-enabled web server.

Fire up your browser and navigate to metatags.html, and you should be confronted with a page like the one in Figure 17.3.

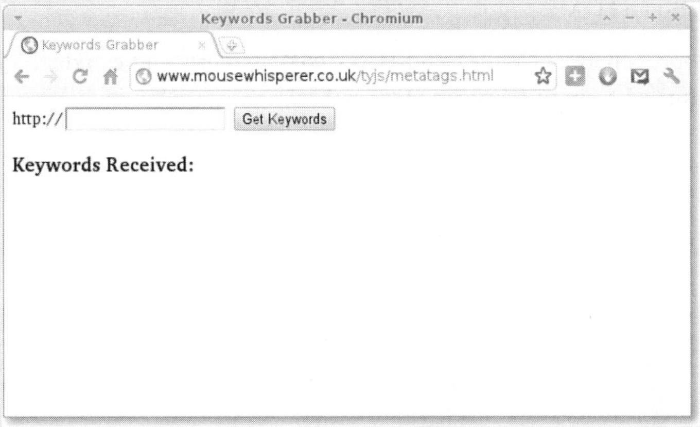

TRY IT YOURSELF ▼

Returning Keyword META Information from Remote Sites

continued

FIGURE 17.3
The Keywords Grabber application

You're invited to enter a URL. Clicking the Get Keywords button causes the doAjax() function to be executed, sending your chosen URL as a parameter to server script metatags.php.

Once the server call has completed, the contents of the responseText property are loaded into the <div> container, producing a display similar to the one in Figure 17.4.

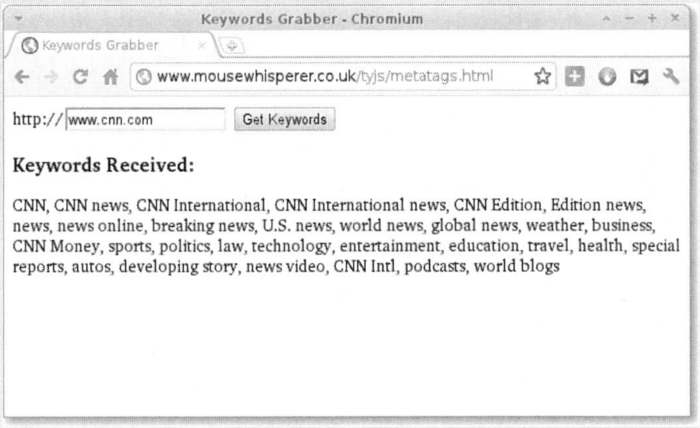

FIGURE 17.4
The keywords are successfully returned.

Note that you can successively enter URLs for different websites, returning the keywords (where keywords are available) without having to wait for your page to be reloaded.

Summary

This hour employed many of the techniques introduced in Hour 16 to produce a compact and reusable JavaScript library for incorporating Ajax capabilities into an HTML page.

The code supports both HTTP GET and HTTP POST requests and can deal with data returned from the server as text or XML.

Q&A

Q. Is there a way to return multiple values via `responseText`?

A. There's nothing to stop you returning serialized data in the `responseText` property and then decoding that information in your application to retrieve the multiple data values. See Hour 8, "Meet JSON," and Hour 10, "JavaScript and Cookies," for examples of data serialization.

Q. Should I use text or XML in preference?

A. For complex applications with sophisticated data structures XML might sometimes be the best option; or you may be stuck with XML if that's the format returned from, say, a third-party application or web service that's providing your data. For simpler applications (and even some more complex ones), though, text parsing may be sufficient and removes some of the potential headaches involved with such things as XML schemas and processor-intensive XML parsing.

Workshop

Try to answer all the questions before reading the subsequent "Answers" section.

Quiz

1. The callback function:

    a. Checks that the Ajax call has successfully completed

    b. Executes after the Ajax call has successfully completed

    c. Executes if the Ajax call does not complete successfully

2. Which Ajax calls need special work to avoid unwanted caching?

    a. GET requests

    b. POST requests

    c. All requests

3. In a POST request the parameter information is passed to the server script

    a. as an argument to the send() method of the XMLHttpRequest object

    b. appended to the target URL as a query string

    c. by the callback function

Answers

1. b. The callback function executes after the Ajax call completed successfully.

2. a. GET requests can suffer from unwanted caching. Our library adds a random value to the query string to help prevent this.

3. a. The parameter information is passed to the server script as an argument to the send() method of the XMLHttpRequest object.

Exercises

See if you can modify the code of Listings 17.3 and 17.4 to present a message to the user while waiting for an Ajax request to complete.

The library doesn't currently do very much to detect and act upon errors. How could you modify it to react to a req.status of other than 200?

Solving Ajax Problems

In an earlier hour, you tried your hand at debugging JavaScript programs using the tools commonly available within, or as extensions to, various modern browsers. Ajax adds a further layer of complexity to code debugging due to the server calls and responses initiated from the page by the XMLHttpRequest object. In this hour you learn how to analyze this traffic to solve program errors. We also discuss some more general problems you might come up against when developing Ajax applications and consider some possible solutions.

Debugging Ajax Applications

Earlier in the book you encountered discussions about debugging your JavaScript code and tried some of the tools shipped with the popular browsers.

Debugging Ajax adds a few more challenges to those encountered so far. To successfully debug your Ajax applications, you need access not only to the current values of variables and expressions, but also to the content of outgoing and incoming data. It's often helpful to have information about the timing of server calls and their responses too.

In this section you see how to look under the hood of your Ajax applications using a variety of popular tools.

Firebug

Mozilla Firefox, like most browsers, is shipped with a number of development tools already installed. In Hour 6, "Scripts That Do More," for example, you used the Error Console to help you debug a simple script, and in

WHAT YOU'LL LEARN IN THIS HOUR

▸ Using browser tools to debug Ajax
▸ Common Ajax errors
▸ Some programming gotchas

Hour 11, "Navigating the DOM," you were introduced to the Mozilla DOM Inspector add-on. Another powerful add-on you should be aware of is Firebug, which is available from http://getfirebug.com/.

Firebug is something of a Swiss Army Knife for JavaScript development and debugging. Some of the additional things that Firebug lets you do include

- Inspect and edit HTML. You can edit HTML "live" and see the changes immediately.

- Inspect and edit CSS. Change the style of any page element on-the-fly.

- Measure and visualize all the offsets, margins, borders, padding, and sizes of page elements.

- Analyze network activity including timelines for the loading of resources, cache activity, and `XMLHttpRequest` actions.

- Profile JavaScript to find and eliminate bottlenecks in your code's execution, making your scripts run faster.

- View, navigate, and edit the DOM tree.

- Log information for later analysis.

▼ TRY IT YOURSELF

Debugging Ajax Using Firebug

When you have installed Firebug into your copy of Firefox, navigate to the keyword grabber script you wrote in Hour 17, "Creating a Simple Ajax Library," (see Listing 17.3). Activate Firebug by pressing F12, and you'll probably see something like the window shown in Figure 18.1.

You'll see that the lower window has a number of tabs; Figure 18.1 shows the Console tab in which various types of messages are collected and displayed. You can tweak Firebug's options to show whatever types of message you find useful, but the default settings should be fine for now.

The Console will probably be empty for the moment.

TIP

The Console also offers a JavaScript command line where you can execute whatever JavaScript commands you want.

Clicking the Net tab opens the Network panel. This panel monitors and displays any HTTP communications initiated from within the web page.

Any HTTP requests will be displayed here, with each line representing a complete round-trip to the server and back. All that's in there at the moment is a record of two files having been loaded; the HTML file metatags.html and your JavaScript Ajax library myAjaxLib.js. Referring to Figure 18.2, you also see a graph to the right of each line showing the timing information for the HTTP request that caused each of these to be loaded.

TRY IT YOURSELF ▼

Debugging Ajax Using Firebug
continued

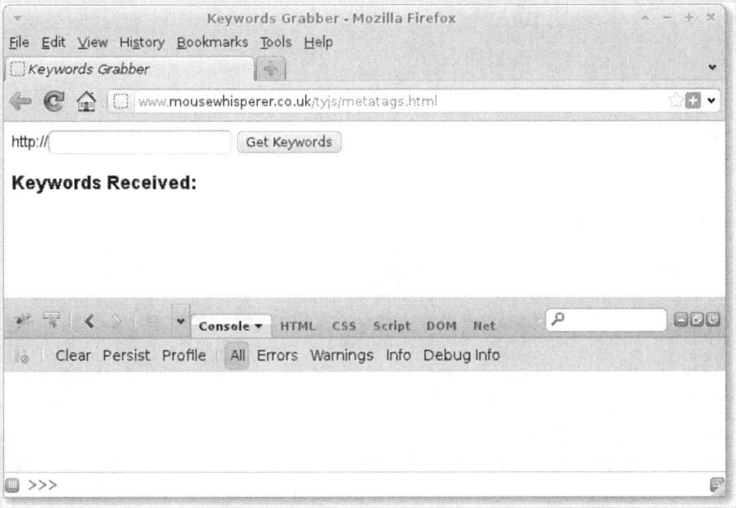

FIGURE 18.1
Firebug in action

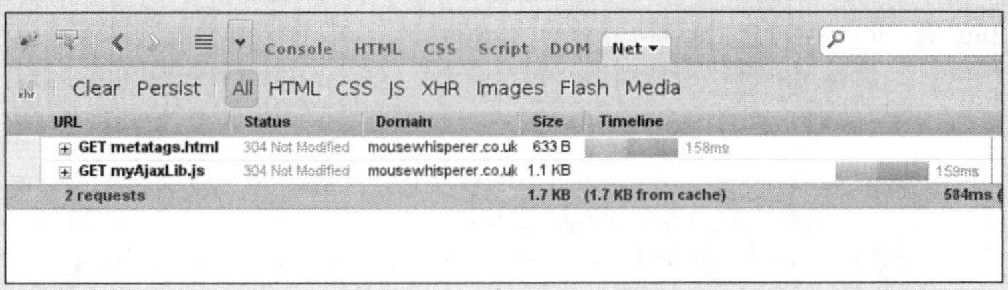

FIGURE 18.2
Firebug displaying HTTP communications

Now let's see what happens when you use the application. Type a URL into the form field and click the Get Keywords button to retrieve some metatag information from a remote site. This additional HTTP round-trip to the server should appear in the list. Clicking the small plus sign in the left-hand column expands the list entry to reveal more information about the Ajax request, including the data sent and returned, the HTTP status returned, and the timing information relating to the server round-trip. Figure 18.3 shows the display.

Some information is fetched not from the server but from the browser cache. The items from cache can be recognized by the status "304 Not Modified," as is the case for the HTML file and the Ajax library entries in the table shown in Figure 18.3.

The status of "200 OK," however, indicates that the information returned by the Ajax call came from the server, as you would want.

▼ TRY IT YOURSELF

Debugging Ajax Using Firebug

continued

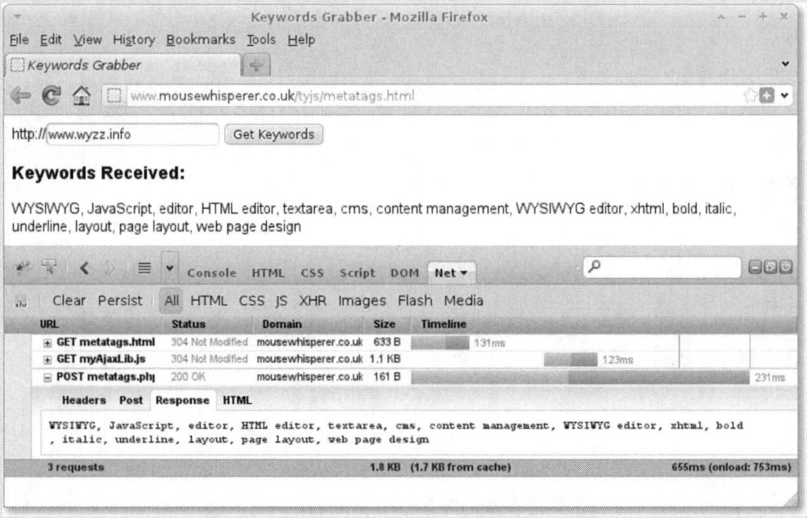

FIGURE 18.3
Information about an Ajax call

Right-clicking any entry in the list opens a content menu that gives you the opportunity to copy parts of the data to the clipboard or open the request in a new tab.

You may be able to make out a small Pause button at the left-hand end of the Net panel toolbar. With this control you can switch on or off a Pause on XHR facility, causing Firebug to pause page execution on each `XMLHttpRequest` call so you can examine the data sent and received. This can be invaluable when you're dealing with complex Ajax applications where a lot of such calls are being made.

Firebug can do much more than this book has space for; if you're serious about Ajax—or simply about JavaScript development—and Firefox is your browser of choice, I recommend you give it a try. You can find plenty of information at http://getfirebug.com/wiki/index.php/Main_Page.

Internet Explorer

With Internet Explorer version 9, Microsoft introduced a set of developer tools with capabilities comparable to those available in Firefox and other contemporary browsers.

If you followed the Try It Yourself section earlier in the hour, the F12 Developer Tools in Internet Explorer 9 will already look fairly familiar to you. Figure 18.4 shows the metatags.html page running in Internet Explorer 9 with the Developer Tools activated.

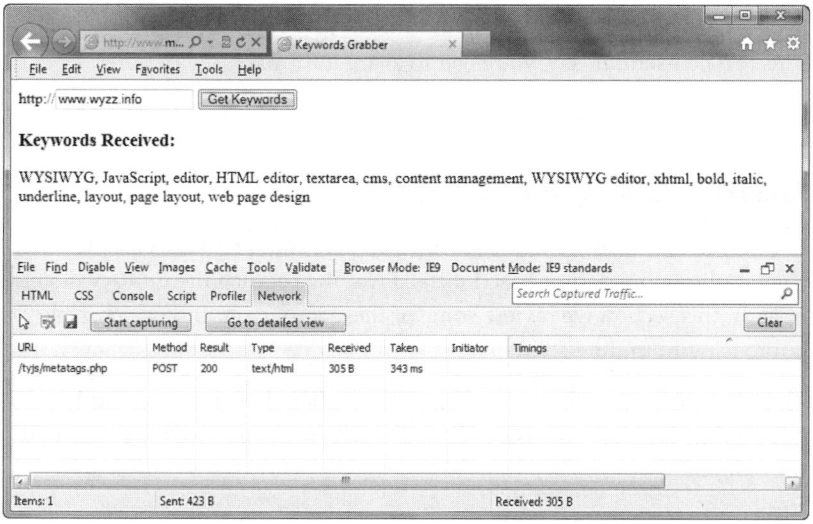

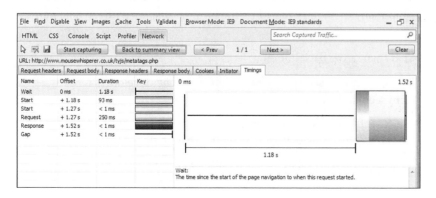

FIGURE 18.4
The Network tab in IE9 Developer Tools

To record Ajax calls and other network events in Internet Explorer, you are required to start and stop the recording activity by means of the Start Capturing button visible in Figure 18.4. This is because the capturing activity itself has a small impact on performance and also uses a little memory.

When events are recorded, they can be double-clicked in the summary view to open a detailed view with a tabbed interface. From here you can analyze the request and response headers, the request and response body, and cookie and timing information. Figure 18.5 shows this panel, with the timing information for our Ajax call currently on display.

FIGURE 18.5
HTTP timing information in IE9

The individual bars of the chart can be clicked to reveal more detailed information.

IE9 Developer Tools also allow you to save information about captured events to a file, in either CSV (comma separated values) or XML format. This can be useful if, say, you need to share information with other developers.

Common Ajax Errors

In addition to the headaches caused by simple coding errors, Ajax has some rather more design-based pitfalls waiting to catch the unwary developer. In this section we review some of these issues and discuss possible approaches to finding solutions.

The list is not exhaustive, and the solutions offered are not necessarily appropriate for every occasion. They should, however, provide some food for thought.

The Back Button

All browsers in common use have a Back button on the navigation bar. The browsers maintain a list of recently visited pages in memory and allow you to step back through these to revisit pages you have recently seen.

Users have become accustomed to the Back button as a standard part of the surfing experience, just as they have with the other facets of the page-based web paradigm.

Ajax, as you have learned, does much to shake off the idea of web-based information being delivered in separate, page-sized chunks; with an Ajax application, you may be able to change page content over and over again without any thought of reloading the browser display with a whole new page.

What then of the Back button?

This issue has caused considerable debate among developers recently. There seem to be two main schools of thought:

▶ Create a means of recording state programmatically and use that to re-create a previous state when the Back button is pressed.

▶ Persuade users that the Back button is no longer necessary.

Artificially re-creating former states is indeed possible but adds a great deal of complexity to Ajax code and is therefore somewhat the province of the braver programmer!

Although the latter option sounds a bit like trying to avoid the issue, it does perhaps have some merit. If you use Ajax to re-create desktop-like user interfaces, it's worthy of note that desktop applications generally don't have—or need—a Back button because the notion of separate "pages" never enters the user's head.

Bookmarking and Links

This problem is not unrelated to the Back button issue just discussed.

When you bookmark a page, you are attempting to save a shortcut to some content. Under the page-based metaphor, this is not unreasonable; although pages can have some degree of dynamic content, being able subsequently to find the page itself usually gets us close enough to seeing what we saw on our previous visit.

Ajax, however, can use the same page address for a whole application, with large quantities of dynamic content being returned from the server in accordance with the users' actions.

What happens when you want to bookmark a particular screen of information and/or pass that link to a friend or colleague? Merely using the URL of the current page is unlikely to produce the results you require.

Although it may be difficult to totally eradicate this problem, it may be possible to alleviate it somewhat by providing permanent links to specially chosen states of an application.

Feedback for the User

This is another issue somewhat related to the change of interface style away from separate pages.

The user who is already familiar with browsing web pages may have become accustomed to program activity coinciding with the loading of a new or revised page.

Many Ajax applications therefore provide some consistent visual clue that activity is happening; perhaps a stationary graphic image might be replaced by an animated version, the cursor style might change, or a pop-up message appear. The means to apply some of these techniques have been taught elsewhere in this book.

Making Ajax Degrade Gracefully

The lessons in this book have covered the development of applications for use in various modern browsers. It's still possible, though, that a user might surprise you by attempting to use your application with a browser that is too old to support the necessary technologies.

Alternatively, a visitor's browser might have JavaScript and/or ActiveX disabled (for security or other reasons).

You would clearly not want your Ajax application to fail completely under such conditions.

At the very least, the occurrence of obvious errors such as the failure to create an instance of the `XMLHttpRequest` object should be reported to the user. If the Ajax application is so complex that it cannot be made to automatically revert to a non-Ajax mode of operation, perhaps the user can at least be redirected to a non-Ajax version.

Dealing with Search Engine Spiders

Search engines gather information about websites through various means, an important one being the use of automated programs called *spiders*.

Spiders, as their name perhaps suggests, "crawl the web" by reading web pages and following links, building a database of content and other relevant information about particular websites. This database, better known as an index, is queried by search engine visitors using their keywords and phrases and returns suggestions of relevant pages for them to visit.

This can create a problem for highly dynamic sites, which rely on user interaction (rather than passive surfing) to invoke the loading of new content delivered on-demand by the server. The visiting spider may not have access to the content that would be loaded by dynamic means and therefore never gets to index it.

The problem can be exacerbated further by the use of Ajax, with its tendency to deliver even more content on still fewer pages. It would seem wise to ensure that spiders can index a static version of all relevant content somewhere on the site.

Pointing Out Active Page Elements

Without careful design, it may not be apparent to users which items on the page they can click on or otherwise interact with to make something happen.

It is worth trying to use a consistent style throughout an application to show which page elements cause server requests or some other dynamic activity. This is somewhat reminiscent of the way that hypertext links in HTML pages tend to be styled differently from plain text so that it's clear to a user that they perform an additional function.

At the expense of a little more coding effort, instructions and information about active page elements can be incorporated in tooltip-style pop-ups. This is, of course, especially important where a click on an active link can have a major effect on the application's state. Figure 18.6 shows an example of such a pop-up information box.

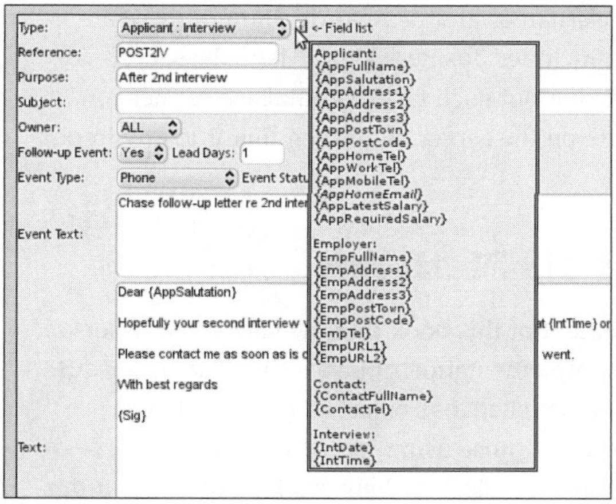

FIGURE 18.6
Pop-up information helps users understand interfaces.

Don't Use Ajax Where It's Inappropriate

Attractive as Ajax undoubtedly is for improving web interfaces, you need to accept that there are many situations where the use of Ajax detracts from the user experience instead of adding to it.

This is especially true where the page-based interface metaphor is perfectly adequate for, perhaps even of greater relevance to, the content and style of the site. Text-based sites with subjects split conveniently into chapter-styled pages can often benefit as much from intelligently designed hyper-linking as they can from the addition of Ajax functionality.

Small sites in particular may struggle to get sufficient benefit from an Ajax interface to balance the associated costs of additional code and added complexity.

Security

Ajax does not itself seem to present any security issues that are not already present when designing web applications. It is notable, however, that Ajax-enhanced applications tend to contain more client-side code than they did previously.

Because the content of client-side code such as JavaScript can be viewed easily by any user of the application, it is important that sensitive information not be revealed within it. In this context, sensitive information is not limited to such things as usernames and passwords (though these are, of course, sensitive), but also includes business logic. Make the server-side scripts responsible for carrying out such tasks as database connection. Validate (or revalidate) data on the server before sending it to any important process.

Test Across Multiple Platforms

It will be clear from the content of this book that the various browsers behave differently in their implementation of JavaScript. The major difference in the generation of XMLHttpRequest object instances between Microsoft's earlier browsers and those using more W3C-inspired approaches is a fundamental example, but there is a host of minor differences, too.

The DOM, in particular, is handled rather differently, not only between browsers but also between different versions of the same browser. CSS implementation is another area where differences remain.

Although it has always been important to test new applications on various browsers, this is perhaps more important than ever when faced with the added complexity of Ajax.

Hopefully browsers will continue to become more standards-compliant, but until then test applications on as many different browsers as possible.

Some Programming Gotchas

Some of these have been alluded to in previous hours, but it's worth grouping them here. These are probably the most common programming issues that Ajax developers bump up against at some time or other.

Browser Caching of GET Requests

Making repeated GET requests to the same URL can lead to the response coming not from the server but from the browser cache. This problem seems especially significant with some versions of Internet Explorer.

Although in theory this can be cured with the use of suitable HTTP headers, in practice the cache can be stubborn.

An effective way of sidestepping this problem is to add a random element to the query string of the URL to which the request is sent; the browser interprets this as a new request and returns data from the server rather than the cache.

In previous hours we achieved this by adding a random number. Another approach favored by many is to add a number derived from the time, which will of course be different on each occasion:

```
var url = "serverscript.php" + "?rand=" + new Date().getTime();
```

Permission Denied Errors

Receiving a Permission Denied error usually means that you've fallen afoul of the security measure preventing cross-domain requests from being made by an XMLHttpRequest object.

Calls must be made to server programs existing in the same domain as the calling script.

Escaping Content

When constructing queries for GET or POST requests, remember to escape variables that could contain spaces or other nontext characters:

```
http.open("GET", url + escape(idValue) + "?rand=" + myRandom, true);
```

CAUTION

Be careful to ensure that the domain is written in exactly the same way. The domain example.com might be interpreted as referring to a different domain from www.example.com, and permission denied.

Summary

Ajax undoubtedly has the potential to greatly improve web interfaces. However, the paradigm change from traditional page-based interfaces to highly dynamic applications has created a few potholes for developers to step into. In this hour we rounded up some of the better-known ones.

Q&A

Q. Is Firebug only available for Mozilla Firefox?

A. Yes,. but there *is* an application called Firebug Lite that works in a broad range of browsers including Internet Explorer, Opera, Safari, and Chrome. It doesn't quite have all the bells and whistles of Firebug, but it's still a very capable tool. You can find out about it at http://getfirebug.com/firebuglite.

Q. What else can I do to ensure that search engine spiders crawl my site correctly?

A. If your site is well designed and built using progressive enhancement, most spiders will be able to find all of your content. If you want to be sure, consider building a sitemap that the robots can access, having simple HTML links to all of your content.

Workshop

Try to answer all the questions before reading the subsequent "Answers" section.

Quiz

1. Firebug is

    a. An extension to the Firefox browser

    b. An Ajax library

    c. A standalone debugger

2. F12 Developer Tools are available in

    a. All modern browsers

    b. All versions of Internet Explorer

    c. Internet Explorer 9 and above

3. A Permission Denied error is usually caused by

    a. Trying to access a server script at the wrong domain

    b. Using a `POST` request instead of a `GET` request

    c. Data not having been escaped correctly

Answers

1. a. Firebug is an extension to the Firefox browser.

2. c. F12 Developer Tools are available in Internet Explorer 9 and above.

3. a. A Permission Denied error is usually caused by trying to access a server script at the wrong domain.

Exercises

Use Firebug or Internet Explorer's F12 Developer Tools to monitor the network traffic for an Ajax-heavy site like Facebook, Gmail, or Twitter.

Find out what sort of response times are typical for the keywords to be returned from remote sites in metatags.html. Why might you need to know this sort of information on likely response times when designing Ajax applications?

PART V
Using JavaScript Libraries

Making Life Easier with Libraries

Libraries are reusable collections of JavaScript code that let you do complicated things by adding only a few lines of extra code to your program.

You already built a simple library for Ajax in Hour 17, "Creating a Simple Ajax Library."

There are many freely available JavaScript libraries that can help you quickly develop capable, cross-browser applications.

Several of the more popular libraries are introduced in this hour.

Why Use a Library?

You'll often see opinions expressed, mainly on the Internet, by JavaScript developers who strongly advocate writing your own code instead of using one of the many available libraries. Popular objections include

▶ You won't ever really know how the code works because you're simply employing someone else's algorithms and functions.

▶ JavaScript libraries contain a lot of code you'll never use but that your users have to download anyway.

Like many aspects of software development, these are matters of opinion. Personally, I believe that there are some very good reasons for using libraries *sometimes*:

▶ Why invent code that somebody else has already written? Popular JavaScript libraries tend to contain the sorts of abstractions that programmers need often—which means you'll likely need those functions too from time to time. The thousands of downloads and pages of online comment generated by the most-used libraries pretty much

WHAT YOU'LL LEARN IN THIS HOUR

▶ Why using a library can be a good idea

▶ The sorts of things libraries can help you do

▶ Library extensions from the user community

▶ Introducing some popular libraries

▶ A quick overview of prototype.js

guarantee that the code they contain will be more thoroughly tested and debugged than your own, home-cooked code would be.

▶ Take inspiration from other coders. There are some *really* clever programmers out there; take their work and use it to improve your own.

▶ Using a well-written library can take away some of the headaches of writing cross-browser JavaScript. You won't have every browser always at your disposal, but the library writers—and their communities of users—test on every leading browser.

▶ Download size for most libraries is not horrific. For the few occasions where you need the shortest of download times, compressed versions are available for most of the popular libraries that you can use in your "production" websites. There's also the possibility of examining the library code and extracting just the parts you need.

What Sorts of Things Can Libraries Do?

The specifics differ depending on the library concerned and the needs and intentions of its creator. However, there are certain recurring themes that most libraries include

▶ **Encapsulation of DOM methods.** As you see later in this hour when you look at prototype.js, JavaScript libraries can offer appealing shorthand ways to select and manage page elements and groups of elements.

▶ **Animation.** In Hour 15, "Graphics and Animation," you animated some page elements using timers. Many of the popular libraries wrap these sorts of operations into convenient functions to slide, fade, shake, squish, fold, snap, and pulsate parts of your page's interface, all in a cross-browser way and with just a few lines of code.

▶ **Drag and drop.** A truly cross-browser drag and drop has always been one of the trickiest effects to code for all browsers. Libraries can make it easy.

▶ **Ajax.** Easy methods to update page content without needing to worry about the nitty-gritty of instantiating `XMLHttpRequest` objects and managing callbacks and status codes.

Some Popular Libraries

New libraries are popping up all the time; others have seen continual development over a number of years. This is by no means a complete list; it simply attempts to point out some of the more popular current players.

Prototype Framework

The Prototype Framework (http://www.prototypejs.org) has been around for a few years now and is currently in version 1.7. Prototype's major strengths lie in its DOM extensions and Ajax handling, though it has many more tricks up its sleeve including JSON support and methods to help with creating and inheriting classes.

Prototype is distributed as a standalone library but also as part of larger projects, such as Ruby on Rails and the script.aculo.us JavaScript library.

NOTE

You look in more detail at the Prototype Framework later in the hour, including some hands-on coding.

Dojo

Dojo (http://www.dojotoolkit.org/) is an open-source toolkit that adds power to JavaScript to simplify building applications and user interfaces. It has features ranging from extra string and math functions to animation and AJAX. The latest versions support not only all major desktop browsers, but also mobile environments including Apple iOS, Android, and Blackberry with their "Dojo Mobile" HTML5 mobile JavaScript framework.

At the time of writing, Dojo is at version 1.7.

The Yahoo! UI Library

The Yahoo! UI Library (http://developer.yahoo.com/yui/) was developed by Yahoo! and made available to everyone under an open-source license. It includes features for animation, DOM features, event management, and easy-to-use user interface elements such as calendars and sliders.

MooTools

MooTools (http://mootools.net/) is a compact, modular JavaScript framework that allows you to build powerful, flexible, and cross-browser code using a simple-to-understand, well documented API (application programming interface).

TIP

You find out a lot about the jQuery library and its associated User Interface library jQueryUI in the following two hours.

jQuery

jQuery (http://jquery.com/)is a fast and compact JavaScript library that simplifies various development tasks including HTML document traversing, event handling, animation, and Ajax calls for rapid development of interactive websites.

Introducing prototype.js

Sam Stephenson's prototype.js is a popular JavaScript library that contains an array of functions useful in the development of cross-browser JavaScript application and includes specific support for Ajax. Shortly you'll see how your JavaScript code can be simplified by using this library's powerful support for DOM manipulation, HTML forms, and the `XMLHttpRequest` object.

The latest version of the prototype.js library can be downloaded from http://prototype.conio.net/.

Including the library in your web application is simple, just include the following in the `<head>` section of your HTML document:

```
<script src="prototype.js"></script>
```

CAUTION

At the time of writing, prototype.js is at version 1.7.0. If you download a different version, check the documentation to see whether there are differences between your version and the one described here.

prototype.js contains a broad range of functions that can make writing JavaScript code quicker and the resulting scripts cleaner and easier to maintain.

The library includes general-purpose functions providing shortcuts to regular programming tasks, a wrapper for HTML forms, an object to encapsulate the `XMLHttpRequest` object, methods and objects for simplifying DOM tasks, and more.

Let's take a look at some of these tools.

The $() Function

`$()` is essentially a shortcut to the `getElementById()` DOM method. Normally, to return the value of a particular element you would use an expression such as

```
var mydata = document.getElementById('someElementID');
```

The $() function simplifies this task by returning the value of the element whose ID is passed to it as an argument:

```
var mydata = $('someElementID');
```

Furthermore, $() (unlike getElementById()) can accept multiple element IDs as an argument and return an array of the associated element values. Consider this line of code:

```
mydataArray = $('id1','id2','id3');
```

In this example:

> mydataArray[0] contains value of element with ID id1.
>
> mydataArray[1] contains value of element with ID id2.
>
> mydataArray[2] contains value of element with ID id3.

The $F() Function

The $F() function returns the value of a form input field when the input element or its ID is passed to it as an argument. Take a look at the following HTML snippet:

```
<input type="text" id="input1" name="input1">
<select id="input2" name="input2">
    <option value="0">Option A</option>
    <option value="1">Option B</option>
    <option value="2">Option C</option>
</select>
```

Here we could use

```
$F('input1')
```

to return the value in the text box and

```
$F('input2')
```

to return the value of the currently selected option of the select box. The $F() function works equally well on check box and text area input elements, making it easy to return the element values regardless of the input element type.

The Form Object

prototype.js defines a Form object having several useful methods for simplifying HTML form manipulation.

You can return an array of a form's input fields by calling the getElements() method:

```
inputs = Form.getElements('thisform');
```

The serialize() method allows input names and values to be formatted into a URL-compatible list:

```
inputlist = Form.serialize('thisform');
```

Using the preceding line of code, the variable inputlist would now contain a string of serialized parameter and value pairs:

```
field1=value1&field2=value2&field3=value3...
```

Form.disable('thisform') and Form.enable('thisform') each do exactly what the name implies.

The Try.these() Function

Hour 14, "Good Coding Practice," discussed the use of try ... catch to enable you to catch runtime errors and deal with them cleanly. The Try.these() function provides a convenient way to encapsulate these methods to provide a cross-browser solution where JavaScript implementation details differ:

```
return Try.these(function1(),function2(),function3(), ...);
```

The functions are processed in sequence, operation moving on to the next function when an error condition causes an exception to be thrown. Operation stops when any of the functions completes successfully, at which point the function returns true.

NOTE

You may want to compare this code snippet with Listing 16.1 to see just how much code complexity has been reduced and readability improved.

Applying this function to the creation of an XMLHttpRequest instance shows the simplicity of the resulting code:

```
return Try.these (
    function() {return new ActiveXObject('Msxml2.XMLHTTP')},
    function() {return new ActiveXObject('Microsoft.XMLHTTP')},
    function() {return new XMLHttpRequest()}
)
```

Wrapping XMLHttpRequest with the Ajax Object

prototype.js defines an Ajax object designed to simplify the development of your JavaScript code when building Ajax applications. This object has a number of classes that encapsulate the code you need to send server requests, monitor their progress, and deal with the returned data.

Ajax.Request

```
var myAjax = new Ajax.Request( url, {method: 'post', parameters: mydata,
onComplete: responseFunction} );
```

In this call, `url` defines the location of the server resource to be called, `method` may be either `post` or `get`, `mydata` is a serialized string containing the request parameters, and `responseFunction` is the name of the callback function that handles the server response.

The `onComplete` parameter is one of several options corresponding to the possible values of the `XMLHttpRequest` `readyState` properties, in this case a `readyState` value of 4 (Complete). You might instead specify that the callback function should execute during the prior phases Loading, Loaded, or Interactive, by using the associated parameters `onLoading`, `onLoaded`, or `onInteractive`.

There are several other optional parameters, including

```
asynchronous:false
```

to indicate that a server call should be made synchronously. The default value for the asynchronous option is true.

TIP

The second argument is constructed using JSON notation, which you learned about in Hour 8, "Meet JSON." Many popular JavaScript libraries have committed to use native JSON if available, including YUI Library, Prototype, jQuery, Dojo Toolkit, and MooTools.

Ajax.Updater

On occasions when you require the returned data to update a page element, the `Ajax.Updater` class can simplify the task. All you need to do is to specify which element should be updated:

```
var myAjax = new Ajax.Updater(elementID, url, options);
```

The call is somewhat similar to that for `Ajax.Request` but with the addition of the target element's ID as the first argument. The following is a code example of `Ajax.Updater`:

```
<script>
    function updateDIV(mydiv) {
        var url = 'http://example.com/serverscript.php';
        var params = 'param1=value1&param2=value2';
        var myAjax = new Ajax.Updater (
                    mydiv,
                    url,
                    {method: 'get', parameters: params}
                )
    }
</script>
<input type="button" value="Go"
onclick="updateDIV(targetDiv)">
<div id="targetDiv"></div>
```

Once again, several additional options may be used when making the call. A noteworthy one is the addition of

```
evalscripts:true
```

to the options list. With this option added, any JavaScript code returned by the server will be evaluated.

Ajax.PeriodicalUpdater

The `Ajax.PeriodicalUpdater` class can be used to repeatedly create an `Ajax.Updater` instance. In this way you can have a page element updated after a certain time interval has elapsed. This can be useful for such applications as a stock market ticker or an RSS reader because it ensures that the visitor is always viewing reasonably up-to-date information.

`Ajax.PeriodicalUpdater` adds two further parameters to the `Ajax.Updater` options:

- ▶ **frequency**. The delay in seconds between successive updates. Default is 2 seconds.

- ▶ **decay**. The multiplier by which successive delays are increased if the server should return unchanged data. Default value is 1, which leaves the delay constant.

Here's an example call to `Ajax.PeriodicalUpdater`:

```
var myAjax = new Ajax.PeriodicalUpdater(elementID, url, {frequency: 3.0,
➥decay: 2.0});
```

Here we elected to set the initial delay to 3 seconds and have this delay double in length each time unchanged data is returned by the server.

Let's use the prototype.js library to build a simple reader that updates periodically to show the latest value returned from the server. In this example, we use the simple server-side script rand.php to simulate a changing stock price:

```php
<?php
srand ((double) microtime( )*1000000);
$price = 50 + rand(0,5000)/100;
echo "$price";
?>
```

This script first initializes PHP's random number routine by calling the srand() function and passing it an argument derived from the current time. The rand(0,5000) function is then used to generate a random number that is manipulated arithmetically to produce phony "stock prices" in the range 50.00 to 100.00.

Now let's build a simple HTML page to display the current stock price. This page forms the basis for our Ajax application:

```html
<!DOCTYPE html>
<html>
<head>
    <script src="prototype.js"></script>
    <title>Stock Reader powered by Prototype.js</title>
</head>
<body>
    <h2>Stock Reader</h2>
    <p>Current Stock Price:</p>
    <div id="price"></div>
</body>
</html>
```

Note that we included the prototype.js library by means of a <script> tag in the document head. We also defined a <div> with id set to "price", which will be used to display the current stock price.

We now need to implement the Ajax.PeriodicalUpdater class, which we attach to the document body element's onLoad event handler. Listing 19.1 shows the complete script.

▼ TRY IT YOURSELF

A Stock Price Reader
continued

LISTING 19.1   Ajax Stock Price Reader Using prototype.js

```
<!DOCTYPE html>
<html>
<head>
    <title>Stock Reader powered by Prototype.js</title>
    <script src="prototype.js"></script>
    <script>
        function checkprice() {
            var myAjax = new Ajax.PeriodicalUpdater('price', 'rand.php',
➥{method: 'post', frequency: 3.0, decay: 1});
        }
        window.onload = checkprice;
    </script>
</head>
<body>
    <h2>Stock Reader</h2>
    <p>Current Stock Price:</p>
    <div id="price"></div>
</body>
</html>
```

Look how simple the code for the application has become through using pro-
totype.js. Implementing the application is merely a matter of defining a one-
line function checkprice() to instantiate our repeating Ajax call and calling
that function from the body element's onLoad event handler.

From the arguments passed to Ajax.PeriodicalUpdater, you see that a 3-
second repeat interval has been specified. This period does not change with
subsequent calls because the decay value has been set to 1.

Figure 19.1 shows the application running. What cannot be seen from the figure, of course, is the stock price updating itself every 3 seconds to show a
new value.

This simple example does not come close to showing off the power and ver-
satility of the prototype.js library. Rather, it is intended to get you started with
your own experiments by offering an easy point of access to this great
resource.

TRY IT YOURSELF ▼

A Stock Price Reader
continued

FIGURE 19.1
Ajax stock reader

Summary

In many instances, writing JavaScript can be made a whole lot easier by using libraries. Such libraries wrap many of the commonly used objects and methods into more user-friendly forms; no longer do you have to remember cross-browser methods to add or remove an event listener or instantiate an XMLHttpRequest object. In this hour you learned a little about some of the more popular JavaScript libraries.

Q&A

Q. How do I include a third-party JavaScript library into my pages?

A. The process varies slightly from library to library. Usually it's simply a matter of including one or more external .js files into the <head> part of your web page. See the documentation supplied with your chosen library for specific details.

Q. Can I use more than one third-party library in the same script?

A. Yes, in theory: If the libraries are well written and designed not to interfere with each other, there should be no problem combining them. In practice, this depends on the libraries you need and how they were written.

Workshop

Try to answer all the questions before reading the subsequent "Answers" section.

Quiz

1. Which of the following objects *is not* a JavaScript library?

    a. MooTools

    b. Prototype

    c. Ajax

2. How can you extend jQuery yourself?

    a. jQuery can't be extended.

    b. By writing server-side scripts.

    c. By writing a plug-in or using a prewritten one.

3. What other JavaScript third-party library does script.aculo.us employ?

    a. Prototype

    b. Dojo

    c. jQuery

Answers

1. c. Ajax is a programming technique enabling your scripts to use resources hosted on your server. There are many libraries to help you employ Ajax functionality, but Ajax itself is not a library.

2. c. jQuery has a well documented way to write and use plug-ins.

3. a. Script.aculo.us uses the prototype.js library.

Exercises

Write a simple script using the Prototype library, or use an example script from the Prototype website at http://www.prototypejs.org.

Visit the Script.aculo.us page at http://script.aculo.us/ and review the complete list of effects made available by this library.

A Closer Look at jQuery

Many JavaScript libraries are available, but jQuery is arguably the most popular and also the most extensible. A huge number of developers contribute open source plug-ins for jQuery, and you can find a suitable plug-in for almost any application you might have. The wide range of plug-ins and the simple syntax make jQuery such a great library. In this hour you learn the basics of jQuery and get a taste of how powerful it is.

Including jQuery in Your Pages

Before you can use jQuery, you need to include it in your pages. There are two main options, as detailed in the following sections.

Download jQuery

You can download jQuery from the official website at http://docs. jquery.com/Downloading_jQuery, where you find both Compressed and Uncompressed versions of the code. The Compressed version is for your live pages, as it has been compressed to the smallest possible file size to download as quickly as possible.

For development purposes, choose the Uncompressed version. Thanks to the well-formatted, commented source, you can read the jQuery code to see how it works.

You need to include the jQuery library in the <head> section of your pages, using a <script> tag. The easiest way is to place the downloaded jquery.js file in the same directory as the page from where you want to use it and then reference it like this:

```
<script src="jquery-1.7.1.js"></script>
```

NOTE

The actual filename depends on the version you download. At the time of writing, 1.7.1 is the current release.

Of course, if you place jQuery in another directory, you'll have to change the (relative or absolute) path in the value you give to the src attribute to reflect the location of the file.

Use a Remote Version

Instead of downloading and hosting jQuery yourself, you can include it from a so-called Content Delivery Network or CDN. In addition to saving you from having to download the jQuery library, using a CDN version has a further advantage: It's quite likely that when users visit your page and their browser requests jQuery, it'll already be in their browser cache. Additionally, CDNs generally ensure that they serve the file from the server geographically closest to them, further cutting the loading time.

The official jQuery site currently lists the following CDNs:

Google Ajax API CDN

http://ajax.googleapis.com/ajax/libs/jquery/1.7.1/jquery.min.js

Microsoft CDN

http://ajax.aspnetcdn.com/ajax/jQuery/jquery-1.7.1.min.js

jQuery CDN

http://code.jquery.com/jquery-1.7.1.min.js (Minified version)

http://code.jquery.com/jquery-1.7.1.js (Source version)

TIP

If you want to make sure your code is always using the latest release of jQuery, simply link to http://code.jquery.com/ jquery-latest.min.js.

You can then modify your <script> tag to suit the chosen CDN, for example:

```
<script
src="https://ajax.googleapis.com/ajax/libs/jquery/1.7.1/jquery.min.js">
➥</script>
```

Unless you have a particular reason for hosting jQuery yourself, this is usually the best way.

jQuery's $(document).ready Handler

At various places through this book you used the window.onload handler. jQuery has its own equivalent:

```
$(document).ready(function() {
    // jQuery code goes here
});
```

Pretty much all the jQuery code you write will be executed from within a statement like this.

Like `window.onload`, it accomplishes two things:

▶ It ensures that the code does not run until the DOM is available, that is, that any elements your code may be trying to access already exist, so your code doesn't return any errors.

▶ It helps make your code unobtrusive by separating it from the semantic (HTML) and presentation (CSS) layers.

The jQuery version, though, has an advantage over the `window.onload` event; it doesn't block code execution until the entire page has finished loading, as would be the case with `window.onload`. With jQuery's `(document).ready`, the code begins to execute as soon as the DOM tree has been constructed, before all images and other resources have finished loading, speeding up performance a little.

Selecting Page Elements

jQuery lets you select elements in your HTML by enclosing them in the jQuery wrapper `$("")`

Here are some examples of sets of page elements wrapped with the $ operator:

```
$("span"); // all HTML span elements
$("#elem"); // the HTML element having id "elem"
$(".classname"); // HTML elements having class "classname"
$("div#elem"); // <div> elements with ID "elem"
$("ul li a.menu"); // anchors with class "menu" that are nested in list
➥items
$("p > span"); // spans that are direct children of paragraphs
$("input[type=password]"); // inputs that have specified type
$("p:first"); // the first paragraph on the page
$("p:even"); // all even numbered paragraphs
```

So much for DOM and CSS selectors. But jQuery also has its own custom selectors, such as

```
$(":header"); // header elements (h1 to h6)
$(":button"); // any button elements (inputs or buttons)
$(":radio"); // radio buttons
$(":checkbox"); // checkboxes
$(":checked"); // selected checkboxes or radio buttons
```

TIP
You can also use single quotes in the wrapper function, `$('')`.

The jQuery statements shown in the preceding examples each return an object containing an array of the DOM elements specified by the expression inside the wrapper function. Note that in none of the preceding lines of code have you specified an action; you are simply getting the required elements from the DOM. In the sections that follow you learn how to work with these selected elements.

Working with HTML Content

One of jQuery's most useful time-saving tricks is to manipulate the content of page elements. The html() and text() methods allow you to get and set the content of any elements you've selected using the previous statements, while attr() lets you get and set the values of individual element attributes. Let's see some examples.

html()

The html() method gets the HTML of any element or collection of elements. It works pretty much like JavaScript's innerHTML:

```
var htmlContent = $("#elem").html();
/* variable htmlContent now contains all HTML
(including text) inside page element
with id "elem" */
```

Using similar syntax, you can set the HTML content of a specified element or collection of elements:

```
$("#elem").html("<p>Here is some new content.</p>");
/* page element with id "elem"
has had its HTML content replaced*/
```

text()

If you only want the text content of an element or collection of elements, without the HTML, you can use text():

```
var textContent = $("#elem").text();
/* variable textContent contains all the
text (but not HTML) content from inside a
page element with id "elem" */
```

Once more you can change the text content of the specified element(s):

```
$("#elem").text("Here is some new content.");
/* page element with id "elem"
has had its text content replaced*/
```

If you want to append content to an element rather than replace it:

```
$("#elem").append("<p>Here is some new content.</p>");
/* keeps current content intact, but
adds the new content to the end */
```

and likewise

```
$("div").append("<p>Here is some new content.</p>");
/* add the same content to all
<div> elements on the page. */
```

attr()

When passed a single argument, the `attr()` method gets the value for the specified attribute.

```
var title = $("#elem").attr("title");
```

If applied to a set of elements, it returns the value for only the first element in the matched set.

You can also pass a second argument to `attr()`to set an attribute value:

```
$("#elem").attr("title", "This is the new title");
```

Showing and Hiding Elements

Using plain old JavaScript, showing and hiding page elements usually means manipulating the value of the `display` or `visibility` properties of the element's `style` object. While that works OK, it can lead to pretty long lines of code:

```
document.getElementById("elem").style.visibility = 'visible';
```

You can use jQuery's `show()` and `hide()` methods to carry out these tasks with rather less code. The jQuery methods also offer some useful additional functionality, as you see in the following code examples.

show()

A simple way to make an element or set of elements visible is to call the `show()` method:

```
$("div").show(); // makes all <div> elements visible
```

However, you can also add some additional parameters to spice up the transition.

In the following example, the first parameter `"fast"` determines the speed of the transition. As an alternative to `"fast"` or `"slow"`, jQuery is happy to accept a number of milliseconds for this argument, as the required duration of the transition. If no value is set, the transition will occur instantly, with no animation.

TIP

The value `"slow"` corresponds to 600ms, while `"fast"` is equivalent to 200ms.

The second argument is a function that operates as a callback, that is, it executes once the transition is complete.

```
$("#elem").show("fast", function() {
    // do something once the element is shown
});
```

Here we have used an anonymous function, but a named function works just fine too.

hide()

The `hide()` method is, of course, the exact reverse of `show()`, allowing you to make page elements invisible with the same optional arguments as you saw for `hide()`:

```
$("#elem").hide("slow", function() {
    // do something once the element is hidden
});
```

toggle()

```
$("#elem").toggle(1000, function() {
    // do something once the element is shown/hidden
});
```

TIP

Remember that the `show()`, `hide()`, and `toggle()` methods can be applied to collections of elements, so the elements in that collection will appear or disappear all at once.

The `toggle()` method changes the current state of an element or collection of elements; it makes visible any element in the collection that is currently hidden and hides any that are currently being shown. The same optional duration and callback function parameters are also available to `toggle()`.

Animating Elements

Some of the standard effects that jQuery offers are powerful. You saw in Hour 15, "Graphics and Animation," how to fade elements in or out using the `opacity` property of the element along with JavaScript timers. Those capabilities are neatly wrapped into a few jQuery methods that you can call for your elements or collections of elements.

Fading

You can fade an element in or out, optionally setting the transition duration and adding a callback function.

To fade out to invisibility:

```
$("#elem").fadeOut("slow", function() {
    // do something after fadeOut has finished executing
});
```

Or to fade in:

```
$("#elem").fadeIn(500, function() {
    // do something after fadeIn has finished executing
});
```

You can also fade an element only partially, either in or out:

```
$("#elem").fadeTo(3000, 0.5, function() {
    // do something after fade has finished executing
});
```

The second parameter (here set to 0.5) represents the target opacity. Its value works similarly to the way opacity values are set in CSS. Whatever the value of opacity before the method is called, the element will be animated until it reaches the value specified in the argument.

Sliding

You can slide elements, or collections of elements, upward or downward. The jQuery methods for sliding an element are direct corollaries to the fading methods you've just seen, and their arguments follow exactly the same rules.

```
$("#elem").slideDown(150, function() {
    // do something when slideDown is finished executing
});
```

And to slide up:

```
$("#elem").slideUp("slow", function() {
    // do something when slideUp is finished executing
});
```

In case you need to slide an element up or down depending on its current state, jQuery also provides a handy `slideToggle()` method.

```
$("#elem").slideToggle(1000, function() {
    // do something when slide up/down is finished executing
});
```

Animation

To animate an element, you do so by using jQuery to specify the CSS styles that the item should have applied. jQuery will impose the new styles but can do so gradually (instead of applying them instantly as in plain CSS/JavaScript), creating an animation effect.

You can use `animate()` on a wide range of numerical CSS properties. In this example the width and height of an element are animated to a size of 400 x 500 pixels; once the animation is complete, the callback function is used to fade the element to invisibility.

```
$("#elem").animate(
    {
        width: "400px",
        height: "500px"
        }, 1500, function() {
                $(this).fadeOut("slow");
    }
);
```

Command Chaining

A further handy behavior of jQuery is that most jQuery methods return a jQuery object that can then be used in your call to another method. You could combine two of the previous examples, like this:

```
$("#elem").fadeOut().fadeIn();
```

The preceding code will fade out all the chosen elements and then fade them back in. The number of items you can chain is arbitrarily large, allowing for several commands to successively work on the same collection of elements:

```
$("#elem").text("Hello from jQuery").fadeOut().fadeIn();
```

Let's use some of what you've learned so far to do a simple animation exercise with jQuery.

Your HTML page will initially display a `<div>` element, styled via CSS, but with no content. Here's the HTML for the page:

```
<!DOCTYPE html>
<html>
<head>
    <style>
        #animateMe {
            position:absolute;
            width: 100px;
            height: 400px;
            top: 100px;
            left: 100px;
            border: 2px solid black;
            background-color: red;
            padding: 20px;
        }
    </style>
</head>
<body>
    <div id="animateMe"></div>
</body>
</html>
```

First you need to add to your page a `<script>` element to link to the jQuery library—in this case, via a CDN:

```
<script src="http://code.jquery.com/jquery-latest.min.js"></script>
```

The first thing to do is add a little text to the `<div>` element using jQuery's `text()` method:

```
$("#animateMe").text("Changing shape...")
```

You can then call `animate()` to change the size (and therefore the shape) of the element:

```
$("#animateMe").animate(
    {
        width: "400px",
        height: "200px"
    }, 5000, function() {
        // callback function
    }
);
```

▼ TRY IT YOURSELF

A Simple jQuery Animation

continued

Of course, because the `text()` and `animate()` methods operate on the same element, you can use command chaining to concatenate the two:

```
$("#animateMe").text("Changing shape...").animate(
    {
        width: "400px",
        height: "200px"
    }, 5000, function() {
        // callback function
    }
);
```

When the animation has completed, let's change the text in the element and then have the element fade slowly away. We'll chain these two commands and use the callback function of the previous call to the `animate()` method to execute these additional commands after the animation is complete:

```
$("#animateMe").text("Changing shape...").animate(
    {
        width: "400px",
        height: "200px"
    }, 5000, function() {
        $(this).text("Fading away ...").fadeOut(4000);
    }
);
```

CAUTION

To use a version of jQuery stored on a CDN, you need your computer to be connected to the Internet. If you have no Internet connection, you need to use a local copy of jQuery to try out these examples.

Note the use of `this`. Because you're currently carrying out methods on the `$("#animateMe")` parent element, using `this` inside the code block refers to that parent element.

Finally, you need to carry out all of this activity when the DOM is ready by wrapping the code inside jQuery's `$(document).ready` handler.

The complete listing is shown in Listing 20.1. Create this page using your text editor and load it into your browser.

LISTING 20.1   A Simple jQuery Animation

```
<!DOCTYPE html>
<html>
<head>
    <style>
        #animateMe {
            position:absolute;
            width: 100px;
            height: 400px;
            top: 100px;
            left: 100px;
            border: 2px solid black;
```

TRY IT YOURSELF ▼

A Simple jQuery Animation
continued

LISTING 20.1   A Simple jQuery Animation

```
          background-color: red;
          padding: 20px;
      }
    </style>
    <script src="http://code.jquery.com/jquery-latest.min.js"></script>
    <script>
      $(document).ready(function() {
        $("#animateMe").text("Changing shape...").animate(
            {
              width: "400px",
              height: "200px"
              }, 5000, function() {
                $(this).text("Fading away ...").fadeOut(4000);
            }
        );
      });
    </script>
</head>
<body>
    <div id="animateMe"></div>
</body>
</html>
```

When the page has loaded, you should see a red `<div>` element with a black border that contains the words "Changing shape...." Once animated to its new width and height, the wording changes to "Fading away...," and the element fades out to nothing. Figure 20.1 shows the animation taking place.

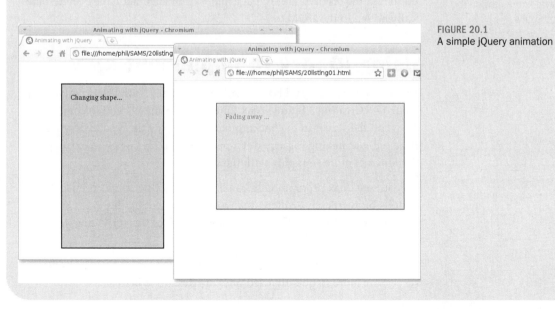

FIGURE 20.1
A simple jQuery animation

Handling Events

You can attach event handlers to elements or collections of elements a number of ways in jQuery. First, you can add event handlers directly, like this:

```
$("a").click(function() {
    // execute this code when any anchor element is clicked
});
```

or with a named function, like this:

```
function hello() {
    alert("Hello from jQuery");
}
$("a").click(hello);
```

In these two examples the function will be executed when an anchor is clicked. Some other common events you might use in jQuery include blur, focus, hover, keypress, change, mousemove, resize, scroll, submit, and select.

NOTE

The on() method was introduced in jQuery 1.7 and is the
recommended replacement for
several previous event handling
methods including bind(),
delegate(), and live(). See
the jQuery documentation for
complete details.

To help you add multiple event handlers, jQuery wraps the attachEvent and addEventListener JavaScript methods in a cross-browser way:

```
$("a").on('click', hello);
```

The on() method can be used to attach handlers both to elements already present in the original HTML page and to elements that have been dynamically added to the DOM.

Using jQuery to Implement Ajax

You learned the nuts and bolts of Ajax in Hour 16, "Introducing Ajax," and Hour 17, "Creating a Simple Ajax Library." Ajax allows you to communicate with the server in the background and display the results on your page without having to carry out a page refresh. This lets you create pages that interact more smoothly with the user.

As you saw, Ajax programming can be a little cumbersome because the various browsers have different ways of implementing the XMLHttpRequest object. Fortunately, jQuery solves this for you, letting you write AJAX routines in few lines of code.

There are a number of jQuery methods for performing Ajax calls to the server; the more frequently used ones are described here.

load()

When you simply want to grab a document from the server and display it in a page element, load() might be all you require. The following code snippet gets the file newContent.html and adds its content to the element with id="elem":

```
$(function() {
    $("#elem").load("newContent.html");
});
```

A neat trick is that you can pass a selector along with the URL and only get the part of the page corresponding to that selector:

```
$(function() {
    $("#elem").load("newContent.html #info");
});
```

Here you have added a jQuery selector after the URL, separated by a space. This causes jQuery to pass back only the content of the container specified by the selector; in this case, the element with id of "info."

Where load() gives you too little control, jQuery offers methods to send GET and POST requests too.

get() and post()

The two methods are similar, simply invoking different request types. You don't need to select a jQuery object (such as a page element or set of elements); instead you can call get() or post() directly using $.get() or $.post(). In its simplest form, the get() or post() method takes a single argument, the target URL.

You'll often want to send data to the server using get() or post(). Such data is sent as a set of parameter and value pairs in a JSON-style string.

In most cases, though, you'll want to do something with the returned data. To do that you pass a callback function as an argument.

```
$.get("serverScript.php",
    {param1: "value1", param2: "value2"},
    function(data) {
        alert("Server responded: " + data);
});
```

> TIP
>
> If you are collecting data from form fields, jQuery offers the handy serialize() method that can assemble the form data for you:
>
> ```
> var formdata =
> $('#form1').serialize();
> ```

The syntax for post() is essentially the same:

```
$.post("serverScript.php",
    {param1: "value1", param2: "value2"},
    function(data) {
        alert("Server responded: " + data);
});
```

ajax()

For the ultimate flexibility, the ajax() method allows you to set virtually every aspect of the Ajax call and how to handle the response. For full details of using ajax() see the documentation at http://api.jquery.com/jQuery.ajax/.

▼ TRY IT YOURSELF

An Ajax Form with jQuery

Let's round off this hour with an example of a simple Ajax form submission powered by jQuery.

We'll work with this simple HTML form:

```
<form id="form1">
    Name<input type="text" name="name" id="name"><br />
    Email<input type="text" name="email" id="email"><br />
    <input type="submit" name="submit" id="submit" value="Submit Form">
</form>
```

You're going to use jQuery to carry out the following tasks:

▶ Check that both input fields contain text.

▶ Submit the form via Ajax using HTTP POST.

▶ Print the data returned from the server into a <div> element on the page.

To check that both fields have had data entered, you use a simple function:

```
function checkFields(){
    return ($("#name").attr("value") && $("#email").attr("value"));
}
```

For the function to return Boolean true, the value attribute of both form fields must contain some text data; if either field is empty, the blank field will be interpreted as "falsy," and the logical AND (&&) operator will cause false to be returned from the function.

TRY IT YOURSELF ▼

**An Ajax Form
with jQuery**
continued

Next, apply jQuery's submit() event handler to detect form submission. If your function checkFields() returns false, the default behavior will be canceled and the form won't be submitted; otherwise, jQuery serializes the data and sends a post() request to the server script.

The jQuery serialize() method is used to collect the form information into a serialized string to send as a data payload with the Ajax call.

For this example, the server script test.php doesn't do anything except format the information it receives and send it back as a little piece of HTML:

```php
<?php
echo "Name: " . $_REQUEST['name'] . "<br />Email: " . $_REQUEST['email'];
?>
```

Finally, the callback function displays the returned information on the page:

```
function(data){
    $("#div1").html(data);
}
```

The code is shown in Listing 20.2.

LISTING 20.2   An Ajax Form

```
<!DOCTYPE html>
<html>
<head>
    <title>Ajax Form Submission</title>
    <script src="http://code.jquery.com/jquery-latest.min.js"></script>
    <script>
        $(document).ready(function(){
            function checkFields(){
                return ($("#name").attr("value") &&
➥$("#email").attr("value"));
            }
            $("#form1").submit(function(){
                if(checkFields()){
                    $.post(
                        'test.php', $("#form1").serialize(),
                        function(data){
                            $("#div1").html(data);
                        }
                    );
                }
                else alert("Please fill in name and email fields!");
                return false;
            });
        });
    </script>
</head>
```

▼ TRY IT YOURSELF

**An Ajax Form
with jQuery**

continued

LISTING 20.2   Continued

```
<body>
    <form id="form1">
        Name<input type="text" name="name" id="name"><br />
        Email<input type="text" name="email" id="email"><br />
        <input type="submit" name="submit" id="submit" value="Submit
Form">
    </form>
    <div id="div1"></div>
</body>
</html>
```

To run this example you need to upload both the file listed in Listing 20.2 and the server file test.php to a web server with PHP support.

Trying to submit the form with one or both of the input fields left blank will cause the script to issue an alert message and prevent the form submission.

A successful form submission should result in the formatted data being presented on the page, as shown in Figure 20.2. The figure also shows Firebug Lite displaying details of the Ajax call and response.

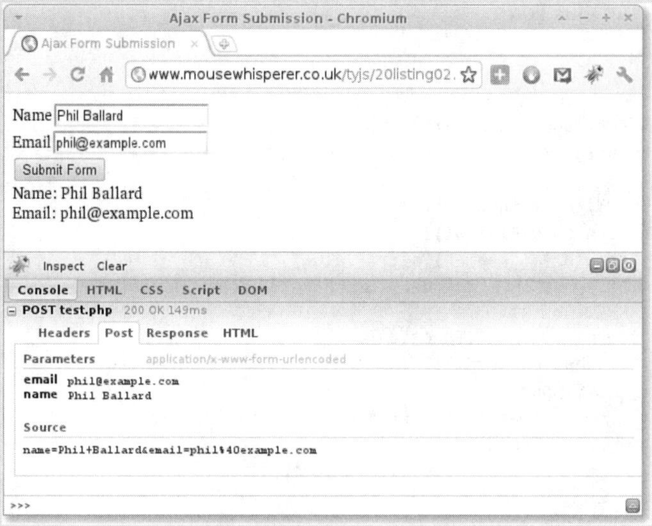

FIGURE 20.2
An Ajax form using jQuery

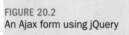

Summary

In this hour you took a good look at the basics of jQuery and learned how it can help you to write concise cross-browser JavaScript applications.

Q&A

Q. Where did jQuery come from?

A. jQuery was written by John Resig and launched in 2006. There are currently several jQuery projects including jQuery Core (used in this hour), and jQuery UI (which you learn about in Hour 21, "The jQuery UI User Interface Library"). These projects are under active development by John and a team of volunteers. You can read about the team and the projects at jquery.org.

Q. Is it possible to use jQuery alongside other libraries? Will there be conflicts?

A. Yes, jQuery can be used with other libraries. jQuery provides a means to prevent conflicts with the jQuery.noConflict() method. You can read about it at http://docs.jquery.com/Using_jQuery_with_Other_Libraries.

Workshop

Try to answer all the questions before reading the subsequent "Answers" section.

Quiz

1. How could you select all page elements having `class = "sidebar"`?

    a. `$(".sidebar")`

    b. `$("class:sidebar")`

    c. `$(#sidebar)`

2. The expression `$("p:first").show()` does what?

    a. Displays paragraph elements before displaying any other elements

    b. Makes the first paragraph element on the page visible

    c. Makes the first line of all paragraph elements visible

3. When applied to fades, slides, and animations, the value "fast" is equivalent to

    a. 1 second

    b. 600 milliseconds

    c. 200 milliseconds

Answers

1. a. $(".sidebar")

2. b. Makes the first paragraph element on the page visible

3. c. 200 milliseconds

Exercises

Review some of the example programs from earlier in the book. Pick a few to rewrite using jQuery and try to do so.

Visit the jQuery site at jquery.com and take a look at the documentation and examples, especially for the many jQuery methods that we didn't have space to discuss here.

The jQuery UI User Interface Library

In the previous hour you learned about the jQuery open source JavaScript library. In this hour you see how to use its companion library jQuery UI.

jQuery UI provides advanced effects and theme-able widgets that help you to build interactive web applications.

What jQuery UI Is All About

The jQuery development team decided to launch an "official" collection of plug-ins for jQuery, bringing together a wide range of popular user interface components and giving them a common interface style. Using these components you can build highly interactive and attractively styled web applications with a minimum of code.

Using jQuery UI in your programs gives you access to

▶ **Interactions.** The jQuery UI library provides support for dragging and dropping, resizing, selecting, and sorting page elements.

▶ **Widgets.** These are feature-rich controls including accordion, auto-complete, button, date picker, dialog, progress bar, slider, and tabs.

▶ **Theme building.** Give your site a coherent look-and-feel across all of the user interface components. A ThemeRoller tool is available at http://jqueryui.com/themeroller/. The ThemeRoller online tool allows you to choose a theme from the gallery of prewritten designs or create a custom theme based on an existing theme as a starting point.

WHAT YOU'LL LEARN IN THIS HOUR

▶ What jQuery UI is all about
▶ Using the ThemeRoller
▶ How to include jQuery UI in your pages
▶ Interactions: drag, drop, resize, and sort
▶ Using widgets: accordions, date pickers, and tabs

In this hour, you see how to use a selection of the more popular plugins. Thanks to the consistent user interface of jQuery-UI, it will then be easy to explore the many other available plugins by using the jQuery documentation.

How to Include jQuery UI in Your Pages

The first step is to visit the jQuery ThemeRoller online application at http://jqueryui.com/themeroller/.

Using the ThemeRoller

The jQuery UI CSS Framework is a set of classes covering a wide range of user interface requirements. Using the ThemeRoller tool, you can build your own interface styles, either from scratch or based on any of the extensive collection of examples available in the gallery at http://jqueryui.com/themeroller/.

Once you've decided on a style, jQuery UI provides a download builder that packages only the components you need. It also handles any dependencies for your selected items so you can't download a widget or interaction without all the ancillary files it requires. All you need to do is then download and unpack the zip file.

After you've unpacked the download, you have the following directories:

```
/css/
/development-bundle/
/js/
```

The `development-bundle` directory holds the jQuery UI source code, demos, and documentation. If you don't intend to change any of the jQuery UI code, you can safely delete it.

Generally, you need to include from the remaining files your theme, jQuery, and jQuery UI on any page that is to use jQuery UI widgets and interactions:

```
<link rel="stylesheet" type="text/css" href="css/themename/
➥jquery-ui-1.8.18.custom.css"  />
<script src="http://code.jquery.com/jquery-latest.min.js"></script>
<script src="http://ajax.googleapis.com/ajax/libs/jqueryui/1.8.17/
➥jquery-ui.min.js"></script>
```

If you use one of the standard gallery themes, you can alternatively link to all of the files you need on a Content Delivery Network:

```
<link rel="stylesheet" type="text/css"
➡href="http://ajax.googleapis.com/ajax/libs/jqueryui/1.8.16/themes/base/
➡jquery-ui.css"/
<script src="http://code.jquery.com/jquery-latest.min.js"></script>
<script src="http://ajax.googleapis.com/ajax/libs/jqueryui/1.8.17/jquery
```

Interactions

Let's take a look at some of the things you can do with jQuery UI to improve how page elements interact with the user.

Drag and Drop

Making an element draggable couldn't be simpler with jQuery UI:

```
$("#draggable").draggable();
```

Listing 21.1 shows how you could achieve this in an HTML page.

LISTING 21.1   Making a Page Element Draggable

```
<!DOCTYPE html>
<html>
<head>
    <link rel="stylesheet" type="text/css"
➡href="http://ajax.googleapis.com/ajax/libs/jqueryui/1.8.16/themes/base/
➡jquery-ui.css"/>
    <style>
        #dragdiv {
            width: 100px;
            height: 100px;
            background-color: #eeffee;
            border: 1px solid black;
            padding: 5px;
        }
    </style>
    <title>Drag and Drop</title>
    <script src="http://code.jquery.com/jquery-latest.min.js"></script>
    <script
➡src="http://ajax.googleapis.com/ajax/libs/jqueryui/1.8.17/
➡jquery-ui.min.js"></script>
    <script>
        $(function() {
            $("#dragdiv").draggable();
        });
    </script>
```

LISTING 21.1   Continued

```
</head>
<body>
    <div id="dragdiv"> Drag this element around the page!</div>
</body>
</html>
```

When the page has loaded, the element <div id="dragdiv"> is made draggable:

```
$(function() {
    $("#dragdiv").draggable();
});
```

You can then drag the item around the page by clicking the mouse on any part of the element, as depicted in Figure 21.1.

FIGURE 21.1
Dragging a page element

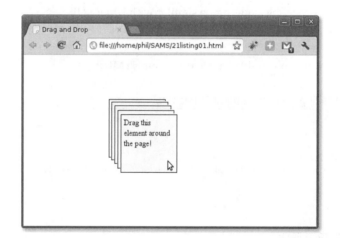

▼ TRY IT YOURSELF

Drag and Drop with jQuery UI

To make an element capable of receiving another element that is dropped on it, you need to use the droppable() method. This method can be specified to act on various events, such as draggable items being dropped, being over the droppable area, or leaving the droppable area.

You're going to modify the code from Listing 21.1 to add a further, larger <div> element as the drop area:

```
<div id="dropdiv">This is the drop zone ...</div>
```

In addition to making the draggable item draggable, you need to specify that the new <div> element is a drop area, like this:

```
$("#dropdiv").droppable();
```

In addition, you're going to make the text on the draggable item change in response to being dropped, or to leaving the droppable area, by adding methods to the handlers of the drop and out events:

```
$("#dropdiv").droppable({
    drop: function() { $("#dragdiv").text("Dropped!"); },
    out: function() { $("#dragdiv").text("Off and running again ..."); }
});
```

Create an HTML page containing the code of Listing 21.2.

LISTING 21.2   Drag and Drop with jQuery UI

```
<!DOCTYPE html>
<html>
<head>
    <link rel="stylesheet" type="text/css"
➥href="http://ajax.googleapis.com/ajax/libs/jqueryui/1.8.16/themes/base/
➥jquery-ui.css"/>    <style>
        div {
            font: 12px normal arial, helvetica;
        }
        #dragdiv {
            width: 150px;
            height: 50px;
            background-color: #eeffee;
            border: 1px solid black;
            padding: 5px;
        }
        #dropdiv {
            position: absolute;
            top: 80px;
            left: 100px;
            width: 300px;
            height: 200px;
            border: 1px solid black;
            padding: 5px;
            }
    </style>
    <title>Drag and Drop</title>
    <script src="http://code.jquery.com/jquery-latest.min.js"></script>
    <script src="http://ajax.googleapis.com/ajax/libs/jqueryui/1.8.17/
➥jquery-ui.min.js"></script>
```

TRY IT YOURSELF ▼

Drag and Drop with jQuery UI

continued

▼ TRY IT YOURSELF

Drag and Drop with jQuery UI

continued

LISTING 21.2   Drag and Drop with jQuery UI

```
<script>
    $(function() {
        $("#dragdiv").draggable();
        $("#dropdiv").droppable({
            drop: function() { $("#dragdiv").text("Dropped!"); },
            out: function() { $("#dragdiv").text("Off and running
➥again ..."); }
        });
    });
</script>
</head>
<body>
    <div id="dropdiv">This is the drop zone ...</div>
    <div id="dragdiv">Drag this element around the page!</div>
</body>
</html>
```

With the page loaded in your browser, you should now find that the draggable page element can be dropped within the droppable <div>, changing its text in response to the drop event.

The text changes once again as you drag the draggable item outside the border of the drop container, as shown in Google Chrome in Figure 21.2.

FIGURE 21.2
Drag and drop with jQuery UI

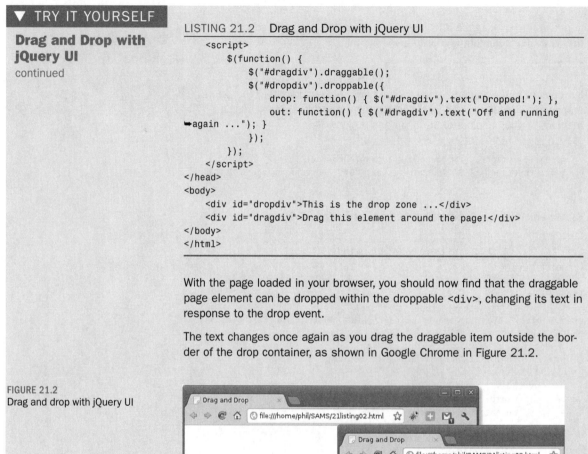

Resize

To add a resizing handle to a block element is equally trivial thanks to jQuery UI (see Figure 21.3):

```
$( "#resizable" ).resizable();
```

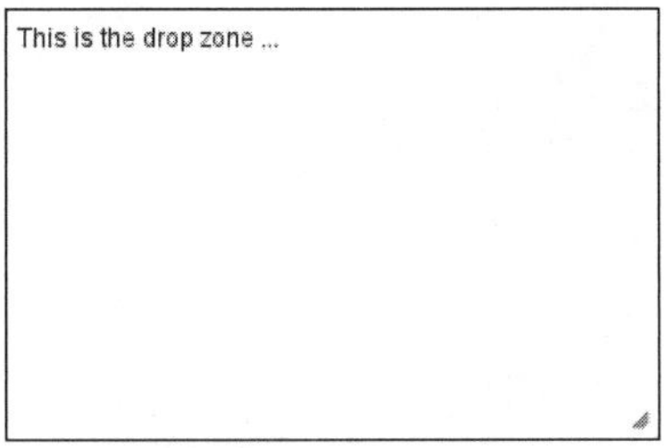

FIGURE 21.3
Adding a resizing handle

To demonstrate, you can chain the `resizable()` method to the droppable container of Listing 21.2:

```
$(function() {
    $("#dragdiv").draggable();
    $("#dropdiv").droppable({
        drop: function() { $("#dragdiv").text("Dropped!"); },
        out: function() { $("#dragdiv").text("Off and running again
➥..."); }
    }).resizable();
});
```

Sort

A further wrapper for drag and drop functionality is the `sortable()` method, which you can add to items in a list to make the list sortable:

```
$("#sortMe").sortable();
```

Listing 21.3 demonstrates how you might apply this method to an unordered list element.

LISTING 21.3   Making Elements Sortable

```
<!DOCTYPE html>
<html>
<head>
    <link rel="stylesheet" type="text/css"
➥href="http://ajax.googleapis.com/ajax/libs/jqueryui/1.8.16/themes/base/
➥jquery-ui.css"/>
```

LISTING 21.3   Continued

```
    <title>Sortable</title>
    <script src="http://code.jquery.com/jquery-latest.min.js"></script>
    <script src="http://ajax.googleapis.com/ajax/libs/jqueryui/1.8.17/
➡jquery-ui.min.js"></script>
    <script>
        $(function() {
            $("#sortMe").sortable();
        });
    </script>
</head>
<body>
    <ul id="sortMe">
        <li>One</li>
        <li>Two</li>
        <li>Three</li>
        <li>Four</li>
        <li>Five</li>
    </ul>
</body>
</html>
```

Dragging elements to a new location in the list causes the list to sort, "snapping" the list into a new order when the drop is made, as in Figure 21.4.

FIGURE 21.4
Sorting a list

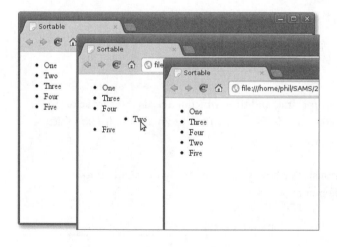

Using Widgets

Widgets are interface items you can drop into your application with a minimum of fuss and complication.

Accordion

The accordion widget lets a user expand a list of `<div>` elements by opening just one at a time, leaving the remaining ones reduced to just a title bar.

First you need to add the data in the semantic layer, using pairs of headers and content panels:

```
<div id="accordion">
    <h3><a href="#">First header</a></h3>
    <div>First content</div>
    <h3><a href="#">Second header</a></h3>
    <div>Second content</div>
</div>
```

Next you can activate the accordion by calling the `accordion()` method on the outer container element:

```
$(function() {
        $( "#accordion" ).accordion();
});
```

Listing 21.4 shows an example application, here dividing the lunch options of a restaurant menu into separate folds of an accordion.

LISTING 21.4   Using the Accordion Widget

```
<!DOCTYPE html>
<html>
<head>
    <link rel="stylesheet" type="text/css"
➥href="http://ajax.googleapis.com/ajax/libs/jqueryui/1.8.16/themes/base/
➥jquery-ui.css"/>
    <title>Menu Choices</title>
    <script src="http://code.jquery.com/jquery-latest.min.js"></script>
    <script src="http://ajax.googleapis.com/ajax/libs/jqueryui/1.8.17/
➥jquery-ui.min.js"></script>
    <script>
        $(function() {
            $("#accordion").accordion();
        });
    </script>
</head>
```

LISTING 21.4   Continued

```
<body>
    <h2>Choose from the following menu options:</h3>
<div id="accordion">
    <h3><a href="#">Starters</a></h3>
    <div>
        <ul>
            <li>Clam Chowder</li>
            <li>Ham and Avocado Salad</li>
            <li>Stuffed Mushrooms</li>
            <li>Chicken Liver Pate</li>
        </ul>
    </div>
    <h3><a href="#">Main Courses</a></h3>
    <div>
        <ul>
            <li>Scottish Salmon</li>
            <li>Vegetable Lasagna</li>
            <li>Beef and Kidney Pie</li>
            <li>Roast Chicken</li>
        </ul>
    </div>
    <h3><a href="#">Desserts</a></h3>
    <div>
        <ul>
            <li>Chocolate Sundae</li>
            <li>Lemon Sorbet</li>
            <li>Fresh Fruit Salad</li>
            <li>Strawberry Cheesecake</li>
        </ul>
    </div>
</div>
</body>
</html>
```

Figure 21.5 shows the accordion widget in action. An accordion doesn't allow multiple content panels to be open at the same time; clicking on the 'Starters' header will open that section, at the same time closing 'Main Courses'.

Date Picker

Expecting visitors to correctly fill out date fields has always been a tricky business, mainly due to the wide range of possible date formats that may be used.

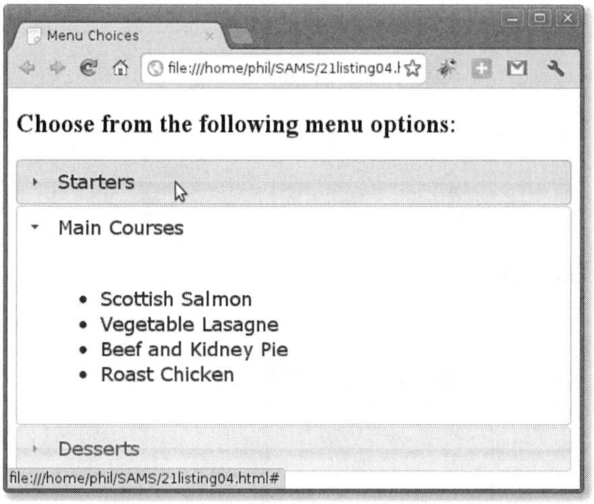

FIGURE 21.5
The accordion widget

A date picker is a pop-up calendar widget that allows the user to simply click on the required day, leaving the widget to format the selected date and enter the appropriate data into the correct input field.

Suppose you have a form field to accept a date:

```
<input type="text" id="datepicker">
```

You can implement a date picker widget for that field with a single line of code:

```
$( "#datepicker" ).datepicker();
```

Listing 21.5 has a complete example you can try.

LISTING 21.5   Using a Date Picker Widget

```
<!DOCTYPE html>
<html>
<head>
    <link rel="stylesheet" type="text/css"
➥href="http://ajax.googleapis.com/ajax/libs/jqueryui/1.8.16/themes/base/
➥jquery-ui.css"/>
    <title>Date Picker</title>
    <script src="http://code.jquery.com/jquery-latest.min.js"></script>
    <script src="http://ajax.googleapis.com/ajax/libs/jqueryui/1.8.17/
➥jquery-ui.min.js"></script>
    <script>
        $(function() {
            $( "#datepicker" ).datepicker();
        });
```

LISTING 21.5   Continued

```
    </script>
</head>
<body>
    Date: <input type="text" id="datepicker">
</body>
</html>
```

Figure 21.6 shows the date picker in action.

FIGURE 21.6
A date picker widget

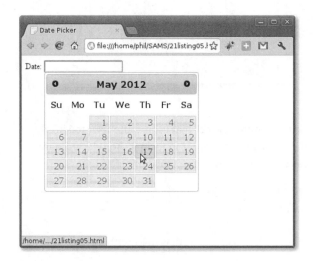

Tabs

Earlier in the hour you saw how to use an accordion widget to save some page area by showing just one panel of information from a list of options.

Another common way to achieve such a saving of space is by using a tabbed interface. Once again jQuery makes it a snap. Take a look at the code in Listing 21.6.

LISTING 21.6   A Tabbed Interface

```
<!DOCTYPE html>
<html>
<head>
    <link rel="stylesheet" type="text/css"
➥href="http://ajax.googleapis.com/ajax/libs/jqueryui/1.8.16/themes/base/
➥jquery-ui.css"/>
    <title>Tabs</title>
    <script src="http://code.jquery.com/jquery-latest.min.js"></script>
```

LISTING 21.6   Continued

```
    <script src="http://ajax.googleapis.com/ajax/libs/jqueryui/1.8.17/
➥jquery-ui.min.js"></script>
    <script>
        $(function() {
            $( "#tabs" ).tabs();
        });
    </script>
</head>
<body>
    <div id="tabs">
        <ul>
            <li><a href="#tabs-1">Home</a></li>
            <li><a href="#tabs-2">About Us</a></li>
            <li><a href="#tabs-3">Products</a></li>
        </ul>
        <div id="tabs-1">
            <p>Welcome to our online store....</p>
        </div>
        <div id="tabs-2">
            <p>We've been selling widgets for 5 years ...</p>
        </div>
        <div id="tabs-3">
            <p>We sell all kinds of widgets ...</p>
        </div>
    </div>
</body>
</html>
```

The tabs are contained in an unordered list:

```
<ul>
    <li><a href="#tabs-1">Home</a></li>
    ...
</ul>
```

The title of each tab is wrapped inside an anchor element, the href of
which points to the id of the <div> containing the content for that panel:

```
<div id="tabs-1">
    <p>Welcome to our online store....</p>
</div>
```

The whole of this is wrapped within a div container with id="tabs", and
to activate the tabbed interface, all you need to do is call the tabs()
method against this container element:

```
$( "#tabs" ).tabs();
```

When activated, the interface looks like the one shown in Figure 21.7.

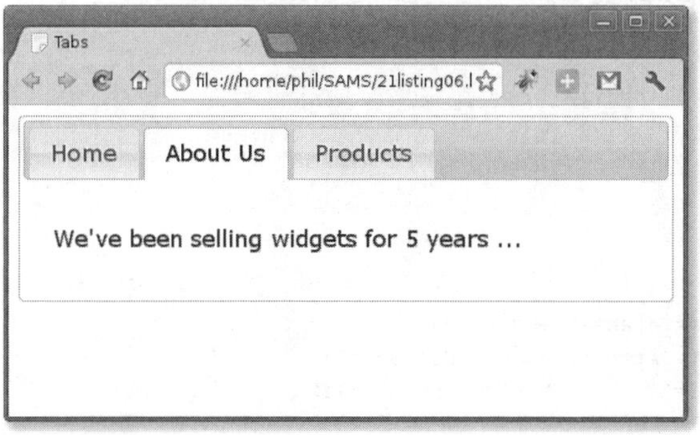

FIGURE 21.7
Tabs

Summary

In this hour you learned how to build slick user interfaces using the jQuery UI library in addition to jQuery. You saw how to quickly add interactions and widgets to your pages and how to set an overall style for your interface items using the ThemeRoller application.

Q&A

Q. Can I further customize these interface elements?

A. Yes you can. Due to the limited space in this book, each of the interactions and widgets demonstrated in this hour used the default settings. In reality, each has a host of customization options to make it work just how you want. You'll find extensive documentation and examples at http://docs.jquery.com/UI/.

Q. How can I make the other elements on my page have the same styles as those generated by jQuery UI?

A. When jQuery UI generates markup, it applies classes to the newly created markup items. These classes correspond to CSS declarations in the jQuery UI CSS Framework. Full details for each widget are given in the jQuery UI documentation.

Workshop

Try to answer all the questions before reading the subsequent "Answers" section.

Quiz

1. To use the jQuery UI in your pages, each page must contain as a minimum

    a. The jQuery and jQuery UI JavaScript libraries and a link to a jQuery UI theme CSS file

    b. Just the jQuery and jQuery UI libraries

    c. Just the jQuery UI JavaScript library and a link to a jQuery UI theme CSS file

2. How can you make a `<div>` element with `id = "parking"` capable of accepting items that are dropped on to it?

    a. `$("#parking").drop()`

    b. `$("#parking").dropzone()`

    c. `$("#parking").droppable()`

3. An accordion widget is capable of displaying

   a. One content section at a time

   b. A definable number of content sections all at once

   c. All content sections at once

Answers

1. a. The jQuery and jQuery UI JavaScript libraries and a link to a jQuery UI theme CSS file

2. c. `$("#parking").droppable()`

3. a. An accordion can display one content section at a time.

Exercises

Use the ThemeRoller to download a jQuery UI theme of your choice. Use it to reproduce some of the example scripts of this hour and compare the appearance of your pages with those displayed in the figures.

Visit the jQuery UI documentation at http://docs.jquery.com/UI/ to investigate how some of these widgets can be further customized with options and try out some examples using the listings in this hour as a starting point.

PART VI
Using JavaScript with Other Web Technologies

JavaScript and Multimedia

The term *multimedia* can include almost anything involving audio or video effects such as images, music, sound effects, speech, video clips, movies, and animations. Nearly all modern web browsers have support for various multimedia formats.

In this hour, you learn about different sorts of multimedia files and how you can control them using JavaScript.

Multimedia Formats

Multimedia content is stored in media files. As with many other types of file, you can usually determine the format being used by the file extension. The following sections describe most of the popular types along with their common file extensions.

Audio Formats

Sound files are created by digitally sampling audio waves. Generally, the more rapidly samples are taken (the sampling rate) and the more precise those samples are (measured in bits), the higher quality the recording[md]and the bigger the resulting file. In an effort to reduce file sizes and bandwidth, many file formats use compression techniques, though this often has a negative effect on audio quality.

The more common audio formats are shown in Table 22.1. Of those listed, WAV is the most-used uncompressed sound format, and is supported by all popular browsers. The MP3 format is currently the favorite format for compressed music and speech, the term *MP3* having become generally associated with digital audio.

WHAT YOU'LL LEARN IN THIS HOUR

- ▶ About multimedia file formats
- ▶ How browser plug-ins are used
- ▶ How to use <embed> and <object>
- ▶ Controlling Flash movie playback in JavaScript

354

TABLE 22.1   Some Popular Audio File Formats

Format	Description
Wave (.wav)	The Wave (waveform) format is developed by IBM and Microsoft. It is supported by all computers running Windows, and by all the most popular web browsers.
WMA (.wma)	The WMA format (Windows Media Audio) can be delivered as a continuous stream of data, which makes it practical for use in streamed applications like Internet radio.
Real Audio (.rm, .ram)	The RealAudio format, developed by Real Media, allows streaming of audio content with low bandwidths but reduced quality.
MP3 (.mp3)	An MP3 file is the sound part of MPEG, a format originally developed for video by the Moving Pictures Experts Group. MP3 is a very popular sound format combining good compression with high quality.

Video Formats

All popular video formats use compression algorithms to reduce bandwidth used and file size. Table 22.2 lists the popular formats.

TABLE 22.2   Popular Video File Formats

Format	Description
AVI (.avi)	Microsoft-developed format supported by all computers running Windows, and by all popular web browsers.
WMV(.wmv)	Microsoft-developed format.
MPEG(.mpg, .mpeg)	Currently probably the most popular format on the Internet. Supported by all popular web browsers.
QuickTime (.mov)	A common, Apple-developed format that on most browsers needs a plug-in to be installed.
RealVideo (.rm, .ram)	This format allows streaming of video with low bandwidths, though with quality reduced.
Flash (.swf, .flv)	The Flash (Shockwave) format was developed by Macromedia (now Adobe). The required plug-in comes preinstalled with most common browsers.

TABLE 22.2   Continued

Format	Description
Mpeg-4 (.mp4)	Mpeg-4 with H.264 video compression is the latest popular format for the Internet, and recommended by YouTube among others.

Browser Plug-Ins

Support for audio and video is handled differently by different browsers. Some of these elements can be handled directly, whereas some require an external program, known as a browser plug-in. A vast number of plug-ins are available for all the popular browsers, some examples being shown in Figure 22.1.

Here are a few of the most widely used:

▶ Macromedia's Shockwave and Flash support both animation and video.

▶ Apple's QuickTime plug-in supports many audio and video formats.

▶ RealPlayer supports streaming audio and video in various formats.

Browsers tend to use different plug-in formats and usually require different versions of a plug-in. Some plug-ins are available only for one platform, such as Windows or Macintosh.

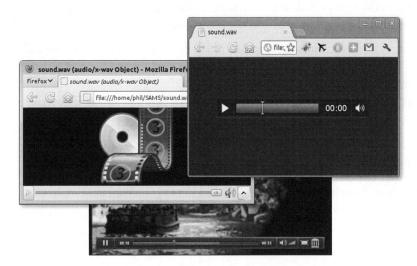

FIGURE 22.1
Many browser plug-ins are available.

Using an Anchor Tag

Probably the easiest way to load and play multimedia content is to link to a multimedia file using the <a> tag, for example:

```
<a href="sound.wav">Play Sound</a>
```

When the user clicks on the link, the browser loads the specified file. If the file is of a type the browser can display, such as a .png image file or an .html page, the browser loads and displays it.

If, however, the file is of a format that the browser needs help to handle, such as an audio or video file, the browser first consults a list of plug-ins registered for that file type. if a suitable plug-in is found, it loads the plug-in and passes it the file. If the file is associated with an external application, it may launch the application and pass it the file if the browser's security settings allow it to do so, or it may first ask for the user's go-ahead.

There are various disadvantages to using the <a> tag, however:

- ▶ If more than one plug-in is registered for the specified file type, you cannot specify what plug-in or application should be used.
- ▶ If no suitable plug-in is installed, the browser simply reports that file X is an unsupported type.
- ▶ You cannot pass attributes to a plug-in via an <a> tag, so you cannot control plug-in operation.
- ▶ Some browsers download the entire file before launching a plug-in, which can cause a delay if the file is large.
- ▶ An <a> tag loads the specified file in its own window or tab, instead of in the same page.

In most situations, using an <a> tag is best avoided. Use one of the following methods instead.

Using <embed> and <object>

Browsers have long supported two different tags for enabling plug-ins, <embed> and <object>.

Using `<embed>`

The `<embed>` element is supported by most browsers, but it is not a standard HTML element and will not validate. It's simple to use, however, and works with common sound file formats:

```
<embed src="music.wav" autostart="true" loop="false">
```

The preceding example uses the music.wav audio file. The parameter `autostart` controls whether playback automatically happens on page load, and `loop` determines whether the sound repeats continuously.

An `<embed>` element can also be used for video playback provided that the browser has support for the file format.

Using `<object>`

Use of the `<embed>` element, as just described, is an old method. The World Wide Web Consortium (W3C) now recommend using the `<object>` element, which became part of the HTML specification in HTML4.

The following code plays the same sound file as in the previous example, but using `<object>`:

```
<object type="audio/x-wav" data="music.wav" width="200" height="75">
    <param name="src" value="music.wav">
    <param name="autostart" value="true">
</object>
```

JavaScript and Plug-Ins

Most plug-ins support scripting with JavaScript.

Normally you would assign an id attribute to the `<embed>` or `<object>` tag, and then use DOM methods such as `getElementById()` to find the object corresponding to the embedded item, before applying methods in the normal way.

What methods you can call depends on the file type and the plug-in. Most sound plug-ins support a `Play()` method. Here's an example that finds an embedded sound file with the id attribute sound1 and plays the sound:

```
document.getElementById("sound1").Play();
```

TIP

Although `<object>` is a more standard way of embedding a file, most current browsers still support `<embed>`.

NOTE

There are now additional elements `<audio>` and `<video>`, which are new in HTML5. The purpose of the `<audio>` and `<video>` tags is to embed multimedia elements in HTML pages. They aren't described here; you learn about HTML5 in the following hour.

Plug-in methods are not part of the standard DOM, so you need to consult the plug-in's documentation to find out what methods are supported.

Plug-In Feature Sensing

When you work with plug-ins, it's important to remember that not all browsers will have the required plug-in installed. You should use feature sensing to use the plug-in only when it is supported. For example, you could check for the `Play()` method like this:

```
var myObj = document.getElementById("sound1");
if (myObj.Play) {
    myObj.Play();
} else {
    alert("Play method is not supported.");
}
```

Flash

Adobe (formerly Macromedia) Flash is a multimedia tool used to add animation, video, and interactivity to HTML pages. As well as vector and raster graphics providing animation of text, drawings, and photos, it also supports streaming of audio and video, and user input via mouse, keyboard, microphone or camera.

Flash files normally carry the .swf extension, and are usually referred to as "ShockWave Flash" or simply "Flash" movies, and may be embedded in web pages. Flash Video files have a .flv file extension and are either used within .swf files, or played through a media player such as QuickTime or Windows Media Player employing external programs called codecs (coders/decoders).

Flash files often tend to be smaller than competing formats for video.

JavaScript can send commands to Flash by calling built-in methods on embedded Flash movie objects. Calling Flash methods is just like making calls to methods of JavaScript objects such as `document.write()` or `window.alert()`. JavaScript methods can control a Flash movie without requiring complementary Flash code in the movie itself.

Table 23.2 lists some of the most useful methods.

TABLE 22.3   Some Flash Methods

Method	Description
Play()	Play the movie.
StopPlay()	Stop the movie.
IsPlaying()	Check if the movie's playing.
GotoFrame (x)	Go to frame x where x is an integer.
TotalFrames()	Count how many frames are in the movie.
Rewind()	Go to frame 1 and stop.
Zoom(percent)	Zoom view. Opposite of what you'd expect: Zoom(50) = 2 times movie size Zoom(200) = 1/2 movie size Zoom(0) = back to original size
PercentLoaded()	Check how much of the movie has downloaded. Returns a value between 0 and 100.

Let's write some code to control the playback of a Flash movie using JavaScript.

First you need to be sure the movie exists and has been fully loaded from the server. We use the PercentLoaded() method as listed in Table 22.3:

```
function flashLoaded(theMovie) {
    if (typeof(theMovie) != "undefined") {
        return theMovie.PercentLoaded() == 100;
    } else {
        return false;
    }
}
```

You can use your flashLoaded() method to check the movie's load status before calling any methods, like this:

```
function play() {
    if (flashLoaded(movie)) {
        ... do something ...
    }
}
```

Controlling a Flash Movie with JavaScript

TIP

To try this exercise you need a Flash movie file. If you have access to a suitable package, feel free to make your own .swf file. If not, you can create a .swf movie online at http://wonderfl.net/.

Controlling a Flash Movie with JavaScript

continued

Now you need to construct functions that wrap the Flash movie's `Play()`, `StopPlay()`, and `Rewind()` methods.

In the cases of `Play()` and `Stop()`, a further check is necessary to see whether the movie is currently playing:

```
function play(){
    if (flashLoaded (document.getDocumentByIdgetElementById('demo')) &&
        !document.getElementById('demo').IsPlaying()){
            document.getElementById('demo').Play();
    }
}
function stop(){
    if (flashLoaded (document.getDocumentByIdgetElementById('demo')) &&
        document.getElementById('demo').IsPlaying()){
            document.getElementById('demo').StopPlay();
    }
}
```

In the case of `rewind()`, the movie is stopped before rewinding by using the `stop()` function:

```
function rewind(){
    stop();
    if (document.getElementById('demo').Rewind()) {
        document.getElementById('demo').Rewind();
    }
}
```

The complete listing is shown in Listing 22.1. Create this file in your editor, being sure to have the .swf movie file in the same directory.

LISTING 22.1   Controlling a Flash Movie with JavaScript

```
<!DOCTYPE html>
<html>
<head>
    <title>Using Embedded Objects</title>
    <script>
        function flashLoaded(theMovie) {
            if (typeof(theMovie) != "undefined") {
                return theMovie.PercentLoaded() == 100;
            } else {
                return false;
            }
        }
        function play(){
            if
➥flashLoaded(document.getDocumentByIdgetElementById('demo')) &&
```

TRY IT YOURSELF ▼
Controlling a Flash Movie with JavaScript
continued

```
            !document.getElementById('demo').IsPlaying()){
                document.getElementById('demo').Play();
        }
    }
    function stop(){
        if
➡ (flashLoaded(document.getDocumentByIdgetElementById('demo')) &&
            document.getElementById('demo').IsPlaying()){
                document.getElementById('demo').StopPlay();
        }
    }
    function rewind(){
        stop();
        if (document.getElementById('demo').Rewind()) {
            document.getElementById('demo').Rewind();
        }
    }
    window.onload = function() {
        document.getElementById("play").onclick = play;
        document.getElementById("stop").onclick = stop;
        document.getElementById("rewind").onclick = rewind;
    }
    </script>
</head>
<body>
    <embed id="demo" name="demo"
        src="example.swf"
        width="318" height="300" play="false" loop="false"
        pluginspage="http://www.macromedia.com/go/getflashplayer"
        swliveconnect="true">
    </embed>
    <form name="form" id="form">
        <input id="play" type="button" value="Start" />
        <input id="stop" type="button" value="Stop" />
        <input id="rewind" type="button" value="Rewind" />
    </form>
</body>
</html>
```

The page, once loaded into the browser, should look something like Figure 22.2 (though you'll no doubt be playing a different movie file, of course!). Check that the three buttons work as you would expect.

▼ TRY IT YOURSELF

Controlling a Flash Movie with JavaScript
continued

FIGURE 22.2
Controlling Flash playback with JavaScript

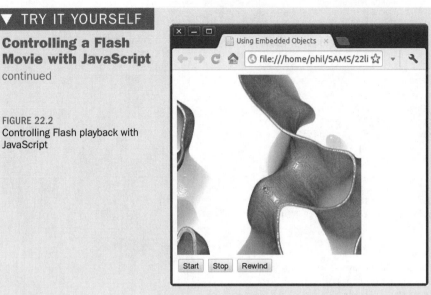

Summary

In this hour, you learned about the different multimedia file formats and how they can interact with JavaScript to help you add audio and video to your pages.

In the following hour, you learn about the up-and-coming methods to control multimedia using HTML5 tags.

Q&A

Q. What is "streaming" audio and video, and what are the most popular streaming formats?

A. "Streaming" allows the browser to play audio and video files before they are completely downloaded. Streaming works by downloading some of the file into memory known as a buffer. The application begins playback using the buffer while downloading the remainder in the background. The buffer allows the browser plug-in to have some material in reserve to compensate for delays in the transmission of the file.

Q. Are there downsides to including multimedia files in my pages?

A. In addition to making you handle the myriad of file formats and plug-in requirements, audio and video files are also generally large, so adding them to your page or site can consume a lot of storage space and available bandwidth.

Workshop

Try to answer all the questions before reading the subsequent "Answers" section.

Quiz

1. Which HTML tag is often used to include a plug-in object within a web page?

    a. `<object>`

    b. `<flash>`

    c. `<stream>`

2. Which of these is a browser plug-in for multimedia files?

    a. Acrobat Reader

    b. QuickTime

    c. Firebug

3. Which of the following is a format for streaming video?

  a. .wav

  b. .mp3

  c. .ram

Answers

1. a. `<object>`

2. b. QuickTime

3. c. .ram

Exercises

Find some Internet sites that embed multimedia content. Examine the source code of the pages to see what techniques they are using to embed the files.

Modify the code of Listing 22.1 to include buttons to increase and decrease the video Zoom level. [Hint: Use the `Zoom(percent)` property listed in Table 22.3.]

HTML5 and JavaScript

The previous version of HTML, HTML 4.01, has been around since 1999.

The XML-based version of HTML, XHTML, had been the subject of various recent W3C efforts, the latest having been moves toward XHTML2. In 2009 the W3C announced that XHTML2 was to be dumped in favor of diverting resources to a new version of HTML, HTML5.

This latest incarnation of HTML concentrates on developing HTML as a front end for web applications, extending the markup language via semantically rich elements, introducing some new attributes, and adding the possibility to use brand new APIs in conjunction with JavaScript.

The HTML5 standard will shortly be finalized as the new standard for HTML, and the major browsers already support many of the new HTML5 elements and APIs.

In this hour, you learn how to control some of these powerful new features with JavaScript.

New Markup for HTML5

Even HTML pages that are well-formed are more difficult to read and interpret than they could be because the markup contains very little semantic information.

Page sections such as sidebars, headers and footers, and navigation elements are all contained in general-purpose page elements such as divs and are only identifiable by the id and class names invented by the page's developer.

WHAT YOU'LL LEARN IN THIS HOUR

- ▶ About the new HTML5 markup tags
- ▶ How to handle video and audio
- ▶ Using the <canvas> element
- ▶ Drag and drop in HTML5
- ▶ Working with local storage
- ▶ How to interface with the local file system

TIP

Note how it's written: HTML5. There's no space between the L and the 5.

HTML5 adds new elements to more easily identify each of these, and more, types of content. Some of the new tags are listed in Table 23.1.

TABLE 23.1   Some New HTML5 Tags

Tag	Description
`<section>`	To define sections of pages
`<header>`	The header of a page
`<footer>`	The footer of a page
`<nav>`	The navigation on a page
`<article>`	The article or primary content on a page
`<aside>`	Extra content like a sidebar on a page
`<figure>`	Images that annotate an article
`<figcaption>`	A caption for a `<figure>` element
`<summary>`	A visible heading for a `<details>` element

Some Important New Elements

While HTML5 introduces a wide variety of interesting new capabilities, this section concentrates on the new tags that help ease some long-standing difficulties.

Video Playback with `<video>`

Video on the Web is extremely popular. However, as you learned in Hour 22, "JavaScript and Multimedia," the methods for implementing video are generally proprietary, reproduction happening via plug-ins such as Flash, Windows Media, or Apple QuickTime. Markup that works for embedding these elements in one browser doesn't always work in the others.

HTML5 contains a new `<video>` element, the aim of which is to allow the embedding of any and all video formats.

Using the new `<video>` tag, you can implement your favorite QuickTime movie like this:

```
<video src="video.mov" />
```

So far there has been much debate about which video formats (codecs) should be supported by the video element; at the time of writing, the search continues for a codec that requires no special licensing terms, though WebM (www.webmproject.org/) is currently looking like the favorite. For the time being, quoting multiple sources gets around the problem and avoids the need for browser sniffing; there are currently three widely supported video formats—MP4, WebM, and Ogg.

```
<video id="vid1" width="400" height="300" controls="controls">
    <source src="movie.mp4" type="video/mp4" />
    <source src="movie.ogg" type="video/ogg" />
    <source src="movie.webm" type="video/webm" />
    <p>Video tag not supported.</p>
</video>
```

It is also a good practice to include width and height attributes for the <video> element. If height and width are not set, the browser doesn't know how much screen space to reserve, resulting in the page layout changing as the video loads.

You are also recommended to place some suitable text between the <video> and </video> tags to display in browsers that don't support the <video> tag.

Some important properties of the <video> tag are listed in Table 23.2.

TABLE 23.2   Some Attributes of the <video> Element

Attribute	Description
loop	Play in a loop
autoplay	Starts video on load
controls	Display playback controls for playback (how they look is browser dependent)
ended	Boolean true if playback has finished (read-only)
paused	Boolean true if playback is paused (read-only)
poster	An optional image that will be displayed while the movie is loading
volume	Audio volume from 0 (silent) to 1 (maximum)

Note that the appearance of the controls added using the controls property will depend on the browser in use, as shown in Figure 23.1.

You can access these properties in the same way as any other JavaScript or DOM object. For the previous video definition, you might use

```
var myVideo = document.getElementById("vid1").volume += 0.1;
```

to marginally increase the volume or

```
if(document.getElementById("vid1").paused) {
    alert(message);
}
```

to pass a message to the user indicating that video playback is currently paused.

Testing Format Support with `canPlayType()`

You can check for support for a particular codec using the JavaScript method

```
media.canPlayType(type)
```

In the preceding example, `type` is a string containing the media type, for example, `"video/webm"`. This method must return an empty string if the browser knows it cannot play the content. The method might also return `"probably"` if the browser is confident it can support the format, or `"maybe"` otherwise.

Controlling Playback

Playback can also be controlled programmatically using the `pause()` and `play ()` commands, as in the following code snippet:

```
var myVideo = document.getElementById("vid1").play();
var myVideo = document.getElementById("vid1").pause();
```

Playing Sound with the `<audio>` Tag

Pretty much everything stated previously about the `<video>` tag applies equally well to the `<audio>` tag. The simple way to use the `<audio>` tag is like this:

```
<audio src="song.mp3"></audio>
```

TIP

Don't abuse `loop` and `autoplay`, or you may find that many of your site visitors don't return!

You can add further attributes to achieve more control over playback, such as `loop` and `autoplay`:

```
<audio src="song .mp3" autoplay loop></audio>
```

As with the earlier examples for video files, you can include alternative formats to help ensure that a user's browser will find one that it can play, as in the following code:

```
<audio controls="controls">
    <source src="song.ogg" type="audio/ogg" />
    <source src="song.mp3" type="audio/mpeg" />
    Your browser does not support the audio element.
</audio>
```

MP3, WAV, and Ogg are typically supported file formats for the `<audio>` element. Controlling an audio file in JavaScript uses the same methods as for the `<video>` tag.

To add and play an audio file via JavaScript, you can treat it just like any other JavaScript or DOM object:

```
var soundElement = document.createElement('audio');
soundElement.setAttribute('src', sound.ogg');
soundElement.play();
soundElement.pause();
```

The `<audio>` and `<video>` tags have many useful properties that you can access via JavaScript. Here are a few useful ones, the meaning of which will be immediately apparent:

```
mediaElement.duration
mediaElement.currentTime
mediaElement.playbackRate
mediaElement.muted
```

TIP

You can find a comprehensive reference to these tags and their properties and methods at www.whatwg.org/specs/ web-apps/current-work/ multipage/the-video-element.html.

For example, to move to a point 45 seconds into a song, you might use

```
soundElement.currentTime = 45;
```

Drawing on the Page with `<canvas>`

The new `<canvas>` tag gives you just that: a rectangular space in your page where you can draw shapes and graphics, as well as load and display image files and control their display via JavaScript. The many practical uses for the element include dynamic charts, JavaScript/HTML games, and instructional animations.

Using the `<canvas>` tag simply allows you to define a region by setting its width and height parameters; everything else related to creating the graphical content is done via JavaScript. There is an extensive set of drawing methods known as the Canvas 2D API.

▼ TRY IT YOURSELF

A Moving Ball Using `<canvas>`

TIP

If you don't set width and height parameters, the canvas defaults to 300 pixels wide by 150 pixels high.

You're going to make a simple animation in a `<canvas>` element—just a red disc (to represent a ball) moving in a circle on the page.

The only HTML markup required in the body of the page is the `<canvas>` element itself:

```
<canvas id="canvas1" width="400" height="300"></canvas>
```

All the drawing and animation will be done in JavaScript.

You first need to specify the *rendering context*. At the time of writing, 2D is the only widely supported context, though a 3D context is under development.

```
context= canvas1.getContext('2d');
```

The only primitive shapes supported by `<canvas>` are rectangles:

```
fillRect(x,y,width,height);        //draw a filled rectangle
strokeRect(x,y,width,height);      //draw an outlined rectangle
clearRect(x,y,width,height) :      // clear the rectangle
```

All other shapes must be created by using one or more path drawing functions. Because you want to draw a colored disc, that's what you need here.

Several different path drawing functions are offered by `<canvas>`:

```
moveTo(x, y)
```

Move to x, y without drawing anything:

```
lineTo(x, y)
```

Draw a line from the current location to x, y:

```
arc(x, y, r, startAngle, endAngle, anti)
```

Draw a circular arc of radius r, having circle center x, y, from `startAngle` to `endAngle`. Setting the last parameter to Boolean `true` makes the arc draw counterclockwise instead of the default clockwise.

To create shapes using these basic commands, you need some additional methods:

```
object.beginPath();
object.closePath();      //complete a partial shape
object.stroke();         //draw an outlined shape
object.fill();           //draw a filled shape
```

To make the ball, you're going to generate a filled circle. Let's make it red, of radius 15, and centered on canvas coordinates 50, 50:

```
context.beginPath();
context.fillStyle="#ff0000";
context.arc(50, 50, 15, 0, Math.PI*2, true);
context.closePath();
```

To animate the ball, you need to alter the x and y coordinates of the ball center using a timer. Take a look at the `animate()` function:

```
function animate() {
    context.clearRect(0,0, 400,300);
    counter++;
    x += 20 * Math.sin(counter);
    y += 20 * Math.cos(counter);
    paint();
}
```

This function is called repeatedly via the `setInterval()` method. Each time it's called, the canvas is cleared by using the `clearRect()` method across the full size of the canvas element. The variable counter is incremented on each loop, and its new value is then used to redefine the position of the disc's center.

The complete code is listed in Listing 23.1.

LISTING 23.1   A Moving Ball Using `<canvas>`

```
<!DOCTYPE HTML>
<html>
<head>
    <title>HTML5 canvas</title>
</head>
<script>
    var context;
    var x=50;
    var y=50;
    var counter = 0;
```

TRY IT YOURSELF ▼

A Moving Ball Using
`<canvas>`
continued

TIP

If you use the `fill` method, an open shape will be closed automatically without you having to use `closePath()`.

▼ TRY IT YOURSELF

A Moving Ball Using
`<canvas>`
continued

LISTING 23.1   Continued

```
function paint()   {
    context.beginPath();
    context.fillStyle="#ff0000";
    context.arc(x, y, 15, 0, Math.PI*2, false);
    context.closePath();
    context.fill();
}
function animate() {
    context.clearRect(0,0, 400,300);
    counter++;
    x += 20 * Math.sin(counter);
    y += 20 * Math.cos(counter);
    paint();
}
window.onload = function() {
    context= canvas1.getContext('2d');
    setInterval(animate, 100);
}
</script>
<body>
    <canvas id="canvas1" width="400" height="300">
        <p>Your browser doesn't support the canvas element.</p>
    </canvas>
</body>
</html>
```

Create this file and load it into your browser. If your browser supports the
`<canvas>` element, you should see a red disc following a circular route on the
page, as in Figure 23.2.

FIGURE 23.2
An animation using `<canvas>`

Drag and Drop

Drag and drop is a part of the HTML5 standard. Just about any element can be made draggable.

To make an element draggable, all that's required is to set its draggable attribute to true:

```
<img draggable="true" />
```

Dragging something, though, isn't much use by itself. To employ a draggable object to achieve something useful, you're probably going to want to be able to drop it somewhere.

To define where an object can be dropped and control the dragging and dropping process, you need to write event listeners to detect and control the various parts of the drag and drop process.

There are a few different events you can utilize to control your drag and drop:

- ▶ dragstart
- ▶ drag
- ▶ dragenter
- ▶ dragleave
- ▶ dragover
- ▶ drop
- ▶ dragend

To control your drag and drop, you need to define a source element (where the drag starts), the data payload (what it is you're dragging), and a drop target (an area to catch the dropped item).

The dataTransfer property contains a piece of data sent in a drag action. The value of dataTransfer is usually set in the dragstart event and read/handled in the drop event.

Calling setData(format, data) or getData(format, data) will (respectively) set or read this piece of data.

TIP

Not all items can be drop targets—an <img>, for example, cannot accept drops.

Drag and Drop in HTML5

You're going to build a demonstrator for the HTML5 drag and drop interface.

Fire up your editor and create a file containing the code listed in Listing 23.2.

LISTING 23.2   HTML5 Drag and Drop

```
<!DOCTYPE HTML>
<html>
<head>
    <title>HTML5 Drag and Drop</title>
    <style>
        body {background-color: #ddd; font-family: arial, verdana,
➥sans-serif;}
        #drop1 {width: 200px;height: 200px;border: 1px solid
➥black;background-color: white}
        #drag1 {width: 50px;height: 50px;}
    </style>
    <script>
        function allowDrop(ev) {
            ev.preventDefault();
        }

        function drag(ev) {
            ev.dataTransfer.setData("Text",ev.target.id);
        }

        function drop(ev) {
            var data = ev.dataTransfer.getData("Text");
            ev.target.appendChild(document.getElementById(data));
            ev.preventDefault();
        }

        window.onload = function() {
            var dragged = document.getElementById("drag1");
            var drophere = document.getElementById("drop1");
            dragged.ondragstart = drag;
            drophere.ondragover = allowDrop;
            drophere.ondrop = drop;
        }
    </script>
</head>
<body>
    <div id="drop1" ></div>
    <p>Drag the image below into the box above:</p>
    <img id="drag1" src="drag.gif" draggable="true" />
</body>
</html>
```

To get the party started, you define a couple of HTML elements on your page. The `<div>` element with id of drop1 is the target area for catching the drop, and the image with id of drag1 is to become your draggable item.

Three important functions are defined in the code. Each of these functions is passed the current event to process. Behind the scenes, ev.target changes automatically for each type of event, depending on where you are in the drag and drop process.

▶ A function drag(ev) that is executed when the drag starts. This function sets the value of the dataTransfer property for the drag to the id of the dragged object:

```
function drag(ev) {
    ev.dataTransfer.setData("Text",ev.target.id);
}
```

▶ Another function allowDrop(ev) that is executed when the drag passes over the intended drop area. All that this function must achieve is to prevent the drop area's default behavior from taking place:

```
function allowDrop(ev) {
    ev.preventDefault();
}
```

▶ Finally, a function drop(ev), executed when the dragged item is dropped. In this function, the value of the dataTransfer property is read to determine the id of the dragged object; then that object is appended as a child object to the drop area object. Once again, the default operation needs to be prevented from taking place:

```
function drop(ev) {
    var data = ev.dataTransfer.getData("Text");
    ev.target.appendChild(document.getElementById(data));
    ev.preventDefault();
}
```

The loaded page should look something like the one shown in Figure 23.3; dragging the small image and dropping it over the white drop area, you should see it "dock" into the `<dive>` element as shown in the figure.

TRY IT YOURSELF ▼

Drag and Drop in HTML5
continued

▼ TRY IT YOURSELF

Drag and Drop in HTML5

continued

FIGURE 23.3
HTML5 drag and drop

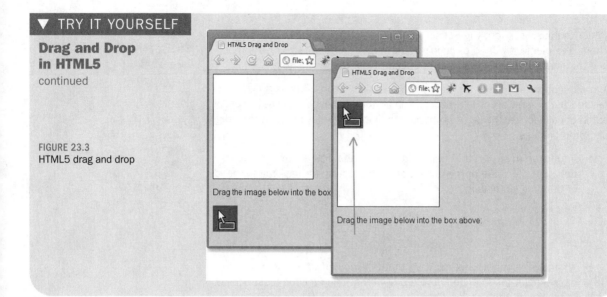

Local Storage

HTML5 pages can store even large amounts of data within the user's browser without any negative effect on the website's performance. Web storage is more secure and faster than doing this via cookies. Like when using cookies, the data is stored in key/value pairs, and a web page can only access the data it has itself stored.

The two new objects for storing data locally in the browser are

▶ localStorage. Stores data with no expiration date.

▶ sessionStorage. Stores data just for the current session.

If you're unsure about your browser's support for local storage, once again you can use feature detection:

```
if(typeof(Storage)!=="undefined") {
    ... both objects are available ...
}
```

To store a value you can either invoke the setItem method, passing to it a key and a value:

```
localStorage.setItem("key", "value");
```

or use the `localStorage` object like an associative array:

```
localStorage["key"] = "value";
```

Retrieving the values can use either of thee methods too:

```
alert(localStorage.getItem("key"));
```

or

```
alert(localStorage["key"]);
```

Working with Local Files

At last HTML provides a standard way to interact with the user's local files, using HTML5's File API specification. There are several ways to access external files:

- ▶ File—provides information including name, size, and mimetype, and gives a reference to the file handle.

- ▶ FileList—array-like sequence of File objects.

- ▶ FileReader—interface uses File and FileList to asynchronously read a file. You can check on read progress, catch any errors, and find out when a file is completely loaded.

Checking for Browser Support

Once more, you can check whether your browser supports the File API by the usual feature detection method:

```
if (window.File && window.FileReader && window.FileList) {
    // we're good
}
```

TRY IT YOURSELF ▼

Interacting with the Local File System

In this example you're going to modify the previous drag and drop example to allow a list of files to be dragged into a web page from the local file system. To do so, you're going to use the FileList data structure.

Take a look at the modified drop(ev) function:

```
function drop(ev) {
        var files = ev.dataTransfer.files;
        for (var i = 0; i < files.length; i++) {
            var f = files[i];
            var pnode = document.createElement("p");
```

▼ TRY IT YOURSELF

Interacting with the Local File System

continued

```
                        var tnode = document.createTextNode(f.name + " (" +
➥f.type + ") " + f.size + " bytes");
                        pnode.appendChild(tnode);
                        ev.target.appendChild(pnode);
            }
            ev.preventDefault();
    }
```

Here, the array-like `FileList` containing information about the dragged files is extracted from the `dataTransfer` object:

```
var files = ev.dataTransfer.files;
```

and then each file is processed in turn by iterating through them individually:

```
for (var i = 0; i < files.length; i++) {
    var f = files[i];
    ...statements to process each file ...
}
```

The complete listing is shown in Listing 23.3.

LISTING 23.3   Interacting with the Local File System

```
<!DOCTYPE HTML>
<html>
<head>
    <title>HTML5 Local Files</title>
    <style>
        body {background-color: #ddd; font-family: arial, verdana,
➥sans-serif;}
        #drop1 {
            width: 400px;
            height: 200px;
            border: 1px solid black;
            background-color: white;
            padding: 10px;
        }
    </style>
    <script>
        function allowDrop(ev) {
            ev.preventDefault();
        }

        function drop(ev) {
            var files = ev.dataTransfer.files;
            for (var i = 0; i < files.length; i++) {
                var f = files[i]
                var pnode = document.createElement("p");
                var tnode = document.createTextNode(f.name + " (" +
➥f.type + ") " + f.size + " bytes");
                pnode.appendChild(tnode);
```

TRY IT YOURSELF ▼

Interacting with the Local File System

continued

LISTING 23.3   Continued

```
                ev.target.appendChild(pnode);
        }
        ev.preventDefault();
    }

    window.onload = function() {
        var drophere = document.getElementById("drop1");
        drophere.ondragover = allowDrop;
        drophere.ondrop = drop;
    }
    </script>
</head>
<body>
    <div id="drop1" ></div>
    <output id="text"></output>
</body>
</html>
```

After creating this file in your editor and loading the resulting page into the browser, you should be able to drag files into the drop area from your local system, and see filename, MIME type, and size listed, as shown in Figure 23.4.

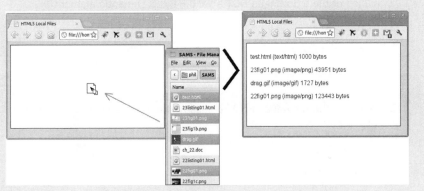

FIGURE 23.4
Interfacing with local files

Summary

HTML5 offers a whole array of new facilities to HTML, enabling the markup language to be used as a much better basis for web applications and allowing JavaScript to exploit some brand new APIs.

In this hour, you had a whistle-stop tour of these new capabilities, including some hands-on coding experience using some of these new APIs.

Q&A

Q. What is the best way for me to learn HTML5?

A. Learn HTML5 by using it. Jump right in and start building pages using HTML5 features. Use the semantic tags; try video and audio playback; play with drag and drop, local storage, and the file API; and build animations using `<canvas>`. When you have questions, many Internet-based tutorials, blogs, and code examples are available.

Q. Are there already real live sites using HTML5?

A. Sure, lots of them. Take a look at http://html5gallery.com/ for some examples.

Workshop

Try to answer all the questions before reading the subsequent "Answers" section.

Quiz

1. Which of the following is NOT a valid HTML5 semantic element?

    a. `<header>`

    b. `<sidebar>`

    c. `<nav>`

2. Which of the following is NOT a valid method for `<audio>` and `<video>` elements?

    a. `play()`

    b. `pause()`

    c. `stop()`

3. Which of the following is NOT a standard drag-and-drop event?

    a. drag

    b. dragover

    c. dragout

Answers

1. b. `<sidebar>` is not a valid HTML5 element.

2. c. There is no `stop()` method.

3. c. There is no `dragout` event; use `dragleave`.

Exercises

Review some of the examples of previous hours and try to rewrite them using some of the new HTML5 interfaces.

HTML5 is pretty new at the time of writing. Check out the current state of browser support for the various aspects of HTML5 at http://caniuse.com/ or http://html5readiness.com/.

JavaScript Beyond the Web Page

Up to now you've learned a wide range of uses for JavaScript in the writing of web pages. However, JavaScript can also be used for extending browsers by building add-ons and extensions. Also, JavaScript interpreters are embedded in a number of tools apart from web browsers. Such applications often provide their own object model representing the host environment, although the core JavaScript language may remain essentially the same in each instance.

In this hour, you learn about uses for JavaScript above and beyond writing simple web content. You also write your own extension for Google's Chrome browser.

JavaScript Outside the Browser

There are a number of applications for JavaScript to control the actions of other applications in addition to web pages:

▶ Browser extensions for Google's Chrome, Opera, and Apple's Safari 5 browsers, and widget/gadget collections for Apple's Dashboard, Microsoft, Yahoo!, and Google Desktop can all be written using JavaScript.

▶ JavaScript is supported in PDF files used by Adobe's Acrobat and Adobe Reader, as well as many third-party applications.

▶ Adobe tools such as Photoshop, Illustrator, Dreamweaver, and others allow scripting via JavaScript.

▶ The OpenOffice.org office application suite (and its sibling LibreOffice) have JavaScript as one of the included macro scripting languages. These suites are written largely in Java and provide a JavaScript implementation based on Mozilla Rhino. JavaScript

WHAT YOU'LL LEARN IN THIS HOUR

▶ Some examples of applications for JavaScript outside straightforward web pages

▶ How to write a browser extension for Google Chrome

macros can access the application's variables and objects, much like web browsers host scripts that access the browser's Document Object Model (DOM) for a web page.

▶ Sphere is an open source and cross-platform program for writing role-playing games, and the Unity game engine supports JavaScript for scripting.

▶ Google Apps Script allows users access and control over Google Spreadsheets and other products using JavaScript.

▶ ActionScript, the programming language used in Adobe Flash, is another implementation of the ECMAScript standard.

▶ The Mozilla platform, which is the basis of Firefox, Thunderbird, and other projects, uses JavaScript for the graphical user interface of these applications.

In this final hour of the book, you're going to try your hand at one of these—writing an extension for Google's Chrome web browser.

Writing Google Chrome Extensions

Extensions are small applications that run inside a web browser and provide additional services, integrate with third-party websites or data sources, and customize the user's experience of the browser application. A Google Chrome extension is nothing more or less than a collection of files (HTML, CSS, JavaScript, images, and so on) bundled into a .zip file (although it's renamed as a .crx file).

The extension basically creates a web page that can use all the interface elements that the browser provides to regular web pages, including JavaScript libraries, CSS style sheets, XMLHttpRequest objects, and so on.

Extensions can interact with web pages or servers and can also interact via program code with browser features such as bookmarks and tabs.

Building a Simple Extension

The first step is to create a folder on your computer to contain the code for your extension.

Each extension has a manifest file, named manifest.json, which is formatted in JSON and provides important information.

Although the manifest file can contain a wide range of parameters and options, the only two required fields in manifest.json are name and version:

```
"name": "My Chrome Extension",
"version": "1.0"
```

In your new folder create a text file called manifest.json and edit it like this:

```
{
    "name": "My First Extension",
    "version": "1.0",
    "description": "Hello World extension.",
    "browser_action": {
        "default_icon": "icon.png",
        "popup": "popup.html"
    }
}
```

Put an icon called icon.png in the same folder—I used a small graphic image of a star, but you can use whatever you want. Create the file popup.html listed in Listing 24.1 and put that in the folder too.

LISTING 24.1   popup.html Google Chrome Extension

```html
<!DOCTYPE html>
<html>
<head>
    <style>
        body {
            width:350px;
        }
        div {
            border: 1px solid black;
            padding: 20px;
            font: 20px normal helvetica, verdana, sans-serif;
        }
    </style>
    <script>
        function sayHello() {
            var message = document.createTextNode("Hello World!");
            var out = document.createElement("div");
            out.appendChild(message);
            document.body.appendChild(out);
        }
        window.onload = sayHello;
    </script>
</head>
<body>
</body>
</html>
```

Display the extensions page by clicking the wrench icon and selecting **Tools > Extensions**.

Click the box next to Developer Mode to show a little more information.

Then click the Load Unpacked Extensions button. Navigate to the folder containing your extension and select it. You should see something like Figure 24.1.

FIGURE 24.1
Your new extension visible on the Extensions page

Make sure the extension is enabled by checking the box next to it. You can now run your extension by clicking the toolbar icon, as shown in Figure 24.2.

FIGURE 24.2
Hello World as a Google Chrome extension

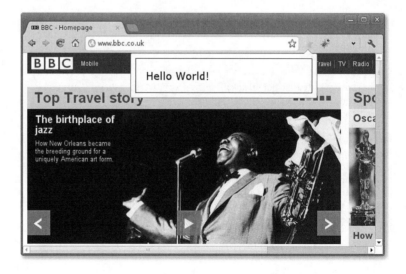

Debugging the Extension

Right-click the icon that launches your extension, and you see a content menu containing options to enable and disable the extension, plus an option Inspect popup. Click that and Chrome's Developer Tools pop open to let you examine the pop-up window, as shown in Figure 24.3.

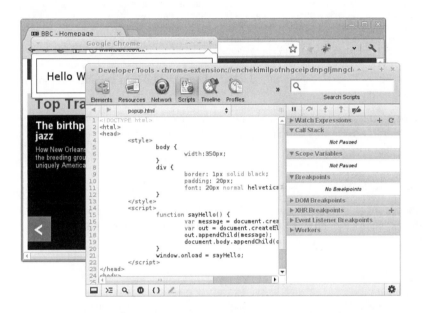

FIGURE 24.3
Inspecting the pop-up window

A Chrome Extension to Get Airport Information

This time you're going to make a Chrome extension that's a little more useful. With the help of the jQuery library, your pop-up is going to retrieve current information about U.S. airports.

To do that, you're going to have your code make an Ajax call to an information feed at http://services.faa.gov/. To demonstrate how this service works, open your browser and navigate to http://services.faa.gov/airport/status/SFO?format=application/json.

SFO is the three-letter code for San Francisco International airport; you can replace it in the preceding URL with the code for another U.S. airport, for example, LAX for Los Angeles International or SEA for Seattle-Tacoma International.

TIP

Refer back to Hour 20, "A Closer Look at jQuery," if you need a refresher on the jQuery library.

▼ TRY IT YOURSELF

A Chrome Extension to Get Airport Information
continued

TIP

You can read the airport codes and see their locations at http://www.fly.faa.gov/flyfaa/usmap.jsp.

The format parameter tells the service that you want to information returned as a JSON string:

```
{"name":"San Francisco
International","ICAO":"KSFO","state":"California","status":{"avgDelay":""
➡,"closureEnd":"","closureBegin":"","type":"","minDelay":"","trend":"",
➡"reason":"No known delays for this
➡airport.","maxDelay":"","endTime":""},"delay":"false","IATA":"SFO","
➡city":"San Francisco","weather":{"weather":"Partly
➡Cloudy","meta":{"credit":"NOAA's National Weather
➡Service","url":"http://weather.gov/","updated":"1:56 AM
➡Local"},"wind":"Southwest at 9.2mph","temp":"44.0 F (6.7
➡C)","visibility":"10.00"}}
```

Your code will parse this returned information and use it to construct a more user-friendly display.

To begin the project, create a new directory somewhere on your computer and call it "airport." In this directory, you need three files, as in the previous example.

An Icon File

Choose an icon to display on your Chrome toolbar and from which to launch the extension. I used a 20 x 20 pixel airplane icon in a file called plane.png, but you can use any icon you have on hand.

The `manifest.json` File

The manifest file will be pretty familiar from the previous example, but with one notable addition: a new parameter permissions. You are going to make an Ajax call to services.faa.gov to retrieve the information you want, and Ajax calls can only be made to pages on the same domain as the caller; adding a permissions value allows Chrome to fulfill this requirement by sending a suitable header to the server. The manifest.json file is shown in Listing 24.2.

LISTING 24.2   The manifest.json File

```
{
    "name": "Airport Information",
    "version": "1.0",
    "description": "Information on US airports",
    "browser_action": {
        "default_icon": "plane.png",
        "popup": "popup.html"
```

TRY IT YOURSELF

**A Chrome Extension
to Get Airport
Information**
continued

LISTING 24.2   Continued

```
    },
    "permissions": [
    "http://services.faa.gov/"
    ]
}
```

The HTML File

Once again the main HTML file will be called popup.html. You can call it something else if you want to, as long as you edit manifest.json and suitably set value of the "popup" parameter.

The simple HTML page is shown listed in Listing 24.3.

LISTING 24.3   The Basic HTML File popup.html

```html
<!DOCTYPE html>
<html>
<head>
    <title>Airport Information</title>
    <style>
        body {
            width:350px;
            font: 12px normal arial, verdana, sans-serif;
        }
        #info {
            border: 1px solid black;
            padding: 10px;
        }
    </style>
</head>
<body>
    <h2>Airport Information</h2>
    <input type=Text id="airportCode" value="SFO" size="6" />
    <input id="btn" type="button" value="Get Information" />
    <div id="info"></div>
</body>
</html>
```

Apart from a little CSS styling, the page only contains a few items: an input field to accept the airport code, with default value set to SFO, a button to request that data is fetched, and a <div> to hold the returned results.

Now you need to start adding JavaScript to the page.

▼ TRY IT YOURSELF

**A Chrome Extension
to Get Airport
Information**

continued

You're going to use jQuery to simplify things, so first you need to include that. Let's use a Content Delivery Network, as discussed in Hour 20:

```
<script src="http://code.jquery.com/jquery-latest.min.js" /></script>
```

When the page has fully loaded, you need to attach code to the Get Information button. The button needs to assemble the required URL based on the airport code value entered in the input field and instigate the Ajax call. Because the remote service may take some moments to respond, it would also be good if the user received a little message to indicate that the program was working.

Here's the code to carry out these tasks:

```
$(document).ready(function(){
    $("#btn").click(function(){
        $("#info").html("Getting information ...");
        var code = $("#airportCode").val();
        $.get("http://services.faa.gov/airport/status/" + code +
"?format=application/json",
            '',
            function(data){
                displayData(data);
            }
        );
    });
});
```

After the page has loaded, jQuery adds code to the onclick event handler of the button.

First it uses jQuery's html() method to add a user message to the output <div> element. This message will later be overwritten when the "real" information is received.

```
$("#info").html("Getting information ...");
```

Next, the desired airport code is retrieved from the input field:

```
var code = $("#airportCode").val();
```

Then the Ajax call is assembled, here using GET:

```
$.get("http://services.faa.gov/airport/status/" + code +
"?format=application/json",
    '',
    function(data){
        displayData(data);
    }
);
```

TRY IT YOURSELF

A Chrome Extension to Get Airport Information

continued

The callback function specified for the Ajax call is `displayData()`, which will format the returned data and display it to the user.

```
function displayData(data) {
    var message = "Airport: " + data.name + "<br />";
    message += "<h3>STATUS:</h3>";
    for (i in data.status) {
        if(data.status[i] != "") message += i + ": " + data.status[i] +
"<br />";
    }
    message += "<h3>WEATHER:</h3>";
    for (i in data.weather) {
        if(i != "meta") message += i + ": " + data.weather[i] + "<br />";
    }
    $("#info").html(message);
}
```

TIP

Look back a few pages to the JSON data returned from the remote server to see how these values were encoded.

Recall from Hour 8, "Meet JSON," that JSON data can be interpreted directly as a hierarchy of JavaScript objects. The `displayData(data)` function takes the returned JSON object data and picks out `data.name` (a string), `data.status`, and `data.weather` (themselves objects) from which to construct the message.

The complete HTML page with code included is in Listing 24.4.

LISTING 24.4   The Complete popup.html for the Extension

```
<!DOCTYPE html>
<html>
<head>
    <title>Airport Information</title>
    <style>
        body {
            width:350px;
            font: 12px normal arial, verdana, sans-serif;
        }
        #info {
            border: 1px solid black;
            padding: 10px;
        }
    </style>
    <script src="http://code.jquery.com/jquery-latest.min.js" /></script>
    <script>
        function displayData(data) {
            var message = "Airport: " + data.name + "<br />";
            message += "<h3>STATUS:</h3>";
            for (i in data.status) {
                if(data.status[i] != "") message += i + ": " +
➥data.status[i] + "<br />";
            }
                message += "<h3>WEATHER:</h3>";
```

▼ TRY IT YOURSELF

A Chrome Extension to Get Airport Information

continued

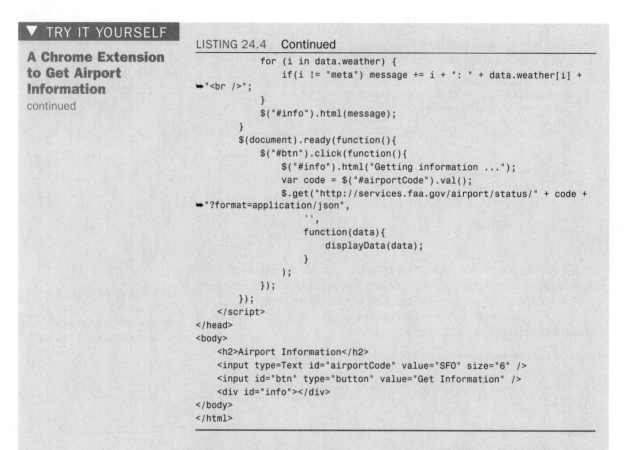

LISTING 24.4   Continued

```
            for (i in data.weather) {
                if(i != "meta") message += i + ": " + data.weather[i] +
➥"<br />";
            }
            $("#info").html(message);
        }
        $(document).ready(function(){
            $("#btn").click(function(){
                $("#info").html("Getting information ...");
                var code = $("#airportCode").val();
                $.get("http://services.faa.gov/airport/status/" + code +
➥"?format=application/json",
                       '',
                    function(data){
                        displayData(data);
                    }
                );
            });
        });
    </script>
</head>
<body>
    <h2>Airport Information</h2>
    <input type=Text id="airportCode" value="SFO" size="6" />
    <input id="btn" type="button" value="Get Information" />
    <div id="info"></div>
</body>
</html>
```

Having assembled the required files in their allocated directory, you can add the extension to Google Chrome exactly as in the previous example.

Clicking the associated icon brings up a small form where you can enter the airport code of your choice. Clicking the Get Information button will cause the program to consult the remote service, assemble the returned information into a readable form, and present it in the pop-up window.

Figure 24.4 shows the extension in operation.

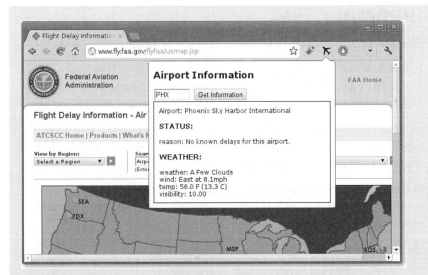

TRY IT YOURSELF

A Chrome Extension to Get Airport Information
continued

FIGURE 24.4
The Airport Information extension

Packaging the Extension

When you've finished developing your extension, click the Pack Extension button in the Extensions page. Your extension will be packed into a .crx file for you. You can serve the .crx file from your web pages, and your visitors will be able to install it on their own copy of Google Chrome.

Going Further

The exercises of this hour barely scratched the surface of what can be done with Chrome extensions. Because Chrome has good support for HTML5 and CSS3, you can use the latest web technologies such as canvas, localStorage, and CSS animations in your extensions, as well as access to external APIs and data sources. Your extensions can even add buttons to the Chrome browser's user interface or create pop-up notifications that exist outside the browser window.

Summary

That brings us to the end of the hour, the section, and in fact the book.

In this final hour, you learned about some applications of JavaScript beyond its use in HTML web pages. As an example, you wrote a small extension for Google's Chrome browser using JavaScript.

In the course of the book, you learned about many aspects of JavaScript, ranging from basic statements to liven up your web pages, through more complex JavaScript techniques used in professional projects.

Hopefully, the material covered in the book will form a sound basis for you to experiment further and develop your coding skills in this fun and useful language.

Good luck with your adventures in JavaScript!

Q&A

Q. Can I write a Firefox extension in a similar way to the Chrome extension described here?

A. The Mozilla way of creating extensions is a little more complex; in addition to JavaScript, you'll have to mess a little with XML too. You'll find some good information to help you get started at https://developer.mozilla.org/en/XUL_School/Getting_Started_with_Firefox_Extensions.

Q. Is it possible to write whole applications in JavaScript that don't have to run inside a browser?

A. Yes it is. As an example, take a look at Node js (www.nodejs.org). Node js is a platform built on top of Google Chrome's JavaScript runtime engine and designed for building server-side network applications such as web servers, chat applications, network monitoring tools, and much more.

Workshop

Try to answer all the questions before reading the subsequent "Answers" section.

Quiz

1. Information about a Google Chrome extension is contained in a file called

    a. manifest.json

    b. manifest.js

    c. manifest.txt

2. A Google Chrome extension is distributed as

    a. A .js file

    b. A .xml file

    c. A .crx file

Answers

1. a. manifest.json

2. c. Google Chrome extensions can be distributed as a .crx file.

Exercises

Browse the available JSON APIs listed at www.programmableweb.com/apitag/weather?format=JSON and try writing your own simple Chrome extension to display the data.

Take a look at the documentation for Node js (www.nodejs.org) to see how JavaScript can be used to write server-side scripts.

PART VII
Appendices

Tools for JavaScript Development

JavaScript development doesn't require any special tools or software other than a text editor and a browser.

Most operating systems come bundled with at least one of each, and in many cases these tools will be more than sufficient for you to write your code.

However, many alternative and additional tools are available, some of which are described here.

TIP

Be sure to check the license terms on the individual websites and/or included in the download package.

Editors

The choice of an editor program is a personal thing, and most program-mers have their favorite. Listed in the following sections are some popular, free editors that you can try.

Notepad++

If you develop on the Windows platform, you're probably already aware of the Notepad editor usually bundled with Windows. Notepad++ (http://notepad-plus-plus.org/) is a free application that aims to be a more powerful replacement, while still being light and fast.

Notepad++ offers line numbering, syntax and brace highlighting, macros, search and replace, and a whole lot more.

jEdit

jEdit is a free editor written in Java. It can therefore be installed on any platform having a Java virtual machine available, such as Windows, Mac OS X, OS/2, Linux, and so on.

A fully featured editor in its own right, jEdit can also be extended via 200+ available plug-ins to become, for example, a complete development environment or an advanced XML/HTML editor.

Download jEdit from www.jedit.org.

SciTE

Initially developed as a demonstrator for the Scintilla editing component, SciTE has developed into a complete and useful editor in its own right.

A free version of SciTE is available for Windows and Linux users via download from www.scintilla.org/SciTE.html, while a commercial version is available via the Mac Apps Store for Mac OSX users.

Geany

Geany (www.geany.org/) is a capable editor that can also be used as a basic IDE (Integrated Development Environment). It was developed to provide a small and fast IDE and can be installed on pretty much any platform supported by the GTK toolkit, including Windows, Linux, Mac OSX, and freeBSD.

Geany is free to download and use under the terms of the GNU General Public License.

Validators

To make sure your pages work as intended regardless of the user's browser and operating system, it's always advisable to check your HTML code for correctness and conformance to standards.

A number of online tools and facilities are available to help you, as discussed next.

The W3C Validation Services

The W3C offers an online validator at http://validator.w3.org/ that will check the markup validity of web documents in HTML, XHTML, SMIL, MathML, and other markup languages. You can enter the URL of the page to be checked, or cut-and-paste your code directly into the validator.

CSS can be validated in a similar way at http://jigsaw.w3.org/css-validator/validator.html.en.

Web Design Group (WDG)

WDG also offers an online validation service at www.htmlhelp.com/tools/validator/.

This is similar to the W3C validator, but in some circumstances gives slightly more helpful information, such as warnings about valid but dangerous code, or highlighting undefined references rather than simply listing them as errors.

Debugging and Verifying Tools

Debugging tools can save you hours when trying to track down elusive problems in your JavaScript code and help you speed up your scripts by analyzing execution timing.

Verifying tools help you to write tidy, concise, readable, and problem-free code.

Numerous debugging and verifying tools are available, including the following.

Firebug

Firebug integrates with the Mozilla Firefox browser to offer excellent debugging, editing, and profiling tools. Go to http://getfirebug.com/javascript.

JSLint

JSLint (www.jslint.com/), written by Douglas Crockford, analyzes your JavaScript source code and reports potential problems, including both style conventions and coding errors.

JavaScript Quick Reference

Tables B.1, B.2, B.3, and B.4 in this appendix contain a quick look-up for some of the more commonly used elements of JavaScript syntax, along with properties and methods for a selection of the built-in objects.

TABLE B.1   The JavaScript Operators

Operator	Description
Arithmetic Operators	
*	Multiplies two numbers.
/	Divides two numbers.
% (Modulus)	Returns the remainder left after dividing two numbers using integer division.
String Operators	
+	(String addition) Joins two strings.
+=	Joins two strings and assigns the joined string to the first operand.
Logical Operators	
&&	(Logical AND) Returns a value of true if both operands are true; otherwise, returns false.
||	(Logical OR) Returns a value of true if either operand is true. However, if both operands are false, returns false.
!	(Logical NOT) Returns a value of false if its operand is true; true if its operand is false.

TABLE B.1   Continued

Operator	Description
Bitwise Operators	
&	(Bitwise AND) Returns a one in each bit position if both operands' bits are ones.
^	(Bitwise XOR) Returns a one in a bit position if the bits of one operand, but not both operands, are one.
|	(Bitwise OR) Returns a one in a bit if either operand has a one in that position.
~	(Bitwise NOT) Changes ones to zeros and zeros to ones in all bit positions—that is, flips each bit.
<<	(Left shift) Shifts the bits of its first operand to the left by the number of places given in the second operand.
>>	(Sign-propagating right shift) Shifts the bits of the first operand to the right by the number of places given in the second operand.
>>>	(Zero-fill right shift) Shifts the bits of the first operand to the right by the number of places given in the second operand, and shifting in zeros from the left.
Assignment Operators	
=	Assigns the value of the second operand to the first operand, if the first operand is a variable.
+=	Adds two operands and assigns the result to the first operand, if it is a variable.
-=	Subtracts two operands and assigns the result to the first operand, if it is a variable.
*=	Multiplies two operands and assigns the result to the first operand, if it is a variable.
/=	Divides two operands and assigns the result to the first operand, if it is a variable.
%=	Calculates the modulus of two operands and assigns the result to the first operand, if it is a variable.
&=	Executes a bitwise AND operation on two operands and assigns the result to the first operand, if it is a variable.

TABLE B.1   Continued

Operator	Description
Assignment Operators (continued)	
^=	Executes a bitwise exclusive OR operation on two operands and assigns the result to the first operand, if it is a variable.
| =	Executes a bitwise OR operation on two operands and assigns the result to the first operand, if it is a variable.
<<=	Executes a left shift operation on two operands and assigns the result to the first operand, if it is a variable.
>>=	Executes a sign-propagating right shift operation on two operands and assigns the result to the first operand, if it is a variable.
>>>=	Executes a zero-fill right shift operation on two operands and assigns the result to the first operand, if it is a variable.
Comparison Operators	
==	(Equality operator) Returns true if the two operands are equal to each other.
!=	(Not-equal-to) Returns true if the two operands are not equal to each other.
===	(Strict equality) Returns true if the two operands are both equal and of the same type.
!==	(Strict not-equal-to) Returns true if the two operands are either not equal and/or not of the same type.
>	(Greater-than) Returns true if the first operand's value is greater than the second operand's value.
>=	(Greater-than-or-equal-to) Returns true if the first operand's value is greater than or equal to the second operand's value.
<	(Less-than) Returns true if the first operand's value is less than the second operand's value.
<=	(Less-than-or-equal-to) Returns true if the first operand's value is less than or equal to the second operand's value.

TABLE B.1   Continued

Operator	Description
Special Operators	
`?:`	(Conditional operator) Executes an "if...else" test.
`,`	(Comma operator) Evaluates two expressions and returns the result of evaluating the second expression.
`delete`	(Deletion) Deletes an object and removes it from memory, or deletes an object's property, or deletes an element in an array.
`function`	Creates an anonymous function.
`in`	Returns true if the property you're testing is supported by a specific object.
`instanceof`	Returns true if the given object is an instance of the specified type.
`new`	Creates an new object from the specified object type.
`typeof`	Returns the name of the type of the operand.
`void`	Allows evaluation of an expression without returning a value.

TABLE B.2   String Methods

Method	Description
`substring`	Returns a portion of the string.
`toUpperCase`	Converts all characters in the string to uppercase.
`toLowerCase`	Converts all characters in the string to lowercase.
`indexOf`	Finds an occurrence of a string within the string.
`lastIndexOf`	Finds an occurrence of a string within the string, starting at the end of the string.
`replace`	Searches for a match between a substring and a string and replaces the substring with a new substring.
`split`	Splits a string into an array of substring and returns the new array.
`link`	Creates an HTML link using the string's text.
`anchor`	Creates an HTML anchor within the current page.

TABLE B.3   The Math Object

Property	Description
Constants	
E	Base of natural logarithms (approximately 2.718).
LN2	Natural logarithm of 2 (approximately 0.693).
LN10	Natural logarithm of 10 (approximately 2.302).
LOG2E	Base 2 logarithm of e (approximately 1.442).
LOG10E	Base 10 logarithm of e (approximately 0.434).
PI	Ratio of a circle's circumference to its diameter (approximately 3.14159).
SQRT1_2	Square root of one half (approximately 0.707).
SQRT2	Square root of two (approximately 1.4142).

Method	Description
Algebraic	
acos	Arc cosine of a number in radians.
asin	Arc sine of a number.
atan	Arc tangent of a number.
cos	Cosine of a number.
sin	Sine of a number.
tan	Tangent of a number.
Statistical and Logarithmic	
exp	Returns e (the base of natural logarithms) raised to a power.
log	Returns the natural logarithm of a number.
max	Accepts two numbers and returns whichever is greater.
min	Accepts two numbers and returns the smaller of the two.
Basic and Rounding	
abs	Absolute value of a number.
ceil	Rounds a number up to the nearest integer.
floor	Rounds a number down to the nearest integer.
pow	One number to the power of another.
round	Rounds a number to the nearest integer.
sqrt	Square root of a number.

TABLE B.3   The Math Object

Method	Description
Random Numbers	
random	Random number between 0 and 1.

TABLE B.4   The Date Object

Method	Description
getDate()	Returns day of the month (1-31).
getDay()	Returns day of the week (0-6).
getFullYear()	Returns year (four digits).
getHours()	Returns hour (0-23).
getMilliseconds()	Returns milliseconds (0-999).
getMinutes()	Returns minutes (0-59).
getMonth()	Returns month (0-11).
getSeconds()	Returns seconds (0-59).
getTime()	Returns number of milliseconds since midnight Jan 1, 1970.
getTimezoneOffset()	Returns time difference between GMT and local time, in minutes.
getUTCDate()	Returns day of the month, according to universal time (1-31).
getUTCDay()	Returns day of the week, according to universal time (0-6).
getUTCFullYear()	Returns year, according to universal time (4 digit).
getUTCHours()	Returns hour, according to universal time (0-23).
getUTCMilliseconds()	Returns milliseconds, according to universal time (0-999).
getUTCMinutes()	Returns minutes, according to universal time (0-59).
getUTCMonth()	Returns month, according to universal time (0-11).
getUTCSeconds()	Returns seconds, according to universal time (0-59).
parse()	Parses a date string and Returns number of milliseconds since midnight of January 1, 1970.
setDate()	Sets the day of the month (1-31).

TABLE B.4   Continued

Method	Description
setFullYear()	Sets the year (four digits).
setHours()	Sets the hour (0-23).
setMilliseconds()	Sets the milliseconds (0-999).
setMinutes()	Set the minutes (0-59).
setMonth()	Sets the month (0-11).
setSeconds()	Sets the seconds (0-59).
setTime()	Sets a date and time by adding or subtracting a specified number of milliseconds to/midnight January 1, 1970.
setUTCDate()	Sets the day of the month, according to universal time (1-31).
setUTCFullYear()	Sets the year, according to universal time (four digits).
setUTCHours()	Sets the hour, according to universal time (0-23).
setUTCMilliseconds()	Sets the milliseconds, according to universal time (0-999).
setUTCMinutes()	Set the minutes, according to universal time (0-59).
setUTCMonth()	Sets the month, according to universal time (0-11).
setUTCSeconds()	Set the seconds, according to universal time 2(0-59).
toDateString()	Converts the date part of a Date object into a readable string.
toLocaleDateString()	Returns date part of a Date object as a string, using locale conventions.
toLocaleTimeString()	Returns time part of a Date object as a string, using locale conventions.
toLocaleString()	Converts a Date object to a string, using locale conventions.
toString()	Converts a Date object to a string.
toTimeString()	Converts the time part of a Date object to a string.
toUTCString()	Converts a Date object to a string, according to universal time.

TABLE B.4   Continued

Method	Description
UTC()	Returns number of milliseconds in a date string since midnight of January 1, 1970, according to universal time.
valueOf()	Returns primitive value of a Date object.

INDEX

Sams **Teach Yourself**

When you only have time
for the answers™

Whatever your need and whatever your time frame, there's a **Sams Teach Yourself** book for you. With a **Sams Teach Yourself** book as your guide, you can **quickly get up to speed** on just about any new product or technology—in the absolute **shortest period of time possible**. Guaranteed.

Learning how to do new things with your computer shouldn't be tedious or time-consuming. **Sams Teach Yourself** makes learning anything **quick**, **easy**, and even a little bit **fun**.

HTML5 Mobile Application Development in 24 Hours

Jennifer Kyrnin
ISBN-13: 978-0-672-33440-5

Java in 24 Hours

Rogers Cadenhead
ISBN-13: 978-0-672-33575-4

PHP, MySQL and Apache All in One

Julie C. Meloni
ISBN-13: 978-0-672-33543-3

Node.js in 24 Hours, Second Edition

George Ornbo
ISBN-13: 978-0-672-33595-6

HTML and CSS in 24 Hours

Julie C. Meloni
Michael Morrison
ISBN-13: 978-0-672-33097-1

Sams Teach Yourself books are available at most retail and online bookstores. For more information or to order direct, visit our online bookstore at **informit.com/sams**.

Online editions of all Sams Teach Yourself titles are available by subscription from Safari Books Online at **safari.informit.com**.

Phil Ballard
Michael Moncur

Fifth Edition
Covers
JavaScript
and Ajax

Sams Teach Yourself
JavaScript™
in 24 Hours

SAMS

FREE
Online Edition

Safari
Books Online

Your purchase of *Sams Teach Yourself JavaScript in 24 Hours, Fifth Edition* includes access to a free online edition for 45 days through the **Safari Books Online** subscription service. Nearly every Sams book is available online through **Safari Books Online**, along with thousands of books and videos from publishers such as Addison-Wesley Professional, Cisco Press, Exam Cram, IBM Press, O'Reilly Media, Prentice Hall, Que, and VMware Press.

Safari Books Online is a digital library providing searchable, on-demand access to thousands of technology, digital media, and professional development books and videos from leading publishers. With one monthly or yearly subscription price, you get unlimited access to learning tools and information on topics including mobile app and software development, tips and tricks on using your favorite gadgets, networking, project management, graphic design, and much more.

Activate your FREE Online Edition at
informit.com/safarifree

STEP 1:   Enter the coupon code: KNXPXAA.

STEP 2:   New Safari users, complete the brief registration form.
Safari subscribers, just log in.

If you have difficulty registering on Safari or accessing the online edition,
please e-mail customer-service@safaribooksonline.com